# Déjà New Marketing:

## *Increase Sales with Social Media, Search Marketing, E-mail Marketing, Blogs, and More*

BY JOHN BRADLEY JACKSON

# Déjà New Marketing:

*Increase Sales with Social Media, Search Marketing, E-mail Marketing, Blogs, and More*

By John Bradley Jackson

First published by Dog Ear Publishing
4010 W. 86th Street, Ste H
Indianapolis, IN 46268
www.dogearpublishing.net

ISBN: 978-160844-464-9

This book is printed on acid-free paper.

Printed in the United States of America

This book is dedicated to all the businesspeople who have braved the new millennium and the all new marketing challenges that it has wrought.

"If you chase two rabbits, both will escape."

**Unknown**

# Reviews

"A few pages into John Bradley Jackson's second book, Déjà New Marketing, the entrepreneur — who faces a withering array of market complexities, competitive and rapidly evolving technological challenges — realizes that he/she has come upon an impressively useful body of information, and is being pulled along to the pages ahead.

While generic marketing tomes are available at any bookstore, Déjà New Marketing prioritizes, defines, segments and demystifies niche marketing challenges that can spell death and/or destruction to the entrepreneur and his career. To successfully market a niche product and create new cash flow, Jackson's thoughts and advice are a must read.

Risk-driven entrepreneurs will find Déjà New Marketing an easy book to read, packed with leading edge concepts, methods and common sense that should be top of mind.

Jackson makes extensive use of his successful sales, marketing, consulting and academic background to provide guidance in analyzing market conditions and create effective marketing plans that are relevant to the entrepreneur's needs.

From his fascinating discussion of the "long tail" market strategy involving personalized or niche products vs. mass markets, to first mover or differentiating strategies, the reader gets a 360 degree view and understanding of the challenges and options for action.

Pick up your copy of Déjà New Marketing and get on with it."

**Frank Sammann, Retired CEO and Current Board Member for Biz360, Incorporated**

"Déjà New Marketing's compendium of short definitions and practical knowledge for the budding entrepreneur, micro and small business is on target. Refreshingly direct and insightful — the book is a delight to read."

**Curtis Chan, President and CEO, CHAN & ASSOCIATES and COGNITIVE IMPACT**

"John Bradley Jackson's new book, entitled Déjà New Marketing should have been titled 'The Marketing Encyclopedia for Entrepreneurs and small business people.'

With more than 190 chapters covering every conceivable subject from 'What to put on your business card' to 'How to have a successful blog' to 'Eight different ways to segment a market', this book has everything you need to know about marketing. In fact, if it's NOT in this book, you don't need to know about it.

This book is a MUST HAVE resource for every entrepreneur who wants to know more about marketing and for every small business owner who wants to do a better job of getting and keeping more customers."

**Tom Patty, Former President, TBWA-Chiat-Day Advertising**

"Every short chapter in Déjà New Marketing is long in benefits. This is not another 'Marketing for Dummies' book that is full of fancy marketing jargon and trite, shopworn without 'dumbing down' the why and how of marketing success. It is about now — how you can be a marketing success today."

**Dr. Michael D. Ames, Professor of Management, Emeritus and Chairman of the Board, CSUF Center for Entrepreneurship**

"John Bradley Jackson's newest book Déjà New Marketing is highly informative and an easy read. It drives home the importance of bringing in the new with the old. The social networking that John writes about and practices is powerful and it has changed the way we connect both personally and professionally.

Through this magic that he writes of in-depth, John and I reconnected on Facebook and classmates.com. We were close childhood friends but only remembered each other through pictures in our high school yearbook. I was delighted to be able to reestablish our friendship. Going our separate ways after high school and moving to another state it would have been impossible to reconnect the old fashioned way.

Only through this new social networking that he refers to in his new book, I am now able to read his fascinating words in print which is helping me as an entrepreneur and business owner. This highly informative book is a must read for anyone that is looking to improve, update, or just stay connected with this fast changing business world.

In the current economy, being "First, Best, or Different" is now more important than ever. Finding new ways to keep our customers and establish new ones is detailed by John.

I have a tendency to jump around in a book and his short chapters that all start with fun and/or poignant quotes makes it a great book and reference guide. Whether you are a student, sales professional or a business owner this book is invaluable. There is a lot of food for thought and you will find yourself referring to it over and over again. It definitely won't be a dust collector and might wear out before it finds its way to your shelf. It is the perfect guide for me as I open a new store.

Being able to reconnect with my friend, tap into his great mind as a professor and marketing guru is priceless."

**Marilyn Darby, Owner and Entrepreneur, D'Juice LLC (Park City, UT)**

"John Jackson is a very effective professor. He fuses Internet Marketing real-time into the classroom. I seldom find faculty working at his speed to follow the constant change of the Internet medium."

**Sinan Kanatsiz, Founder, Internet Marketing Association**

"John Bradley Jackson has again written a concise handbook of new millennium business and marketing thinking for first-time entrepreneurs or experienced small business owners who want to get it right the first time, or this time around, in the information age where the rules have changed. If you plan to be successful with your new business, this essential book is required reading. Keep it handy, you will return to it frequently. I do."

**Ken James, Founder and President, Clearly Innovative Home Office Products**

"Jackson's new book is a step-by-step guide about the essentials skills of sales, marketing, and entrepreneurship. His proven real-world success and candid storytelling techniques serve the reader in a way that most books cannot. Rather than relying on theory, Jackson uses real lessons, learned and shared by real people."

**William Taormina Jr., Entrepreneur, Clean City Inc.**

# *Preface*

"Déjà New Marketing: Increase Sales with Social Media, Search Marketing, E-mail Marketing, Blogs and More"—OK, why this title?

Let's first look at the familiar term "déjà vu." Wikipedia, the free encyclopedia, defines it as "the experience of feeling sure that one has witnessed or experienced a new situation previously (an individual feels as though an event has already happened or has happened in the near past). The term was coined by a French psychic researcher, Émile Boirac (1851–1917) in his book "The Future of Psychic Sciences." The experience of déjà vu is usually accompanied by a compelling sense of familiarity and also a sense of eeriness, strangeness, or weirdness. The previous experience is most frequently attributed to real life, although in some cases there is a firm sense that the experience "genuinely happened" in the past."

Thus, I coined the term "Déjà New Marketing" and defined it as the experience of feeling sure that you have witnessed or encountered a marketing situation previously. Yet, with this recognition is the knowledge and acceptance that new methods of marketing such as social media, search marketing, e-mail marketing, and blogs are required to maximize this new opportunity or address the problem. These new techniques involve the whole marketing mix: price, promotion, product, and place. But, these techniques may need to be used or applied differently than before, or you may need to use entirely different techniques. Put another way, the old tools don't work as well anymore, if at all. It is a new ballgame.

My research and consulting work with entrepreneurs and marketing executives, along with my own experience in niche market environments, has taught me about the great significance that an innovative and properly executed marketing plan has on the success of a venture. In practice, most entrepreneurs and marketing executives have had precious little marketing training. Instead, they have learned on the job. While some may have succeeded, many struggled with the art of niche marketing and were overwhelmed by the choices offered in the marketing mix.

Unfortunately, too many firms race forward without defining their target market or taking the time to truly understand and stay in touch with the customers' needs and problems. In a desperate attempt to create cash flow, they run from one customer to another, offering the same old solution, which is often off the mark. Statistically, most businesses fail in the first few years due to the absence of a concrete marketing strategy and to a lack of capital. If they had only slowed down long enough to create substantive marketing plans, they might have avoided frustration and, possibly, failure.

I have written this book to help the entrepreneur reinvent his or her marketing tool kit. Along the way I hope to demystify the sometimes overly complex nomenclature of marketing by writing this book in plain English, by using easy-to-read short chapters, and by offering ideas on how to market better and sell more. Absent from the book is any tedious debate on what the various marketing terms mean; instead, you will find short definitions and practical insight. All these suggestions come from successful entrepreneurs that I have known and from my personal experiences.

As in my previous book, "First, Best, or Different: What Every Entrepreneur Needs to Know About Niche Marketing," I struggled with the word "entrepreneur" which is French for someone who creates or operates a business, is personally accountable for the success or failure of the business, and contends with risk. A common usage today of the word "entrepreneur" is someone who has vision or is innovative, whether in a small or a large organization. Small businesses may or may not be innovative, but they certainly contend with risk. You will note that I sometimes use "entrepreneur" and "small business" interchangeably, which is not technically correct. I defend myself by aligning with the others in the business press who also use the terms interchangeably.

One more thing—this book is a compendium of ideas, stories, anecdotes, algorithms, and strategies, and musings. While it is protected by copyright, I encourage you to pass it on to others. That is why I wrote the book. I have learned that when I help others unconditionally, I am helped in return. And, for that I am grateful.

# *Acknowledgments*

I am forever thankful for the support from Jeff Abraham, Merv Adrian, Tisa M Aley, Mark Aloise, Danhya Alvarez, Jose Alvear, Michelle Anderson, Casey Annis, Greg Arbues, Mark Arenal, Dr. Melissa A. Arizpe, Frank Arredondo, Carmen and Denis Axen, Andrew Baker, Jerry Banks, Aaron Barkenhagen, Ben Barns, Jeff Barovich, Brad Barrett, Brian Batte, Benjamin Baumgardner, Niki Dal Bello, Dave Bellon, Kevin Bellwood, Sue Bendheim, Rip Benson, Shelly Berggren, Alison Bergquist, Norm Bianchi, Jannine Bielesch, Jeff W. Black, Stuart Blake, Dr. Lawrence Blocher, Daniela Anavitarte Bolzmann, Neil Bradford, Dr. Tami Brady, John Broussard, Mike Bry, April Buchner, Hector M. Calderon, Jose Calero, Tyler Cameron, Sean Cantelon, Mary and Earl Carbone, Jim Carr, Rob Carrillo, Terry Carter, Jim Case, Ray Cerulli, Greg Chagaris, Young Chai, Curtis Chan, Rudy Chavarria Jr., Edward Chiu, Elaine Chu, Don Collier, Brian Collins, Jerry Conrey, Steve Cooper, Ken Crooks, Linsey Crow, John Curtis, Dick Dadamo, Valerie Danzig, Zack Dafaalah, Marilyn Darby, Mary Dean, Robb Dorf, Stephen Duarte, Ryan Dudley, Randolf Dupree, Bill Dyer, Wally Eater, Kevin Eikenberry, Paul Estrada, Brent Evans, Angelo Farro, Len Feldman, Alan and Gail Fernandez, Manny Fernandez, Reuben Fine, Steve Forell, Don Gage, Matthew Gallizzi, Mike Gancar, Lawrence Gasman, Duane Gomer, Claudia Gonzalez, Carolina Grechuta, David Gross, Kenneth W Guchereau, Jeannie Hankins, Neil Harle, Tom Hartley, Jason Hartman, Michael Harnetiaux, Steve Hawley, Russ Hearl, Chick Hearn, Judy Herrick, Alfred Herzing, Wally Hicks, Len Hills, Bob Hooven, Jeanne Hopkins, Blake Hoss, Andrea Hurt, Davis H. Ikemiya, John Ishimaru, Bob Jackovich, Steve Jaksch, Ken James, Stephen Jester, Melinda Johnson, Valerie Johnson, Bo Jones, Sharon Kaak, Michelle Kabahit, Lyle Kan, Sinan Kanatsiz, Yumi Kaneko, Don Kasle, Ross Kaufman, Naseef Kazi, Jim Kelton, Linda Kebrea, Dave Kinnear, Tom Kirksey, Chuck Kissel, Nancy Knapp, Guy Knuf, Zain Kolsy, Garrett Kop, Linda Krall, Bob Kreisberg, Ron LaRosa, Tom Lazear, Tina Le, Kevin Leibl, Nick Leighton, Randy and Kitty Lesage, Robert Lescaille, Qevin Leung, Liz Levy, Barry Lieberman, Randy Likas, Cris Lins, Maria Lizarraga, Kristen Llorente, Curtis Ludlow, Ciao Luu, Kathy Ly, Dennis Lyftogt, Victor Macias, Paul Magargee, Dan Mahoney, Raj Manek, Alan Mannason, Rey Marques, Lane Mason, William McClennen, Sue Pearson McCowan, Paul McKinney, Craig McLaughlin, Charlesetta Medina, Lynn and Gary Melton, Dr. Nancy A. Merlino, Bonni Montevecchi, Chad Morgan, Nick Morgan, Bill Morland, Mike Murray, Garrett Myklak, Jack

Napoli, Alison Nasisi, Mark Newcomb, Bruce Nguyen, Robert Nolan, Gene Norrett, Jan Norman, Tom Northrup, Scott and Donna Olpin, Jan Oncel, Paul Oronoz, Andrew Pardo, Zachary Parker, Gary Parks, Clifton A. Passow, Urva Patel, Tom Patty, Ryan Paules, Jeff Paulin, Charles Pavia, Andy Paz, Mike Paz, Rod and Robin Peacock, Tom Pearson, Brian Pendarvis, Doug Pennington, Dr. J. Mitchell Perry, Jarrett Pflieger, Vi Pham, Hazel Phillips, Tom Power, Dave Primac, John Primac, Arunk Puri, Jerry Ramos, Srinivas Rao, Azuma Reiji, Laurie Resnick, Tyler Richardson, Ray Robinson, Edward Rogoff, Joseph Rosenzweig, John Rosica, Chia Rowan, Krystle Rowry, Jennifer Rudd-O'Neil, Doug Rugg, Joseph Saadi, Mike Sadeghpour, Ron Saetermoe, Alan Safahi, Teresa Saldivar, Shaun Salvino, Barbara J. Samara, Frank Sammann, Hector Sanchez, Candace Santos, David Scott Savlowitz, Michael Sawitz, Ron Schott, David Meerman Scott, Marisa Sherb, Steve Shields, Charles Simon, Earl Skakel, Brad Smith, Bill Smyth, Lisa Spillone, Bernie Spear, Terry Splane, Doug Sproal, Malcolm Stanley, Ronald Stein, Jim Stewart, Eric Stockton, Anthea Stratigos, Scott Stratton, Dan Struve, Rick Sturdivant, Andrew Sundstrom, Sylvan Swartz, William Taormina, William Taormina Jr., Thien Tat, Sheridan Tatsuno, Mel Thomsen, Oli Thordarson Vince Tjelmeland, Ken Townsend, Larry Trujillo, Paul Ulyett, Tom Underhill, Karenna Vasquez, Ali Vaziri, Fritz Von Coelln, Robert Wagner, Greg Wallace, Bruce Welch, Bruce Wells, John Wetteland, Denise Westcott, Dave Wheeler, Robert Willey, Craig Willison, Greg Winston, Carl Woodard, Julie Woods, Yau Tze Yip, Christina Zazueta, and many others.

I am deeply appreciative of the support from my marketing mentors Dr. Irene Lange, Dr. Ellen Dumond, Dr. Anil Puri, and Dr. Michael Ames at California State University, Fullerton; all inspired me to make this book a reality.

Additionally, I want to thank all my students at the Center for Entrepreneurship at California State University, Fullerton, who braved my classes and challenged me to write this book. Entrepreneurs themselves, the students were a constant inspiration to write this book so that we could better help our entrepreneur clients. Frankly, we learned a lot from each other, and I may have learned the most from them. I count many of them as my friends and trusted advisers.

The staff at the CSUF Center for Entrepreneurship has also been most supportive including Andrea Hurt, Marisa Sherb, Charlesetta Medina, and Urva Patel. Thanks for your patience and daily inspiration.

Also, at CSUF I would like to thank Michele Cesca, Dr. Peng Chan, Kathy Drake, Brent Evans, Dr. Joe Greco, Dr. Wayne Jones, Rick Lamprecht, Matty Li, Guy Knuf, Ligaya Lim, Dr. Dmitry Khanin, Jeff Miller, Alicia Maciel, Pamela McLaren, Bene Lusk, Ginny Pace, Paula Parker, Karl Seppala, Dr. Tom Schwarz, Mike Trueblood, Kit Richard, and Emeline Yong.

Thanks also to my in-class coaches whose time-tested experience as entrepreneurs and marketers helped guide my students and me. My appreciation also goes out to our consulting clients who welcomed the students into their businesses and gave us the opportunity to better understand the marketing challenges with new ventures.

Special thanks to the MRG staff including Gary Schultz, Jose Alvear, Grace Moyles, Michelle Kabahit, and Mike Galli. The folks at MRG helped me look into the future — and the future looks bright.

My friends at AppSoft Web Design were also inspirational to me including John Widdows, David Freeman, Peter Roesler, Rachel Kuncicky, and Craig Heineman. This team helped me understand search marketing and why it matters.

I owe a big thank you to the readers of my first draft including my Frank Sammann, Sinan Kanatsiz, Ken James, Marilyn Darby, Scott Olpin, Curtis Chan, William Taormina Jr., Tom Patty, Dr. Michael Ames, and Zachary Parker. This group of contributors helped make the book better.

I am appreciative of the many creative inputs from Greg Jordan, my friend and collaborator. He helped me understand the web and how search marketing really works.

A very special thank you must go to my colleague, editor and collaborator Travis Lindsay. His special aptitude for grammar, detail, and style made this book a most pleasurable experience. It is an understatement to say that I could not have done it without him. In fact, the book would not have been finished had he not stepped in and pushed me along.

Also, a very special posthumous thank you goes to my life long friend Doug Rogers who recently passed away unexpectedly. He was a constant source of inspiration and I miss him terribly.

Additionally, another very special posthumous thank you goes to my recently passed brother-in-law Bert Berschauer who always challenged me to try harder and set my goals higher. He was my hero. I love you Bert.

I am also thankful for the support of my brothers and sisters Craig, Clark, Bruce, Marlys, Gail, Jess, and Ross along with their spouses and children. Their encouragement was critical to the book's completion.

Most of all, I must thank my lovely supportive wife Janet and my beautiful children Beth, Tom, and Valla. I love you forever.

# Table of Contents

# 1. Déjà New Marketing

"This is like déjà vu all over again."

**Yogi Berra (1925 – present) Professional Baseball Player**

Do you ever get the feeling that you have experienced something before, but you are not sure what to do about it?

If you are like me, it happens a lot. This happens when I confront a familiar marketing problem or opportunity. While I may have experienced or witnessed a similar marketing challenge before, my previous responses or reactions just don't seem to work so well any more. For whatever reason, new marketing solutions are needed if I am to remain competitive, let alone meet the challenge. I call this phenomenon "Déjà New Marketing."

For example, a proven promotional method for many businesses is print advertising. Traditionally, print advertising has been an effective tool and one that virtually all marketing executives and entrepreneurs under-stood. You know the drill. You place the ad in the newspaper, directory, or magazine, and then you wait for the customers to respond. You pay the bill and hopefully you get rewarded.

Sadly, print advertising is becoming less and less effective in the new millennium. Driven by the pervasiveness of the web, print advertising is quickly losing its grip on the customer. While I feel pity for my friends in the print advertising business, as a buyer of print advertising it is clear that the web has quickly become a more efficient and cost effective channel to get your message out to your customer. This stunning change in print advertising revenues and effectiveness is only one example.

Consider the recent changes in selling goods and services. For the last 100 years, salespeople have used face-to-face presentations and the tele-phone to build relationships and push products. During the last decade, customer purchasing behavior has dramatically changed. It's as if cus-tomers have gone into hiding!

Today, personal selling often seems reduced to e-mail and voicemail with a customer who no longer has the time or the desire to talk with sales-people. When you do get to talk to a customer they are often just as informed as the sales rep about the product specifications, the competition, and the pricing. Small talk is not necessary and they are ready to negotiate. Once again, the web has changed the landscape for the buyer and the seller; in this case, the buyer seems to know too much, while the seller is reduced to a price and delivery information exchange.

Bricks and mortar store fronts are now being trumped by websites that require ecommerce applications. Sparkling website sales copy has grown ineffective, if not inadequate, since visitors tend to scan rather than read. Visitors don't want to be bothered with details or trite sales pitches; instead visitors want to find help with their problems or needs.

Search engines have grown increasingly sophisticated and now prefer copy that is written by an SEO copywriter rather than a traditional copy writer or journalist. Getting found on the internet is now the priority for the website owner. After getting found on the web, the goal then is to get the visitor to respond to your call to action (CTA), which may be for them to contact you for more information or to buy now.

Facebook, MySpace, LinkedIn, Twitter, and the other social networking websites have supplanted the water cooler as the place to go when you need a break from your work day. Emails almost seem passé in comparison to these social networks. For some, these social networking sites are the only way to connect.

Similarly, landline telephones are quickly becoming old fashioned with many "twenty somethings" using cell phones only. Text messaging is the new telegraph or shortwave radio, which has created a new language of sorts or certainly a new way of spelling.

Thus, familiar marketing challenges require new and different responses. The same old marketing techniques don't work as well as they did a few years ago, or even a few months ago. Do you want your business to survive in the new millennium? Then you better get with the program and embrace "Déjà New Marketing."

*Answer this: What marketing tools are you using today that seem less effective than they did in the past?*

# 2. Markets, Market Segments, and Target Markets

"The odds of hitting your target go up dramatically when you aim for it."

**Anonymous**

Simply put, a market is a group of buyers that are willing and able to buy your product or solution. A market is made up of sub-markets or "market segments" which are groups of potential buyers who have similar wants, needs, experiences, and/or problems. As a wise man once said, "There is no market; there are only market segments."

Your target market is the customer group that will buy and/or use your product or solution. Historically, marketers have defined target markets using factors or demographics such as age (I.E. 18- to 33-year-old men and women). For example, it was commonly thought that someone in their late twenties was an adult, likely married with children, and quickly headed to middle age.

In the new millennium we find that while some people in their late twenties fit this profile, many others of the same age group still live at home and remain dependent on their parents for financial support. Often, they are unmarried and have no children. Yet, the old age based segmentation lumps these two disparate groups into one bucket. This simplistic type of segmentation in the consumer marketplace is now considered inadequate, because of the new sophistication of the consumer and of our increased knowledge of segmentation.

Thus, your target market is the market segment that you choose to serve and know. To truly understand your target market you need to answer these questions:

- Who are they?
- What do they want to buy?
- How do they want to buy?
- When do they want to buy?
- Where do they want to buy?
- Why do they want to buy?

You need to be able to answer these questions fully; if not, you don't deserve their business.

Additionally, "cohort marketing," a term originating in consumer marketing circles, defines customer segments using a common experience or multiple experiences shared by a group of people. They have a bond and a common set of needs or interests. For example, Apple computer users who choose not to follow convention with the Windows operating systems; instead, they take pride in the cult-like creativity and independence that Apple products offer.

So, what does this segmentation mean to the entrepreneur? It means that the target market needs to be carefully defined and understood, which insures that your offering matches precisely with the market's wants or needs. If you define your market too broadly, you might find yourself with a customer who is indifferent to your offering and may be willing to move to the competitor that better understands his or her needs.

Successful entrepreneurs target the under-served or overlooked markets where there is little or no competition. This segment, while small, is still big enough for the entrepreneur to make a profit—this is niche marketing. The key to niche marketing success is the intimacy that you have with the customer needs, problems, and issues. I call this being a "knowledge broker" or someone who is an expert about the customer's day-to-day life.

This knowledge allows you to create a dialog with them. In time you can build a constituency made up of customers who believe in what you do. If they refer you to other customers you have achieved an advocacy which sustains your business. This is when you know that you have made it.

Turning your customers into your advocates is not easy. It can take blood, sweat, and tears to get them. Your referrals are the best indicator of a bull's eye hit of your product in your target market. Interesting enough, you may be surprised when you get them since they may not be who you targeted in the first place.

For example, when I wrote my first book "First, Best, or Different" (shameless plug) I figured my book would appeal to a broad spectrum of readers including small business owners, marketing executives, and avid business book readers. While this has proven true, many of my fans are not people that I had necessarily targeted.

My longtime landscaper, Tom Hartley, may be my biggest advocate. He so enjoyed my book that he has been trading his services for my books: which he gives to friends, family, and other customers. Although I had heavily researched the business book market, I had no idea that a small business owner like him would connect with my message. The lesson was simple. It is not what you think that counts. It is what the customer thinks, feels, and does.

Another example of market segmentation is a market made up of coffee buyers, but it can be divided into many different market segments. One coffee buyer market segment is the group of coffee drinkers who will pay two times the normal price of a regular cup of coffee to enjoy the coffee and experience found at Starbucks. Starbucks has a grip on its market segment that is so powerful that coffee drinkers endure long lines and ridiculous prices for the chance to drink an overly bitter and burnt cup of coffee.

Think I am full of it? Consumer Reports just completed an independent test comparing the coffee at Burger King, McDonald's, Starbucks, and Dunkin' Donuts. Guess what? McDonald's won! But I digress. It does not matter what I think; it is what the Starbucks market segment thinks since they vote with their dollars.

To truly understand a market segment (I.E. why Starbucks buyers must have their "Grande Latte" every morning) you need to know who they are and what they want.

*Question: Who is your customer and why do they buy?*

# 3. Strategy or Tactic?

"A sly rabbit will have three openings to its den."

**Ancient Chinese Proverb**

Strategy is an overused if not abused word in the business community. People use the word strategy when they are in trouble or desperately need to change or do something new. Lost a key customer market and have a bad quarter? Most people will tell you to get a new strategy.

In reality, strategy is a process that is about choice, which affects long-term outcomes. Wikipedia defines strategy as "a long-term plan of action designed to achieve a particular goal, most often winning." Practically speaking, strategy is driven by long-term planning and not by a reflex action to the ups and downs of the market. Thus, strategy involves a long-term plan coupled with critical thought.

Day-to-day decisions might be better described as tactics. Tactics are the actual means used to gain an objective. Strategy is the overall plan, which may involve complex activities and decision-making. Thus, changing a price for a product is a tactic. A price reduction in response to a competitor's advance is a tactic. Planning to diversify the company product line by entering new markets over the next five years is a strategy.

The point is that most marketing executives and entrepreneurs manage tactical activities on a day-to-day basis, while most references to strategy are just lip service. This is because most small to medium sized firms don't have strategic plans—they just wing it.

For example, a while back a good friend of mine asked for my opinion about the 2008 stock market decline. His 401K had lost over 40% of its value in a few months and the market still seemed in a free fall. He asked me if he should sell before it was too late.

While I don't pretend to be a financial adviser, I do know a few things about strategy. In my friend's case, his long-term strategy was to earn a 6-8% annual return on this 401K hoping to retire in ten to fifteen years. Capital preservation and safety was and remains his priority. His investment vehicle was corporate stocks and bonds.

Selling on the way down or at the bottom would be a lousy decision for my friend and I told him so. I reminded him that the stock market is volatile and that if he cannot tolerate that volatility he should invest elsewhere. Despite the recent slide of the stock market, his long strategy had not changed a bit. His long-term goal for retirement remained the same and he still had ten to fifteen years to go before he would make his first withdrawals. I told him to hold and wait for the market to return.

Got a good strategy? Stick with it.

*Homework assignment: Review your most recent strategic plan. Don't have one? Write one.*

# 4. Sell Aspirin, Not Vitamins

"One of the greatest pains to human nature is the pain of a new idea."

**Walter Bagehot (1826 – 1877) Businessman and Journalist**

Given the many options for new products and new ventures, why not create an offering that solves a problem or relieves a pain for your customer—a problem that the customer wants to fix right away.

When people have headaches they reach for aspirin or other pain relievers. The need is clear and immediate. The value proposition is pain relief (I.E. no more headaches). Price is not an issue. Just get me the pill!

Vitamins are different. The need to purchase generally needs to be created and marketed. The purchase can always be done later or not at all. Vitamins are nice to have but are not really needed.

When contemplating new ventures or new products, stick with solutions that address known problems or real issues. The time to market is much quicker, the selling is easier, and the cost of promotion is far less.

Thus, the likelihood of success is greater than when selling vitamins.

*Deep thoughts: What causes you the most pain?*

# 5. *Strategic Marketing in Plain English*

> "Do not go where the path may lead, go instead where there is no path and leave a trail."

**Ralph Waldo Emerson (1803 – 1882) Transcendentalist**

There are many books written about strategic marketing and the authors seem to delight in making it look really sophisticated and complex. In actuality, strategic marketing is really pretty simple.

Strategic Marketing is about analyzing opportunities while answering three basic questions:

- What might we do?
- What do we do best?
- What must we do?

So, why change your marketing strategy? Most of the time companies change because they have no choice. They are forced to change because of factors such as declining profitability, environmental changes, outright failure, political or legal changes, advances by the competition, socio-economic change, and population shifts.

The word strategy is generally used when people want to change things rather than maintaining the status quo. While there may be many potential marketing strategies, pragmatism generally rules the day and companies will focus on what must be done to make a profit today.

Generally speaking, there are only four types of marketing strategy:

1. Market Penetration Strategy: Sell existing products to existing markets. This presumes that there is still more opportunity available.
2. Market Development Strategy: Sell existing products to new markets. This presumes that other markets have similar wants or needs.

3.  Product Development Strategy: Create new products for existing markets. Your past success encourages you to boldly strike out for new opportunities.
4.  Diversification Strategy: Create new products for new markets.

Marketing strategy involves the selection of markets and the development of programs to reach those markets. The programs that help reach those markets are the venerable 4 Ps of Marketing: Price, Place, Product, and Promotion.

What factors drive a company to change or modify their strategy? The list is long, but here are a few of the drivers of strategic decisions:

- Make more profits; money is good and more would be better.
- Balance risk with reward; successful firms can become adventuresome.
- Environmental changes such as global warming.
- Fear, failure, or doubt; nothing wakes you up like lost money or decreasing market share.
- Competitor actions including price changes or new products.
- Greed and more greed.
- Technological changes such as the pervasiveness of the Internet.
- Political changes such as emission controls.
- Socio-economic changes such as women becoming the dominant consumer force.
- Population shifts such as our aging population.

For some firms, the status quo dictates their decision and they will choose to not modify their strategy; this may work for a while, but not for long. Thus, with marketing strategy you only have four options—choose wisely.

*Think about your new product plans: Which type of marketing strategy are you deploying? Why?*

# 6. *Crowds Can Be Dumb*

"If everyone is thinking alike, then somebody isn't thinking."

**George Patton (1885 – 1945) US General during WW II**

Please extend my apologies in advance to James Surowiecki, the author of "The Wisdom of Crowds." His best selling book suggests that groups make better decisions than any decision made by a single member of the group. To this notion I say "bull hockey" (note that I am expressing this opinion as an individual and I belong to no partisan group).

"Group-think" is flawed for a number of reasons. The chief flaw is the raw emotion of the crowd or "mob." Call it herd instinct, but the weak and intellectually inferior will follow the strong and manipulative. Think of the failure of the crowd to second guess the lunacy of Nazi Germany during World War II. Of course, fear was a factor for many who blindly followed the crazed leadership in Germany.

By examining current events in business, we can find the same blind subservience to the wisdom of the crowd. Consider that General Motors has been given market feedback for two decades that the US auto consumer prefers small, fuel efficient vehicles such as those offered by Honda, Toyota and Nissan. Despite this consumer demand, GM decided to build large SUVs and full sized trucks. When the price of oil jumped, GM had no choice but bleed red ink.

Entrepreneurs are often rejects from large corporate culture—they cannot follow the crowd, so they choose to do it on their own. Abandoned or fired by the crowd, entrepreneurs take it upon themselves to create better products or services. They may deserve the reputation of "control freaks" for their compulsion to do it their way but, at least, they won't be lead by the crowd, goose stepping off into oblivion.

Other examples of dumb crowds: Enron, the New York Knicks, AOL merges with Time Warner, IBM rebuffs startup Microsoft, Ford and the Edsel, Napoleon and the Louisiana Purchase, etc, etc.

Think differently. Reject the crowd.

*Come clean on this one: Name a recent decision where you just followed the crowd. Did it work out?*

# 7. Confronting New Problems and Opportunities

"In the middle of every difficulty lies opportunity."

**Albert Einstein (1879 – 1955) Nobel Prize Laureate for Physics**

When confronted with a new problem or a new opportunity, a common reaction is to do what you have done before or do nothing. While thinking before you leap is prudent, you still need to get started or else the problem may fester or the opportunity may pass you by.

For those moments of indecision, I offer the following simple tool to get you started. Ask yourself the following three questions:

- What do I know?
- What do I want to know?
- How will I find it out?

Yes, these are simple questions. But, by simply writing down the answers to these questions (or, at least what you know at the time) you can uncover the depth of the problem in front of you or the magnitude of the opportunity. I suggest using an outline approach or bullets for the answers to each of these questions. (By the way, thanks to Dr. Michael Ames for creating this simple but effective three question approach.)

With this simple statement and top-of-mind facts, you can begin your research or problem solving. A good next step might be to seek out the help of a colleague or mentor to discuss the same three questions. It is my experience that others will see things that you overlooked. Add these inputs to your list and soon you will have a statement of work on how to proceed.

The key is to get started.

*Put down this book: Write down your most significant problem that you are facing in your business today. Ask yourself the following three questions: What do I know? What do I Want to Know? How Will I find it out?*

# 8. *The Long Tail Wags the Dog*

"However beautiful the strategy, you should occasionally look at the results."

**Winston Churchill (1874 – 1965) British Statesman and Nobel Laureate for Literature**

Clever title, huh? Whoops, not so clever. I just "Googled" the title and got 462 exact hits (more on this later).

But, let me first admit the truth. I just now got around to reading Chris Anderson's best seller "The Long Tail." It truly is an eloquent work: scholarly, footnoted, indexed, and a bit long-winded. A New York Times best seller! Everyone has read this book or says that they have. If you have not yet read it I recommend that you do. And just about every speaker at a trade show or conference these days will throw in a couple of obligatory "long tails" to show that he or she is up-to-date.

What does the "long tail" really mean to you and me?

OK, here goes. The long tail describes a new economy that provides an economic incentive for firms to offer many personalized or niche products instead of mass market products. This new economy exists because of technological advancement in the supply chain including manufacturing and distribution, along with new efficiencies in marketing largely due to the Internet. Think of an expanded market where there is more opportunity for little products.

Although Wal-Mart is currently a monolith as a mass marketer because of superior supply chain management and store management practices, the "new" marketplace is fragmenting into a giant virtual swap meet (I.E. the Internet) with sellers who are targeting very specific niche markets. This change is being driven by pent up consumer wants and needs for specificity, which is a rejection of the mass market products offered by Wal-Mart today. This means that over time (and Anderson thinks it will be soon or maybe now) more and more of Wal-Mart's customers will seek the eminently available and preferable niche products offered by new long tail marketers.

The best example of a long tail marketer today is Amazon who sells tens of thousands of products one by one including my book. Anderson feels that Amazon is blazing the trail for large-scale long tail marketing. Implied in this theory is that Wal-Mart is the dinosaur of the future unless they join the long tail bandwagon. Further, this new economy is creating endless opportunities for small firms or entrepreneurs like you and me who understand niche market needs and wants.

But, one inherent weakness in Anderson's theory is the issue of profitability. Most long tail businesses struggle to break even, if not just survive. One might argue that those struggling niche businesses are delivering inferior goods or services, that some are poorly managed, and that some are poorly capitalized. This may be true in many cases or even in most cases.

Fundamentally, it is hard for a long tail provider, big or small, to make money since the economies of scale are not there to leverage. It is hard to make money when you sell "onesies-twosies" (a technical term for selling or making stuff one at time). Although Amazon sells a ton of stuff, they really have not returned profits like Wal-Mart or Exxon or Home Depot or Microsoft. All these firms are mass marketers with massive economies of scale. They do a few things very well.

The small niche (long tail) players are lucky to just stay in the game. Being unique is a tough business. Try Googling a great idea like my blog title sometime. All the great ideas seem to be taken already. And if you do create something special, try making money at it with a small business.

Long Tail? Woof. Woof.

*When you have some free time: Go visit Amazon.com. Think about a consumer product that you want and see if it is there.*

# 9. Product Positioning Strategies

"The best way to predict the future is to create it."

**Peter Drucker (1909 – 2005) Management Legend**

Positioning is what the customer believes about your product's value, features, and benefits; it is a comparison to the available alternatives offered by the competition. These beliefs tend to be based on customer experiences and evidence rather than awareness created by advertising or promotion.

Positioning is what the customer believes and not what the provider wants them to believe. Positioning can change due the countermeasures taken by the competition. Managing your product positioning requires that you know your customer and that you understand your competition. Generally, this is the job of market research and not just what the entrepreneur thinks is true.

Most of the successful small firms that I have studied have successfully positioned themselves in a market segment where they have little significant competition. This allows room for a decent profit margin and focuses the firm's efforts on pleasing the customer, while not worrying about what the competition will do next.

While this is true, some experts suggest that you should literally hide from competitors. The problem that I have with hiding from competitors is that you may also be hiding from customers. It is hard to create a market for a new product or service if no one knows about you. You need to make a lot of noise.

Marketers manage product positioning by focusing their marketing activities on a positioning strategy. Pricing, promotion, channels of distribution, and advertising all are geared to maximize the chosen positioning strategy.

While there are many product positioning strategies, here are eight basic strategies to be considered:

1. By attribute or benefit: This is the most frequently used positioning strategy. For a light beer, it might be that it tastes great or that it is less filling. For toothpaste, it might be the mint taste or tartar control.

2. By use or application: The users of Apple computers can design and use graphics more easily than with Windows or UNIX. Apple positions its computers based on how the computer will be used.

3. By user: Facebook is a social networking site used by college students and young adults. Facebook is too cool for MySpace and serves a hipper, more sophisticated cohort.

4. By product or service class: Margarine competes as an alternative to butter. Margarine is positioned as a lower cost and healthier alternative to butter, while butter provides better taste and wholesome ingredients.

5. By innovation: A common positioning strategy is based on an innovative product. Innovation is cool, but it requires a special customer who wants to be innovative, too. You can burn a lot of rubber trying to find that innovative customer. If you cannot find any competitors who are making money in your market segment, you may want to ask yourself if there is really a business there anyway.

6. By brand: BMW and Mercedes often compare themselves to each other segmenting the market to just the crème de la crème of the automobile market. Ford and Chevy need not apply.

7. By size: Another approach that is successful and can provide a possible exit down the road is to compete against big and dumb companies or institutions. Competing against smart and big competitors can be hard; when they have seemingly endless resources, it can be lethal. Big and dumb firms allow you the chance to steal their customers without them even knowing it. Since your firm is small by comparison, they probably don't even know that you exist. To do so requires specialization that your customer values. The best example of big and dumb that I can think of is the U.S. Postal Service. Two centuries of tradition and bureaucracy have made the U.S. Postal Service one of the most lethargic and disconnected institutions on earth. By providing a similar service without the lethargy and bureaucracy, FedEx grew into a marketing giant. FedEx delivers the next day with greater than 99% accuracy, which is something that the U.S. Postal Service still cannot figure out.

8. By price or quality: Tiffany and Costco both sell diamonds. Tiffany wants us to believe that their diamonds are of the highest

quality, while Costco tells us that diamonds are diamonds and that only a chump will pay Tiffany prices.

While there are many product positioning strategies, successful niche market players target the under-served or overlooked market.

*Think back: What product or service did you need recently but could not find?*

# 10. First, Best, or Different

"Not all those who wander are lost."

**J. R. R. Tolkien (1892 – 1973) Writer**

The entrepreneur, who targets a customer segment that has been underserved or overlooked, can earn extraordinary rewards. Niche marketing requires that you focus on customers who cannot get what they want or need from their existing providers. For various reasons, mainstream firms will often innocently overlook or deliberately pass over customers with special needs; instead, they will choose to market to the larger, more homogeneous customer groups. These underserved or overlooked segments can be very fertile ground for the entrepreneur to exploit, since they need a provider who truly understands their requirements.

By focusing on these customer segments the entrepreneur can differentiate their offerings from that of the competition while creating loyal customers which will be a source of referrals. Additionally, the entrepreneur may be rewarded with higher margins and longer product life cycles. Every entrepreneur needs to know that to be successful in niche marketing you need to be first, best, or different.

Being first can be enough in some markets to capture a great reward. A business can differentiate itself by being the first to solve the customers' needs; these customers and their unique needs may have been passed over by other firms. Unfortunately, it is hard to defend that position long-term, presuming the market is big enough for more than one competitor. Sometimes being first creates a loud "buzz," a public relations euphoria associated with the new solution. You may have witnessed this buzz in the software industry when innovative products hit the market. The product is the "new thing" and everybody seems to want it, at least until something faster or better comes along. When a second player enters the market with a better product, and this is often the case, the buzz for the first product goes silent, making the first firm a "one-hit wonder."

Many times the "second-to-market" or "later-to-market" firms make the bigger profits. For example, Apple's iPod followed Rio and Eiger Labs after the market was created. Both had fully functioning MP3 players long before the iPod hit the scene. Ever heard of them? Amazon.com founder

Jeff Bezos recently warned his workers "being first isn't necessarily enough." For the entrepreneur in a smaller market, the impact of the second-to-market players may be less of an issue, but the same math still applies. Being first is expensive and difficult. Thus, being first is seldom sustainable in the long-term.

Being the best may be the optimum state for the entrepreneur. This implies that the solution provides exactly what the customers need today; most often this fit is derived from an intimate understanding of the customers' wants and needs while offering a perfect or best solution. The customers value the solution above all others and may tolerate paying a higher price. Because of their loyalty, they may even be a source of referrals for your firm which helps create market-share dominance. The challenge in this case is how to stay on top. If the market is big enough, other firms will eventually want a piece of this market. If the competitors have sufficient capital and the barriers to entry are low, the first entrepreneur may struggle to defend its best position. Being best is easier when the market niche is very small and your firm is the only significant player. This positioning may be the "Nirvana" of niche marketing but I don't know of many of them.

This leaves being different as the remaining option for most entrepreneurs. In this environment, the solution offered is unique enough to be a better choice for the customers; an example of this might be the Ferrari. The Ferrari, with its unique styling and high-end performance, is considered different to the point of being exotic and is highly valued by a special segment of automobile buyers. Ferrari has a loyal following, has few real competitors, and commands a very special price for the car's unique attributes.

Alternatively, things can be done differently. My favorite example of doing the same thing differently is Starbucks, where a pedestrian product like a cup of coffee is delivered, packaged, and sold as a lifestyle item. In return, Starbucks commands a premium price and is rewarded with incredible brand equity. We can argue about their product quality but, essentially, they are doing things differently rather than offering something different. Being different or doing things differently tends to be the domain of many successful entrepreneurs.

To be successful, an entrepreneur has to be first to market, has to be the absolute best, or has to be demonstratively different from the competition. While it may be "possible" to be all three (first, best, and different), the challenge for the business is to be sustainable over the long-term. Can you name any businesses that are first, best, and different and have stood the test of time? It is truly a short list and subject to great debate.

Coca-Cola comes to mind as a firm that might be first, best, and different but some would argue about the firm being first, best, or different. Coca-Cola was actually beat to market by a "coca-wine" which was initially sold as a headache medicine but Coke was the first mass-marketed soft drink. Pepsi drinkers might argue that Coke is not best by citing the "Pepsi Challenge," which was a blind taste test that showed that cola drinkers had a preference for Pepsi over Coke. Is Coke different? People have voted yes with their dollars with Coca-Cola topping $43 billion in 2005 revenues; remember, "Coke is It." There is no doubt that Coca-Cola has been a sustainable brand; it was founded in 1886 and has been a cultural phenomena. It must be said that Coca-Cola is not exactly a niche player, but it illustrates the point that it is hard to be all three: first, best, and different.

Thus, the choices that remain for the successful entrepreneur tend to favor the creation of a unique offering for a special customer that has not been served well or at all by the other providers; this is the essence of niche marketing. As for which niche market to choose, that is up to you.

*One more comment: Underserved or overlooked customer groups make for great niche markets but make sure that the market segment is big enough to make a profit. If there are truly no competitors serving this segment it may mean that the opportunity is too small. For more on this subject see my first book, "First, Best, or Different."*

# 11. You Are Going to End Up Somewhere…

"The essence of strategy is choosing what not to do."

**Michael Porter (1947 – present) Management Professor**

You are going to end up somewhere, so why not end up where you want to be? Organizations (and people) all have a purpose or a reason for being. Many call it a mission. That mission helps the firm to make good decisions that are consistent with its purpose. With a well written "mission statement" to guide you the little decisions for your firm become easier and you have a better chance of getting to your desired destination.

A mission statement is a proclamation about why the firm exists and what really matters. It should speak about the firm's values and describe what the business hopes to achieve while describing the nature of the business. A mission statement can provide a compass during times of uncertainty or strife by reminding the employees at the firm about what really matters.

The mission statement should be a few sentences up to a brief paragraph that is simple, clear, and jargon free. No Shakespeare needed here. Thirty words or less should do the trick. It should be memorable and motivating to the firm's employees. If properly written, the mission statement can be displayed proudly on the company website, brochures, and business cards.

Your mission statement should include some or most of these elements:

- Who is your customer?
- What business are you in?
- What are your products or services?
- What is your geographic domain?
- What is your commitment to ownership?
- How is your firm different from the competition?
- What are the opportunities available for the firm?
- What is your company philosophy?

- What are the firm's core beliefs and values?
- What is the essence of your brand?
- What do things look like when things go well?

A vision statement, while similar to a mission statement, is more of a proclamation of what the firm should be; it is an image of the desired future, almost Utopian in its grandeur. Typically, a vision statement is no more than a short sentence. Some say that a vision statement is a description of an ideal and, thus, it will never be achieved. Most vision statements are imaginative and hope to inspire others.

So, what is your purpose?

*A sobering exercise: You have just died and you have been given a chance to write and present your own eulogy. Describe to your family and friends what your life was all about and what truly mattered. What would you say was your purpose while on earth?*

# 12. Business Concept

"Think left and think right and think low and think high.
Oh, the thinks you can think up if only you try!"

**Dr. Seuss (1904 – 1991) Writer and Cartoonist**

A "business concept" is the first step in the process of starting a new venture. It typically describes a vision of what might be. It generally precedes the business plan and it begs feedback on the merit of the idea.

A business concept speaks about the customer, the product or service, the value proposition, and the distribution channel:

- Who is your customer?
- What is the product or service you are offering?
- What is the value proposition? The value proposition is the benefit that is being provided to the customer. In other words, why will the customer buy from you—what's in it for them?
- How will the benefit be delivered to the customer? That's how you reach the customer and deliver the benefit. Entrepreneurs often confuse benefits with features but the decision to buy is usually based on the benefits provided by the service or product.
- How do they want to buy this offering?
- When will they want to buy it?
- Where will they want to buy it?

The business concept defines strategies for successfully implementing the product in the marketplace. This includes pricing, revenue, and distribution models. A business concept is a way to define an opportunity so that it can be tested through a process known as feasibility analysis.

A feasibility analysis is a process whereby you can test your business concept and arrive at the conditions under which you are willing to go forward with this business. No matter what type of business you start or intend to start you will go through the same feasibility process. This is also called a concept test. The purpose of this step is to go out and start selling your product or service.

Money is important but comes later. For now you need to find out whether you have a business that has customers.

Next you need to determine what makes your company unique or different. Customers buy because of your offering's differences not because it is the same as others. These unique competencies become the core of your competitive advantage.

A feasibility test acts as a reality check for your idea. A feasibility test weighs the validity of your business concept by examining the following factors:

- The product your firm will offer.
- The customer you will target.
- Your value proposition.
- How you will get the product to its intended users.

With your idea tested, the next step is to begin the business planning process.

*Idea: What new business would you start if money was no object? What is appealing to you about it? Why aren't you doing it?*

# 13. Goal Setting

"It is better to light one small candle than to curse the darkness."

**Confucius (551 BC – 479 BC) Chinese Philosopher**

Study after study shows that people who set goals accomplish more, achieve greater success, and accumulate greater wealth than people who don't.

Let's examine sales goals. Setting your sales goals for next year should begin with a review of how you did in the last year. Did you achieve your last year sales goal? If so, what went well? Ask yourself what sales techniques, marketing campaigns, or promotional strategies worked best and which might you use again next year?

If you missed your sales goal last year ask yourself why? What didn't work? What should you do differently or better next year? Were there any major uncontrollable forces that impeded your ability to hit your goal such as the economy, government regulation, or the weather? Or, was the goal unrealistic?

So much for being analytical—it is now time to move forward.

Good goals have a few basic components:

- They must be specific and definite such as "I will sell $10,000,000.00."
- They must be measurable such as "I will measure my success in billings."
- Good goals are attainable and realistic, not just wishful thinking. Challenging yourself to improve is terrific but asking yourself to do the impossible is silly.
- Finally, good goals are bound by a specific time frame; for example, you could use the period that begins on 1/01/09 and ends on 12/31/09?

These goals must be put in writing and posted where you can see them such as on your office bulletin board or on your PDA. Tell your friends and colleagues about your goal and seek their assistance and feedback. Who knows? Maybe they can help you.

*You should try this: I suggest a monthly review of your progress on your goals as a minimum; this will keep the goals alive and allow you to take corrective action if you falter.*

# 14. New Venture Sales Forecasting

"The weather forecast for tonight: dark."

**George Carlin (1937 – 2008) Comedian**

Forecasting sales requires in-depth research along with educated guess work. There is no substitute for knowing your customers and why they will buy your offering. Buyers will choose your product over the competition because it is different or better. They buy for their own reasons and not yours.

Presuming your offering is competitive and is desired by the target market, here are the basic steps in developing a sales forecast:

- Develop a profile of your target market: Who are your customers and why do they need your offering?
- Determine the trends in your industry: What is unique about the purchasing cycle in your space? Are there any anticipated future trends such as changes in government regulations, economic changes, or environmental changes?
- Define the size or boundaries of your market: This market sizing could be by geography such as North America, by vertical such as healthcare, or by technology such as Apple users.
- Identify your competitors: Which competitor supplies your customer today? What is the sales volume? What is the channel of distribution?
- Estimate an average sales price for your offering: This price should be conservative and may increase or decrease in years two or three. Note that discounting may be needed in year one.
- Calculate monthly sales: Prepare sales estimates by month. Be sure to assess how seasonality may impact your sales cycle; this includes holidays, summer versus winter, or specific industry buying trends.
- Compare your annual forecast to other similar companies: Consider using Risk Management Association (RMA) data to determine if your forecast is reasonable? If it varies from the industry norm how will you explain this variance to investors or bankers?
- Be prepared to change and modify this forecast: As you build your financial plan, it is normal for your forecast to change. Stay flexible.

New venture Sales forecasting is a best guess, but if you know your customer it is an educated guess and you are the best one to do it.

*Google this: Risk Management Association (aka RMA). Check out how your company financials compare to similar companies.*

# 15. Business Plan Blunders

"The only true wisdom is in knowing you know nothing."

**Socrates (469 BC – 399 BC) Classical Greek Philosopher**

Business plans are like a compass—they point the way for the company and explain the business to the investor. Yet, business plans can tell the wrong story and may even kill the deal with the investor.

Here are some examples of business plan blunders to avoid:

- Lousy Writing: Nothing kills a plan more quickly than poor grammar, incorrect punctuation, and spelling errors.
- Lack of Value Proposition: Inability to define and defend why your customers need your product or service is a major red flag.
- No Feasibility Testing: No matter how amazing your business concept may seem to be if you don't have customers it will be a tough sell to investors.
- Poorly Defined Target Market: A product that fits everyone is a prescription for disaster. Don't go there. Be very specific in your definition of your customer.
- Incomplete Plan: Missing key elements or an incomplete plan tells the reader that the plan is half baked or not well thought out.
- Too Technical: An obsession with technical details often is done at the expense of the business model. The investor wants to know how the business will make money.
- Blue Sky Sales Projections: Although it is true that plans should be optimistic, a hockey stick growth curve needs to be backed up with strong assumptions and facts.
- Risk Unaddressed: Not addressing risk in the plan is a major flaw—bankers and investors want to know what the downside risk is in the plan.
- Ignoring the Competitive Environment: Ignoring or dismissing the competitive environment is a common blunder by business plan writers. Who is the competition and what do they do right and wrong?
- Non-disclosure Agreement Required: Don't obsess about confidentiality since most investors won't sign a Non-disclosure Agreement anyway. You need to tell your story to as many

people as possible. Privacy is a modest concern at best if you want to get funded.

- First to Market Claims: There are not many rewards for being first in a market; in fact, the opposite is generally true. Being first is very expensive and investors know this.
- Business-Speak: Say what you mean and leave the big words for the lawyers. Be deliberate and concise. Avoid business clichés such as "think outside of the box."
- Plan Too Long: The one inch thick business plan does not get read. Keep it below 50 pages.
- Business Plan Services: Don't even consider the use of cheap business plan services which outsource to India or other exotic places. This is very tacky.
- Business Plan Pre-made Templates: These templates are the pre-made plans you edit to fit your business. They are pure garbage. This is the domain of the lazy entrepreneur.
- Business Plan Software: I am not sure why but most business plan software programs are bug-ridden. Be sure to double check the financials.
- Hidden Profits: Investors want to know how the business will make money and what the return on investment will be. Address it in your plan.
- Unclear Valuation and Exit Strategy: What is the cost of ownership and how will the investor get their money out? This must be spelled out clearly or there is no deal.

If you avoid these pitfalls, your plan will be better than 95% of the others out there.

*Late night reading: Consider buying the book "Bankable Business Plans" by Edward Rogoff. It can help you write a better business plan.*

# 16. Sometimes Plans Change

"We are not retreating - we are advancing in another direction."

**Douglas MacArthur (1880 – 1964) US General**

A good business plan makes a great compass to guide a firm's daily decisions but you must be flexible about reviewing the goals and initiatives associated with them. Just because you wrote, sold, and implemented the plan doesn't make it "right" or everlasting. In fact, most plans are short-lived.

Writing a business plan is easy while implementation is the most challenging part in the strategic planning process. The most common time-frame for a strategic plan is one to five years. The first key task is to effectively communicate and get input from your employees as much as possible in the planning process. Monitoring it and taking corrective action is another matter entirely.

Changing markets will mean changing plans. This is when most companies under react and hold to the plan (since the plan is in writing and everybody is sold on the tactics and goals). This is particularly true for sales goals. With forecasted revenue driving staffing and product decisions sales goals become "gospel" instead of an estimate.

When the sales force comes back with customer feedback that the business is "soft," invariably the sales representatives are told to get back out there and sell harder. Seldom are the representatives listened to nor are their goals changed. How absurd is that? The sales force which has the best pulse of the customer and the market are told to go back and read the plan. My bet is the representatives will go back and update their resumes instead.

Good plans need to be reviewed and changed quarterly. While this might be stressful to the CFO, this is reality. Companies need to monitor key metrics for their industry and at the firm. Internal metrics could include book to bill ratios, customer cancellations, sample requests, email click through rates, etc. External metrics could include interest rates, housing starts, new product announcements at the competition, etc.

When the market changes up or down, plans need to be modified. A good plan is a fluid, living document while a bad plan is a stake in the ground that is static.

*Think about this: When was the last time you changed your plans?*

# 17. A Business Plan Is Like a Compass

"A good plan today is better than a perfect plan tomorrow."

**George S. Patton (1885 – 1945) US General during WW II**

Show me a startup without a business plan and I will declare it a "rudderless" ship. For without a business plan to guide you, a business will just float along chasing one opportunity after the next, while ending up nowhere special.

Business plans are not hard to write, but they do challenge you to think things out ahead of time, while asking you to address the hard questions about who you are and what you really want to do.

The basic elements include:

The Title Page: This includes all the basics such as name of the business, logo, your contact info (such as your address, phone, and website), and the date that the plan was prepared. Be sure not to clutter this page up with too many details.

The Executive Summary: This is the single most important part of the plan; virtually all readers (who actually read the plan) read this section. I recommend writing this section at the very end. Wordsmith it to death since it is your principle sales document.

Outline or Table of contents: You know what to do here.

The Marketing Plan: If you piqued the reader's interest with the executive summary, then this section is typically the next section that he or she will read. If it says one thing, it needs to tell a story about your strategic competitive advantage or how you are doing things differently than your competition. This is a statement about how your business does things differently or how it does different things. If you can't position your business as unique, you might as well break camp and head home.

People and Organization: This section says who you are and why you are qualified. It also reveals who is needed to get the job done. It should say who is on board today and give a vision of what the organization might look like in the future.

Financial: You may think that this section is boring and nobody reads it. Wrong! The person who might fund you will most definitely read this section. Often this is the weakest section in most plans. This is caused by creating the numbers using a "top-down" methodology. A much better practice is to start at the bottom with your product, create a time line for product development and launch, figure how many people are needed to manage and sell the products, and then create your forecast. This approach creates a more realistic plan which will be believed by your banker or investors.

Everything Else: All the other stuff (references, technical specs, mockups, etc.) goes in the appendix and is used only when it is needed and should be bound separately. Present this second volume only when asked.

*Tip: Most business plans should be no more than 50 single spaced pages. In fact, there is a trend for shorter and shorter plans with 25-30 pages as the new maximum page count. Long plans don't get read.*

# 18. The Executive Summary Sells the Business Plan

"Somewhere there is a map of how it can be done."

**Ben Stein (1944 – present) Actor and Pundit**

The "executive summary" is the first part of the business plan that gets read and may be the only part of the plan that actually gets read. Its job is to get the plan funded whether by an investor or by a banker. Perfecting this one to two page document is ultra-critical to the entrepreneur. Some say that if you cannot write your business plan in two pages or less it is an indication to the reader that you are indecisive and can't set priorities.

While there is no one formula for writing an executive summary, all executive summaries should address the following:

- What is the purpose of this business? What is the mission?
- How is this business different from others?
- Does this business have a sustainable competitive advantage? If so, what is it?
- Describe your offering?
- What is your target market?
- Why will this target market want your offering?
- How will you market to your customers?
- How will you organize your workforce?
- What will you require to get started in cash, people, and resources?
- What is the competitive environment like?
- What are the financial projections for your firm?
- Why should someone invest in your firm?
- Why are the founders a good fit for this business?

If you can answer these questions in your executive summary with clarity then the heavy lifting of the business plan is already done.

*I am not kidding: Venture capitalists have been known to separate business plans into "read later" and "trash" piles based on nothing more than reading the executive summary.*

# 19. *Writing Business Plans That Sell*

"My aim is to put down on paper
what I see and what I feel in the best and simplest way."

**Ernest Hemingway (1899 – 1961) American Writer**

Business plans have three main purposes: to guide the operation, to secure loans from the bank, and to secure new investments. Regardless of the application or use, the plan must sell the reader on why this business concept works.

The most basic use of the plan is for internal use at the company. In this case, business plans are best written in a collaborative fashion by the team rather than by one individual or visionary. By writing in a collaborative approach, the plan receives the benefit of the diversity of the authors while securing the buyoff of the team itself. By writing the plan, the individual authors take ownership in the vision of the firm and take responsibility for its implementation. Plans should be reviewed quarterly because plans will change and are subject to outside influences that are hard to forecast or even anticipate.

A business plan that is part of a loan package has a different mission. The reader, which in this case is the banker, wants to know if the business creates sufficient "cash flow" to cover the debt and basic expenses of the operation. Beyond that, the banker wants to know if the business will be self-sustaining. For the lender to offer funding, the bank needs to feel comfortable that the business will survive and be financially viable.

The investor has different motivations. Investors want to own the company and be a part of a successful enterprise. Admittedly, that ownership may not be long-term since the investor ultimately wants to exit with a strong return on investment (ROI). Thus, the investor needs a plan that describes a firm that has a sustainable competitive advantage over the competition. The investor is looking for a solid management team, a winning marketing strategy, and an aggressive growth path.

Regardless of the type of plan being written, the plan should be written in a business voice with a deliberate style. The plan's messaging should be positive but reasonable; blue sky plans with unrealistic expectations will be tossed aside.

You should always write in the third person. Avoid the use of "I" or "we"; instead refer to the firm or the company. Support key points with expert opinion or outside sources. Photos can help communicate products and graphics help the reader understand key concepts. With that said, avoid overly artistic or overly clever graphics and images which make the plan look comical or simple.

Pay special attention to timelines and milestones. Far too many business plans preach vision and goals but lack the nuts and bolts of how things will get done. Keep exhibits to a half a page. If more detail is needed, put it in the appendix. The appendices are found in a second volume which should be made available upon request.

Write your business plan for your reader. Help them understand your plan so that they can help you achieve your objectives.

*Read this: Lynn Gaertner-Johnston, founder of Syntax Training, has a blog dedicated to business writing at http://www.businesswritingblog. com/. Check it out.*

# 20. Solve Your Customer's Problems (Not Yours)

"We try very genuinely to design products that solve problems.
They are not about self-expression. What we are trying to do is design
something that when you see it you really wonder if it's been designed at
all because it seems so obvious and so inevitable and so simple."

**Jonathan Ive (1967 – present) Apple,
at the 2006 Radical Craft Conference**

Designing new and innovative products is very hard to do. All too often egos, expectations, and compromises get in the way when you design new things; sometimes the customer gets a backseat in this process. This can be true for a large firm such as Apple or even in a startup.

New product design is first and foremost about solving your customer's problems. For the niche player, this requires an intimate understanding about the target market and the problem itself. Intensive market research and study is mandatory. Often called concept testing, this research verifies the product definition and fit of the solution with the prospective customer.

Good product design is not about using idle labor, spare parts, or excess materials. These unused resources can be a great impetus to find a new customer problem, but the orientation is all wrong.

Worse may be the role of history in product development. In this case, the manufacturer designs new widgets because the firm has always made widgets. But, as the financial guys say, "past performance is not a good indicator of future success."

Finally, ego can get in the way when the leadership team desires an image turnaround. Often new product design is pushed to create a "disruptive technology," whether or not the market wants it or not.

The moral is simple: fix customer problems, not your own.

*You might consider: Invite your customers to suggest new product ideas. They might know something that you do not.*

# 21. Which Niche?

"Once you make a decision, the universe conspires to make it happen."

**Ralph Waldo Emerson (1803 – 1882) American Philosopher**

Having thoroughly researched the topic of niche marketing and having written a book on the subject, I can tell you with some authority that there is no algorithm for finding a niche business that is perfect for you. Making that choice is art rather than science.

My research did uncover some commonalities among the successful niche businesses and the entrepreneurs themselves. While I did not uncover a secret formula for success, here are a few of my findings:

- Many successful niche businesses started accidentally. Sometimes a hobby grew into something bigger. Other times a small idea took on a life of its own.
- Most niche businesses started slowly with a lot of trial and error. The entrepreneur kept improving the offering until he or she got it right.
- Most of the entrepreneurs had a special connection to the market. They were intimate with the customers and extremely knowledgeable about their wants and needs.
- Making money was not the key determinant in choosing the business. In fact, it was initially pretty low on the list of priorities. The rewards came later.
- The competition was never an issue since the competition typically did not serve the target market or did not serve it well. Most successful niche businesses have little real competition.
- Most successful entrepreneurs had personal talents and interests that nicely aligned with the niche business. They liked what they did.
- During the early stages of the business, they somehow found enough capital to survive. Most were self-funded.
- Contrary to popular opinion, most entrepreneurs were conservative and avoided unnecessary risks. They were frugal and made very calculated decisions.
- Many of the entrepreneurs were sons and daughters of entrepreneurs. It seems to run in families.

- The niche market served was big enough for the niche business to make a good living, but was not big enough to draw the attention of the bigger firms.

*Food for thought: Ask a friend who owns a successful business how they got into the business. You might be surprised at their answer.*

# 22. Innovation in Niche Markets

"It's really hard to design products by focus groups. A lot of times, people don't know what they want until you show it to them."

**Steve Jobs (1955 – present) Apple CEO in Business Week, May 25, 1998**

Innovation is the mainstay of niche marketing; yet your customer may not be able tell you what products they will need in the future. And this makes sense if you think about it. Invariably, your customers are focused on the here and now. Future needs make great cocktail conversations, but invariably they get put on the backburner. Making payroll and shipping product are just higher priorities.

This is the dilemma of market research and product development. As Steve Jobs infers, customers don't always know what new products that they will need in two years. Most market research methods, such as focus groups, rely heavily on customers' opinions about future products. With many industries having product development cycles that require the providers to think two and three years ahead, the challenge becomes even more complex.

So how do you develop future products? According to "Creating a Killer Product" by Clayton M. Christensen and Michael E. Raynor, "To create products that customers want to buy—ones that become so successful they "disrupt" the market? It's not easy. Three in five new-product-development efforts are scuttled before they ever reach the market. Of the ones that do see the light of day, 40% never become profitable and simply disappear."

So, on top of everything else, it is easy for new products to fail. The authors additionally said, "Managers need to segment their markets to mirror the way their customers experience life–and not base decisions on irrelevant data that focus on customer attributes. Managers need to realize that customers, in effect, 'hire' products to do specific 'jobs.' That's one reason why retail formats like Home Depot and Lowe's have become so successful: Their stores are literally organized around jobs to be done."

The lesson is to not build products that are cool or easy to make; instead, you need to look for jobs that need to get done tomorrow.

*Keep your eyes open: What jobs are getting done?*

# 23. Customer Choices

"The strongest principle of growth lies in human choice."

**George Eliot (a.k.a. Mary Anne Evans) (1819 – 1880) English Writer**

The choice is yours.

Choice is the process of deciding between new options. Many people think that having choices are a positive thing since they give you a feeling of control. Yet, choices can be confusing or frightening. This can be particularly true when choosing between many options.

If you have too many choices it can be daunting. What if you choose the wrong the option? Will you regret not taking one of the other options? Too many options can confuse or even paralyze a decision maker. Consumer products makers know this and try to eliminate buyer confusion by bundling features into a product. Japanese auto makers sell cars with many standard features such as leather interior or air conditioning. When your choices are limited or you have to choose between unattractive options, you may feel frightened or angry. Despite having a choice, you may not like either which makes you feel out of control. An employee working for a failing firm might have to choose between a demotion and a severance package—neither option may sound good.

The question becomes how do you make the choice? One way to choose is to evaluate the merits or attributes of the options. Most options have positive and negative attributes. This analytical approach is appropriate for the customer with time and resources. A purchasing manager will create a spreadsheet that compares product features and pricing from vendors participating in a bid.

Some buyers are intuitive and make the decision based on past experience and by feel. When you are in a restaurant and need to choose between fish or fowl, there is little time to analyze the options. Since you got sick on the fish last time, tonight it will be the chicken. The decision is made quickly.

For the marketer, the challenge is to provide as much choice as the buyer needs without confusing them or making them feel trapped. The choice is up to you.

*Question: How many choices are too many for your customer?*

# 24. Dumpster Diving for Niche Market Products

"Not knowing when the dawn will come, I open every door."

**Emily Dickinson (1830 – 1886) American poet**

Dumpster diving for niche market products is my way of describing the process of creating new niche market products. I read once that for every 3,000 new product ideas you get one successful product. Obviously, this was a six figure study funded by the federal government for some university research lab, but I digress.

Three thousand new product ideas is a very believable number if you think of the giant mass marketers, which have precise criterion for fitting into their existing product families.

New product ideas can be tossed into the dumpster for a variety of reasons:

- Is the new product idea compatible with the company strategy?
- Is the new product idea compatible with the existing market or consumption behavior?
- Does the product offer an advantage over existing products?
- Is the product simple for the buyer and user to understand?
- Does it stand up to the test of market research?
- Is their a need for the product?
- Is the market big enough to make a profit?

At a mass market firm, a lot of good ideas get dumped in the dumpster; some deserve to be thrown away while others just did not fit the company strategy or did not serve a big enough market for the company to support it. Additionally, Netscape says it takes 32 months to gestate a new product, which may not necessarily be successful. Behind this product launch are all the failed product ideas.

This is where the niche marketer comes into play. What does not fit the mass marketer may nicely fit into the entrepreneur's domain. The optimum situation for the entrepreneur is an overlooked or underserved market segment that has a customer base big enough for the smaller firm to make a profit but small enough that the mass marketer will pass on it.

This allows the entrepreneur to focus on the customers' wants and needs, rather than always worrying about the competition. Successful niche marketers become experts or "knowledge brokers" about their customers' problems and issues; the customers learn to depend on them for answers and advice.

The best niche products are not cool or easy to make; they are solutions to real problems that people will have tomorrow. Often mass marketers will fixate on doing what they know best or on doing what is easy to build or to design. They play it safe by leveraging existing resources. A better approach is to think in terms of work processes for your customer; if you can, project into the future and try to anticipate problems or jobs that will need to be done. Help your customer solve these problems or get the job done.

It could be that cool new ideas may have been tossed in the dumpster by the big guys. You know the expression: one man's trash is another man's treasure.

*Crazy Idea: Read "The Wild Idea Club" written by Lee Silber, Andrew Chapman, and Linda Krall.*

# 25. Failure Enables New Products

"Only those who dare to fail greatly can ever achieve greatly."

**Robert F. Kennedy (1925 – 1968) Statesman**

Many "wannabe" entrepreneurs struggle with the idea of coming up with the perfect product or solution. This obsession with being the best keeps them from launching the product. Instead, they stay sequestered in the pre-launch stage trying to perfect the concept by tweaking the product feature set.

Contrast this behavior to successful entrepreneurs who choose to launch their products and fail openly and often in front of God and country. For example, Thomas Edison pushed the envelope when it came to failure. He literally created thousands of filaments for his light bulb before he found one that had a sustainable life. He was undaunted by his repeated failures. He did not fear failure—he relished it since he knew that each time he failed he was one step closer to success.

This fearlessness is a key component of innovation. You can also argue that these reckless innovators are just plain uninformed about the prospect of failure or they don't really care what people think. It is my contention that this "just do it" mindset works given the alternative of doing nothing.

My advice to entrepreneurs is to welcome failure by launching your products early. Failure is a catalyst for success.

*Make a list of your failures: Congratulate yourself for trying.*

# 26. *Creating Innovative Products*

"You can't sit around and wait for inspiration.
You have to go after it with a club."

**Jack London (1876 – 1916) American Author**

Creating innovative products can come via sheer serendipity, but most of the time they are the result of hard work and taking deliberate steps in an innovation process.

Here are the basics steps for inventing new products:

- Awareness: A problem, idea, or random thought jumps up and bites you and it makes you think to yourself, "There has got to be a better way" or "Hey, this is a great idea."
- Incubation: The light is now on and you think about the issue—you might even obsess over it. You may lie in bed at night thinking of it.
- Visualization: Solutions and options start to emerge but they lack structure or form. You may start to write things down.
- Illumination: Your ideas are starting to take shape and you are able to articulate them to others. It takes some bravery to do this since many people greet new ideas with skepticism.
- Verification: You start to detail the solution or solutions into concrete prototypes.
- Alpha Offering: You create a working prototype to prove to yourself and your colleagues that it can be done. It is not ready for customer review since it may be full of bugs and is untested.
- Beta Offering: Your solution is ready for some real world testing so you let a few special customers try it out. You can expect some harsh feedback and criticism at this stage.
- Redesign: The feedback was valuable no matter how much it hurt to hear it. Many times this feedback sends you back to the drawing board, but it is worth it. Sometimes, this kills the idea off.
- Pre-release: A new and improved offering goes back for additional testing by the customer. Your fingers are crossed but often you get even more feedback.
- Release: Your offering is now debugged and is ready for customer usage. Now the big question is: "Will it be accepted? Will it sell?"

Although some innovative solutions come from a moment of inspiration, I have found that most great products come from hours of perspiration.

*Sweaty thoughts: Go back to your list of failures and try again.*

# 27. Dream Big and Think Small

"Nothing happens unless first we dream."

**Carl Sandburg (1878 – 1967) American writer**

Dream big thoughts but it is better to build businesses upon little ideas. The most common strategic marketing mistake is to think too big. The answer is think small, think niche.

By focusing on a niche, you become an expert at providing your product or service. Because you understand the needs of this niche, your marketing message resonates with truth and your target market will buy from you. Your customer is happy because of your expertise and product quality. Your happy customers gladly refer you to other prospective customers who have the same need. This referral process lowers the cost of sales since you have to do less prospecting and qualification.

Conversely, the more general your solution and the less specific your customer, the more likely you are to fail. The more you diversify your efforts, the less centered you become. An overly broad charter keeps you from gaining customer knowledge and from gaining operational efficiencies. Your marketing message is weakened by your lack of focus. You get fewer references. Selling is harder and keeping your customers is more difficult. Your customers are not as happy either.

Niche marketing makes finding the customer easier. You can cull out the customers that don't fit with your plan since not everyone gets the honor of being your customer. Successful niche firms say "no" frequently and won't waste their time on customers that do not fit their niche. The wisdom in knowing what business to avoid is critical to a niche play.

It is OK to dream big, but you need to think small.

*Dreaming: Keep a notepad or a digital recorder on your nightstand to capture those late night creative ideas.*

# 28. Niche Marketing Versus Mass Marketing

"Small is the new big."

**Seth Godin (1960 – present) Marketing Expert**

What's the difference between niche marketing and mass marketing? I get asked this question a lot. The answer is actually fairly simple.

Niche marketing is about serving a unique market segment that is underserved or overlooked by the other providers. The customers in this market segment have special needs that are not being addressed by current providers. They are ignored because the other providers don't know about the segment's unique needs or the providers just don't care. Often the market segment is too small for a bigger provider to make any money.

An example of a niche market would be the "exotic" automobile segment served by the automaker Ferrari; they offer a highly specialized product for a very few, unique customers. Competition and price is not an issue for Ferrari, since their focus is on the users' very unique "needs." Ferrari perennially sells everything it can manufactures with waiting lists of six to twelve months considered normal.

Mass marketing focuses on serving as much of the market as possible. As Mr. Spock of Star Trek fame says, "It is logical. The needs of the many outweigh the needs of the few or the one." Generally, mass marketing involves providing the same solution to many customers with little personalization. The emphasis is on volume, cost, and efficiency. This is the domain of large providers such as consumer product firms.

A good example of a mass marketed product is a Snickers candy bar, which sells in the millions of units and is not personalized for its users. The parent, Mars Incorporated, must worry about price, channels of distribution, the cost of sugar, and the competition at all times. Maintaining market share is their mantra. The customer can get lost in all this worrying about the competition.

*Ask yourself: What niche marketer do you admire? Why?*

# 29. Square Watermelons and Glass Floor Mats

"If you build a better mousetrap, you will catch better mice."

**George Gobel (1919 – 1991) Comedian and Actor**

Yes, there are still things to be invented. How about square watermelons and glass floor mats?

Japanese urban dwellers live in notoriously small houses and apartments which in turn have tiny refrigerators. Watermelons are considered a delicacy in large part because of their size and storage issues. Because of this storage issue, watermelon is a favorite at Japanese restaurants, but they are seldom served on the kitchen table.

A farmer from Zentsuji in the Kagawa prefecture has solved the problem by growing the round fruit while still on the vine in a square "Plexiglas" box. When full grown, the square melon is removed from the box and harvested. Note that all the melons are the same uniform size.

These easily stored watermelons are sold in upscale markets for three times the price of conventional round melons. By North American standards, the watermelons are small (10 inches square). But for many, the price premium is worth it since otherwise they probably would not buy the larger round variety.

What I love about this story is the new twist on an old idea. Here is another new look at an old idea.

I have a friend named Ken James who has a startup company which makes chair mats out of tempered glass. Similar to the round watermelons, conventional chair mats are pervasive but problematic for many people. The traditional plastic chair mat ages quickly, develops ruts, and becomes difficult for the chair to move. Because of this wear and tear they need to be replaced every few years. Frankly, as a person who sits at his desk all day long, I hate plastic chair mats.

Ken's floor mats are made of tempered glass providing an ageless surface which allows your chair to move easily with no ruts and no replacement needed. I suppose you could say that they are beautiful when compared to plastic floor mats after a couple of years of use. Like the square melon, the glass floor mats sell at a premium but from my perspective they are well worth it.

Both the square watermelon and glass floor mats are perfect examples of niche marketing—they both target a customer who was overlooked or underserved by the bigger players. The happy customer gladly pays the price premium to get what they want.

To be successful in niche marketing, you need to practice the following:

- Define your purpose: What do you want to achieve? What is important?
- Define your customer or niche: What is unique about your customer? What do they want that they cannot get from the competition?
- Conduct market research before you build your product: What are the unique specifications of the product needed? How will your product be used? Why will it be valued?
- Build a unique product: Marketing is about making connections, specifically between a customer's unmet needs and the solutions you provide. Have the courage to create products that are different.
- Test the market: Start by sending out samples to your customers and get feedback from them. Go back and make the necessary changes.
- Create a mantra: Create a three or four word phrase that describes your product that is memorable, easy to say, and spell.
- Market the "benefits": Always market the benefits of your product, not the details.
- Get the message out: Frequency of contact is the number one criteria in the decision to buy your product.
- Promote the product in unusual ways: Go viral. Find out where your customer lives and go meet them there. Promote the product in unusual ways and in unusual places. Try new methods and get a little crazy.

- Always measure your success: How did you do? What did not work? What would you do different? Test and measure every aspect of your marketing? Always try new ideas.
- Do it again, but do it better.

*While surfing the web: Go visit Clearly Innovative Home and Office Products at www.chairmatsofglass.com.*

# 30. Only Dead Fish Swim with the Current

"Don't think you're on the right road just because it's a well-beaten path."

**Anonymous**

It is time for you to go fishing.

A Sustainable Competitive Advantage (SCA) is a unique offering that is valued by your customer and is not readily available from the competition. Michael Porter, the lauded Harvard Professor, coined the term in the eighties and it lives on as an iconic business term. In fact, it has become a cliché, since its usage often is mangled and misapplied. It is not what you think it is or what you want it to be. It is what your customer believes and that is what counts—this perception is everything.

Your SCA is made up of your distinctive competencies, which are unique attributes or benefits that are valued by the customer. Simply stated, this means that you do different things or that you do things differently from your competition. These distinctive competencies are so valuable to your customer that they will choose your offering instead of the competition. These benefits could be unique product features, product design, method of delivery, or even your brand.

A competitive advantage is sustainable if others can't copy or deliver the same thing, or if the cost or the time to develop a competing solution is very significant. Porter suggests that a SCA is achieved when you do different things that are valued by your customer and are not available from the competition. Alternatively, you can create a SCA by doing things differently, which are valued by the customer and are not available from the competition.

An example of doing things differently is Starbucks. They serve coffee, which is hardly unique, but they make the coffee buying experience almost a lifestyle. Have you seen the lines at this place? And, people go to Starbucks just to hang out and be seen. An example of doing different things might be MySpace; although not the first social networking site, they targeted the younger crowd and created an environment to connect with 100 million other individuals. They reinvented how people stay in touch with other people.

In some industries, being first allows for a competitive advantage, but seldom is it sustainable in the long run. Invariably the word gets out and the competition joins the market erasing whatever advantage there was for the first entry. Apple was enormously innovative with their early personal computers which offered a graphical user interface and a mouse. IBM later entered the market and grabbed a commanding market share; all Apple could do was watch.

I have found that specialization in a niche business helps ensure the sustainability of the SCA. This specialization is achieved by having expert knowledge of the target market and by fully understanding the wants and needs of your customer, your offering is better than your competitors. This can be true if your product is different or you do things differently. Being the same as your competition is a dead-end street littered with price reductions, canceled orders, and missed sales forecasts.

For example, Apple created the iPod, which allowed the consumer to inexpensively download music on a mobile device. We can debate whether they were first (they were not), and whether this advantage is sustainable (not really), but Apple did energize the MP3 movement for the mass consumption market. This is an example of doing something different and specialization in a niche.

On the other hand, Starbucks sells coffee, which is not exactly a new product, but Starbucks markets coffee in a different way than others have. They market "premium coffee," although some might argue that point. Moreover, they charge a premium for this difference. Thus, Starbucks is an example of how you can achieve a competitive advantage by doing something differently.

Not surprisingly, I have witnessed that a tight geographic focus helps create a strong competitive advantage for niche businesses. The sheer constraint on geography allows for excellence and bars competitors from getting a toehold. This goes counter to the thinking of many entrepreneurs who are tempted to stretch their geographical boundaries for additional cash flow.

Participating in a niche market with few competitors helps create a sustainable SCA. With fewer competitors, the provider can capture higher margins and profits, which allow the entrepreneur to invest more in the firm.

Of course, brilliant designs that are patented can provide competitive advantages but, in our global economy, patents are increasingly difficult to defend. Talk to someone who competes with Asian firms in a global market and you will find that good ideas or products are quickly cloned. Catch them if you can.

*Action: To determine your SCA and distinctive competencies you need to identify the unique attributes or benefits that are valued by your customers, and then list your chief competitor's distinctive competencies. Compare both lists. Delete the attributes or benefits from your list that you share with your competitor since they are not truly unique. The remaining items on your list make up your competitive advantage. Next, ask yourself if this SCA is really sustainable? Can this competitive advantage be duplicated and, if so, how soon? If your competitive advantage is easily cloned then you had better come up with some new attributes.*

# 31. Have You Heard About My Disruptive Technology?

"If you are going to walk on thin ice, you might as well dance!"

**Anonymous**

What is disruptive technology? With increasing frequency, the technology crowd has liberally branded new products as "disruptive technologies." I think it is fair to say that most of these new offerings are not disruptive or even interesting for that matter. They are new products, plain and simple.

The term "disruptive technology" was first used by Harvard Business School professor Clayton M. Christensen in his 1997 book "The Innovator's Dilemma." He actually divided new technologies (I.E. innovations) into two buckets: one called disruptive and the other called sustaining.

According to Christensen, a disruptive technology is unrefined and may not even have a practical use at the beginning, or ever. The invention of the innovation may be largely accidental and its value may not be recognized at first. In fact, these innovations are typically laughed at and tossed aside. He cites the example of the telephone by Alexander Graham Bell which actually took decades before it was adopted for everyday use. Bell was considered an eccentric at best.

Sustaining technologies are a different beast altogether. Christensen describes it as improvements to an existing technology or process that are made sequentially over time. You could say that Intel has made continued improvements to its microprocessor technology and, thus, is a maker of sustaining technologies. Intel is a good example of the type of firm that is expert at sustaining technologies.

Intel's heritage encourages continuous improvement. Additionally, this type of innovation is culturally consistent with Intel and its goals. On the other hand, innovation for innovation's sake has little cachet at Intel since they hope to capitalize on all new research and development.

A true disruptive technology shocks the status quo and needs an evangelist who can withstand the laughter and ridicule. And, besides being tough skinned, this evangelist must be patient since disruptive technologies are embraced very slowly, if ever.

*Beware the marketer that shouts disruptive technology: It probably is just a pathetic cry for attention.*

# 32. Is Different Better?

"Different isn't always better, but better is always different."

**Marshall Thurber, Entrepreneur**

I like this quote because it sums up my thinking about how customers will buy an offering because of its differences—not because it is like other offerings. This is true even if the offering is a commodity or is nearly the same as the competition. Invariably, the customer buys because of the product's differences not because of its similarities.

Think about it. When a buyer is deciding between two seemingly identical products, the buyer instinctively looks for differences in price, quality, or delivery. With some perception of a difference, the buyer chooses one offering over another. The operative word in that sentence is perception.

It is my contention that buyers buy for the following underlying reasons:

- "Needs" are things that you must have to survive and to function; this includes shelter, food, clothing, and medicine. These purchases are easily justified and are basic motivations for a buyer.
- "Wants" are things that are desired, but not necessary such as wanting an iPod. Wants are tougher for the buyer to justify, but people will buy them because of an innate ability to rationalize most any purchase. If I buy an iPod I will be happier and more popular.
- "Desires" are wishes or dreams, which can be powerful motivators. You can desire to be famous and this can motivate you to take action or not to take action. Desires can motivate people to change or modify their behavior. If you lose weight, you will be more attractive and this can help make you famous.
- "Fear" can motivate the buyer to take action or not to take action. Fear can create barriers to success by holding people back from taking a promotion. Or, fear can also keep people safe by keeping them from taking unnecessary risks; if you don't buy this book, you will not be successful, so you buy it out of fear.

With these underlying reasons driving them, customers then seek to justify their decisions with their perception of the differences in the offerings available.

The essence of niche marketing is presenting your product as different while fulfilling the buyer's underlying reason for buying the offering in the first place.

*Be Different: Write down five ways in which you differentiate yourself from the competition.*

# 33. *Market Research Methods at Small Companies*

"There is much pleasure to be gained from useless knowledge."

**Bertrand Russell (1872-1970) Humanitarian,
Philosopher, Mathematician**

Market research can be one the best uses of funds at a small firm. However, more often than not, it seldom gets done. The reasons include lack of funds, little or no experience with market research, no time to do the research, and, often, the autocratic styles of entrepreneurs don't allow for third party feedback.

There are many uses of market research including competitive analysis, customer satisfaction, brand awareness, message testing for advertisements, employee satisfaction, and new product development. Generally speaking, all research requires the help of a third party since a third party conducts the research without bias. This is often hard for entrepreneurs to understand.

The best place to begin when you need market research is with secondary research, which is simply pre-existing research. Already prepared, secondary research is on the shelf and can be inexpensive or even free. Sources include:

- Trade journals (a good source of technical trends)
- Market research firm publications
- Trade associations
- Magazines
- Internet resources
- Conferences
- Multi-client studies
- Subscription services

When more specific research is needed, custom or primary research is the preferred choice. Primary research is original research that is conducted for one client. Primary research can use qualitative and/or quantitative techniques.

Most primary research starts with qualitative market research techniques to determine the key issues or problems. Qualitative research uses open-ended questions that "fish for answers" using techniques such as:

- Focus groups with a professional moderator.
- Intercept interviews at the place of business or point of purchase.
- Telephone interviews seeking opinions.
- Pre-arranged interviews with target executives.
- Email focus groups for the convenience of the participant.

Once the key issues or problems are identified, quantitative market research techniques are typically employed to verify the qualitative findings by polling a sample of the population to give a statistically significant picture. Quantitative techniques may include computer aided telephone interviews, in-person interviews, mail surveys, and e-mail surveys.

Market research is money well spent by the entrepreneur.

*When market research firms call: Don't hang up. Instead listen to the sequence of questions that they ask.*

# 34. Bright Ideas

"First Thoughts Are Not Always the Best."

**Vittorio Alfieri (1749 – 1803) Italian Dramatist**

OK, I have never seen an "Italian tragedy," but this quote reminded me that while inspiration may be an important part of marketing and entrepreneurship, no idea is so great that it cannot be verified or tested. Maybe the biggest mistake that entrepreneurs can make is to love their ideas too much. In fact, loving the idea or thought too much is exactly the wrong orientation since it is not about what the entrepreneur thinks or loves. It is what the customer thinks or believes that nothing else matters.

Entrepreneurs need to divorce themselves from the emotion of the first idea and become more deliberate and analytical. New products need to withstand a feasibility test, also known as a concept test. This feedback is critical for a new offering.

Maybe the smartest money ever spent by an entrepreneur is to conduct a concept test, which is basic market research on an offering before you go to market. Concept testing can use qualitative or quantitative research methods; most commonly, qualitative tools such as in-person interviews and focus groups are chosen for their expediency and live feedback.

Essentially, prospective customers are given an early viewing of an offering to assess their reactions before the provider invests more money in the new offering. It forces the entrepreneur to expose the offering to the prospective customer base to solicit real feedback. The test verifies that the benefits of the offering are recognized and valued by the customer. This feedback is essential but sometimes difficult for the entrepreneur to accept, particularly if the feedback is negative. Often the best concept test is done with focus groups.

The purpose of a focus group is to help find answers to difficult questions. A consumer research technique that uses open-ended questions, focus groups can quickly discern key issues and determine why the issues are important. Focus groups are moderator-led discussions of six to ten people randomly selected from a sample list comprised of participants in your target market.

An independent, third party moderator who is trained at managing the complex interpersonal dynamics of a group discussion best conducts "true" focus groups. The goal of a focus group is to smoke out hidden issues, test ideas, and seek feedback. The group discussion environment can be a very powerful tool for determining how people feel about a new offering or idea.

The client who sponsors the focus group predetermines the objectives of the session, but the format is flexible enough to accommodate the serendipity of qualitative research. You never know exactly what you will learn in a focus group. Most moderators prefer to follow a discussion outline, but they ultimately let the discussion lead the way.

A focus group that is poorly or unprofessionally moderated is a waste of time. Generally speaking, focus groups are best left to the professionals. Often small firms will attempt to moderate focus groups by themselves; this is often a poor choice since the entrepreneurs are inherently biased about their businesses and will only hear what they want to hear.

Sadly, most entrepreneurs don't properly test their ideas. Former Apple evangelist Guy Kawasaki joked that in the "old days" at Apple that new products only required a funky name, a few thousand t-shirts, and a media blitz—then they would figure out what the product's specifications would be. Apple is greatly admired for innovation, but I wonder if they might even be more successful if they did more concept testing.

Sometimes, the concept test identifies problems such as possible confusion about how the product is positioned with competing products. Often the marketing messages are still in draft form, so this concept test also assists in refining the basic messaging. In fact, concept tests are frequently performed for advertising campaigns to verify that the target customer can understand the benefits of the products.

However, concept testing may not be a good indicator of purchasing behavior. Just because someone understands the benefits of a new product and even admits to liking the product, it does not mean that they will buy it. Additionally, concept testing may identify product attributes that are significant but this type of research can struggle to assess which attribute is more important.

Concept tests typically try to answer the following questions:

- What is unique about this new product or service concept?
- How does it compare to competitive offerings?
- How might it benefit the customer?
- What are the relative strengths and weaknesses of the new product or service concept?
- Would the customer buy the product?

Ironically, many startups and entrepreneurs go to market without conducting a concept test. Instead, because of their strong belief in the product or service concept they often elect to skip this step. The ramifications are many, including failure.

First thoughts and new products should be tested since they are not always the best.

*Say yes: The next time you get asked to join a focus group, go ahead and try it.*

# 35. The Inconsistent Wisdom of Crowds and Market Research

"Nobody goes there anymore. It's too crowded."

**Yogi Berra (1925 – present) Baseball Great**

James Surowiecki wrote "The Wisdom of Crowds: Why the Many Are Smarter than the Few and How Collective Wisdom Shapes Business, Economies, Societies and Nations" back in 2004. The book reinforced the now ubiquitous term called the "wisdom of crowds." Used by academics and marketing gurus alike, the cliché tells us to listen to the needs, or better said the rants of the crowd rather than the reason of a single member of a group.

Crowds can be great at determining a consensus view where the right wing cancels out the left wing and we are left with the middle ground occupied by the statistical mean, or the "silent majority" as former US President Nixon called it. In politics and other venues this type of group thinking can be powerful and correct.

Surowiecki actually argued that crowds are often wrong, but that message seems to have been lost on most readers (remember the average North American buys only one book a year and seldom finishes it). He suggests that crowds can get it wrong by listening to gossip or innuendo, instead of objectively looking at the facts. Sometimes a pretty face or a charismatic leader can sway the crowd and lead them to a disastrous conclusion such as riots, Nazi Germany, and conclusions from market research studies.

Crowds and market research sample groups are wrong for the same reasons:

- They are too much alike and lack the diversity of the population; the sample was not random or representative.
- There is regional bias such as only doing focus groups in Manhattan; the people in Chicago and LA may feel very differently than the folks in the Big Apple.

- The respondents don't tell the truth; instead they say what they think the researcher wants to hear.
- Respondents can be like sheep in that they follow the flock; they can be heavily influenced by others. They read it in People Magazine so it has to be true.
- Focus group participants can be overpowered by a biased moderator (they are not supposed to be biased, of course).
- Their decisions can be selfish or fear based, rather than what is good for the group.

So, when doing market research, pick the crowd carefully to insure that it is representative of the total population. Ask the questions without bias or influence. Probe deeply to understand why people answer as they do. Avoid biases in the sample.

Listen to the crowd, but beware of the mob.

*Crowdsourcing: Giving a task normally done by an individual or a group to a very large group of people or a community such as on a forum or social network.*

# 36. *Net Promoters Recommend You to Friends*

"Do what you do so well that they will want
to see it again and bring their friends."

**Walt Disney (1901 – 1966) Visionary**

If you can only ask your customer one question to determine his or her level of satisfaction with your product or service, you need to ask him or her "How likely would you be to recommend our company to a friend?" This question comes from loyalty expert Fred Reichheld's book "The Ultimate Question: Driving Good Profits and True Growth."

He suggests that customers that become your advocate and are willing to risk their reputation by recommending you to a friend are unquestionably loyal. This is the type of customer that a company can build long-term growth upon. They typically will pay a higher price and they will forgive an occasional error or quality problem. In fact, he suggests that this is the only kind of growth that can be sustained over the long-term. He calls this type of customer a "Net Promoter."

Reichheld feels that the real challenge for companies is to make employees just as accountable for providing a superior customer experience as they now feel for delivering superior profits. And that message starts at the top with key executives touting customer service over profits.

Implementing this approach is simple according to Reichheld. Companies need to ask this all-important question in a regular, systematic, and timely fashion. They need to regularly track the answers, publish the results, and they need to put the information to work immediately. Companies that actively use this process can manage customer loyalty and the growth it produces just as rigorously as they can manage profits.

I agree with the concept, but I think he is asking the wrong question. The question should be, "Have you recommended our company to a friend?" It is one thing to say that you will do it and another to actually do it. Real advocates are people who actually recommend your firm to their friends. They are not people who just talk about it.

*Loyalty: Means actually referring a product, service, person, or company to a friend. What products or services have you referred lately? Why?*

# 37. Things to Know About the Competition

"There is only one good, knowledge, and one evil, ignorance."

**Socrates (469 BC – 399 BC) Philosopher**

You and your competitors have a common goal—all of you want to outsell the others in the marketplace. But, do you really know your competition?

Here are things that you must know about your competition:

- Who are your major competitors? This could be by product, so you might have many competitors.
- What does your target market think about your competitors?
- What are your competitors doing right and wrong?
- How do they do business?
- Do they use direct sales, manufacturer representatives, distributors, or affiliates?
- Are they easy to work with?
- What is their marketing strategy and how is it different than yours?
- Do they use a similar pricing method?
- How do they advertise?
- Is their website up-to-date?
- What is their competitive advantage, if any?
- What makes them unique or better?
- How do customers describe them?
- What are their weaknesses?
- What don't they do well?
- What do customers complain about?
- Who are their major customers?
- Are they the same as yours or is it a different list?
- Do you see any commonality with their major customers: geography, vertical, size, or other characteristic?
- What are their long-term goals?
- Are they hoping to exit soon or do they intend to stay in the market for the long haul?

- What are their financials like?
- Are they making money or are they cash poor?
- What type of financial terms do they offer?

*Do it yourself: Can you answer these questions about your competitors? If not, you need to get started.*

# 38. Behavior Predicts Behavior

"If you know the enemy and know yourself, you need not fear the result of a hundred battles. If you know yourself but not the enemy, for every victory gained you will also suffer a defeat. If you know neither the enemy nor yourself you will succumb in every battle."

**Sun-Tzu (544 B.C. – 496 B.C.) Author of "The Art of War"**

What this means to the modern marketer is that competitive analysis is a critical factor when planning marketing strategy. Knowing your competitor's history gives you insight to their future strategy. Essentially, behavior predicts behavior. This is the essence of competitive analysis.

While it seems a simple conclusion, companies tend do the same thing over and over even when it is wrong. Change is hard and people will change only when they really have to change. This means that the behavior and the strategies of your competitors are largely predictable.

To predict the future, all you have to do is to look backwards. Here are a few ideas:

- Talk with your customers who are doing business with the competition or previously did business with the competition.
- Visit your direct competitor's stores and talk to the sales staff; it is amazing what people will say.
- Websites can be a treasure trove of information, so dig deep; register on their websites.
- Suppliers often have keen insight on the health and strategy of your competition; take your suppliers out to lunch but beware what you reveal since the door swings both ways.
- You can gather secondary data on the competition from trade associations and publications. These member fees can give great access to low cost industry data.
- Have lunch with former employees of the competition—they often sing like canaries.
- Watch for press releases, radio commercials, and TV spots.
- Save print advertising and promotions used by the competition.
- If feasible, buy your competitors' products or services.

When this is complete, analyze your competitor's products regularly for improvements, weaknesses, and quality trends. Make a short list of anticipated competitor strategies and tactics for the current year. Map out your retaliatory strategies and tactics, including situations to which you will not respond. He or she who is most prepared wins.

Oh, and one more thing. Try to learn from your own mistakes and don't repeat them if you can.

*Easy to do: Put a team member in charge of gathering this data; I bet your team has a great deal of information which has never been collected in one spot.*

# 39. Barriers Are Mostly Psychological

"If you find a path with no obstacles, it probably doesn't lead anywhere."

**Anonymous**

Have you ever confronted a barrier or a problem that stopped you from going forward with your goals and objectives? Maybe it was because you did not have the support from your friends or family. Maybe the task itself just seemed insurmountable. Whatever the barrier, it was big enough to stop you in your tracks.

In reality most barriers are psychological in nature. They may seem real, but most exist only in your mind. More often than not, we consciously or unconsciously give theses obstacles more power than we should.

Psychological barriers can be categorized into three basic buckets:

1.  Trying to please everyone
2.  Trying to be perfect
3.  Fear of failure

Trying to please everyone is not possible and it does not make good business sense. This behavior manifests itself as being unable to say no to an unreasonable request, or not fighting back when confronted with aggressive behaviors in others. The key to overcoming this self-destructive behavior is to monitor your own behavior and catch yourself in the act. Saying "no" is the best method to stop being a people-pleaser.

Perfectionism is rooted in a deep seated feeling of never being satisfied with what you have done or with yourself. This higher self-standard causes you undo stress and, ironically, can decrease your productivity and quality. More often than not, your initial effort on a task is just fine; further refinement or effort won't make it appreciably better. Give yourself a break and be content with your initial efforts. For example, novelist Norman Mailer wrote with a pen on a yellow pad of paper and did not rewrite or edit his work—his first draft was always his best.

Fear of failure may be the biggest enemy of success. For many of us, failure is often avoided by doing nothing. Of course, doing nothing often just insures failure. Instead, welcome failure as a way to improve yourself rather than looking at it an exposure of your weaknesses. Confront fear of failure by determining the worst case scenario—while this scenario is highly improbable, it is empowering to know that even if the perfect storm happens you will survive or even thrive.

Finally, consider reaching out for help when the barriers seem insurmountable. Sometimes we are just too close to the situation and do not have the skills, training, or awareness to fully diagnose and overcome our own barriers. A third party such as a coach, boss, or friend can see things differently and provide strong counsel. Listen to them.

*No worries: I have yet to see a barrier so big that I could not walk around it and continue the journey.*

# 40. Great Brands Promise Value

"Act the part and you will become the part."

**William James (1842 – 1910) Philosopher and Psychologist**

Your brand is what people think you are. Successful brands are authentic, differentiated, and consistent.

Brands are authentic when they are perceived as real and natural. Fabricated brands seldom live for long. No pretense or fibs allowed here. You cannot make up a brand since a brand must have integrity to be believed. When a brand is based on falsehoods or exaggerations, no one will believe you, nor will they continue to buy from you (not for long anyway).

Brands are differentiated when they say what is unique or special about the business or product. A differentiated brand answers why and how the firm delivers value. A good brand describes what makes your firm different from the competition. It describes the uniqueness of your product; this is what the customer remembers.

Consistency is the commitment from the brand that the purchase experience will be the same each time. Otherwise, why would anyone buy the same product or service again? Consistency allows the brand to live on beyond the first impression and the hope for the brand is that it will eventually take on a life of its own that could live on without your company. Customers buy brand name products because they know that these products are reliable enough.

Let's look at the world famous brand Coca-Cola. While the exact formula of Coca-Cola is a trade secret, we all understand that it is carbonated sugar water. Coca-Cola has marketed Coke with a variety of slogans such as "The pause that refreshes," "I'd like to buy the world a Coke," and "Coke is it." The underlying message has been a simple one: drink this carbonated sugar water and you will have fun. This honesty rings true for the consumer.

Differentiation is what the customer believes to be special or unique about the brand. While it could be argued that colas are very similar or even the same, Coke drinkers think otherwise by choosing it over the many other cola alternatives. Coke has extended its brand to include many different flavors including Diet Coke, Cherry Coke, and Vanilla Coke (to name a few). These spin off products have proven to be wildly successful even though they are similar to the original product.

Brands are built on consistency, which means that your customer gets the same product or service each time they choose to do business with you. For example, no matter where you buy a Coca-Cola, you know that it will taste the same. Even the packaging will be same. This reliability makes buying a Coke an easy decision.

Your brand is a promise of value that separates you from your peers. Branding is not about building a new image, but it is a statement about your uniqueness. Successful brands know their target market; they know what the customer needs and they deliver on that promise time and again.

Still, you must be careful not to dilute your brand by trying to be something you are not. For example, I read recently that Buick has been marketing the Buick Lucerne in China as a luxury automobile brand and has had considerable success in selling to upper class business executives. You may be surprised to know that China is now the world's second-largest auto market with 250 million members of its emerging middle class owning a car or planning to buy one within the next two years.

Encouraged by their success in the luxury market, Buick extended their brand with an economy model selling for $12,000. Unfortunately, this brand extension backfired. The luxury car buyer was left confused by the economical image of the new cars; the China luxury car buyer deserted the Buick brand for other upscale automobiles.

The Buick lesson is simple: don't confuse your customers with high, medium and low quality offerings. Instead, be like Coca-Cola and be true to your brand even if it is just carbonated sugar water.

*Branding quiz: What is unique about your brand?*

# *41. Keep a Brand Handbook*

"We are always in our own company."

**Friedrich Nietzsche (1844 - 1900) German philosopher**

Your brand is your promise of value. It is often said that good brands have three primary characteristics: they are authentic, consistent, and differentiated. Of the three characteristics, staying consistent may be the hardest thing to do.

With that said, the biggest internal challenge for a brand is with people and discipline. Unfortunately, as your firm grows it becomes harder and harder to keep your brand consistent. All employees must sing the same song, so to speak. They must honor the brand by using the same tag line, by treating customers with the same level of respect, by using the same logo, and by dressing appropriately in the work environment. In practice, it is a lot like herding cats.

Discipline in this case means that people need to know what to do. Of course, the brand starts with the leadership of the company and the vision communicated. Yes, all employees need to be on board with the company mantra. But it goes beyond cheer leading and mission statements. You need to document the essentials of your brand, if you want people to honor the brand with consistency.

Your company name, logo, and tag line must be consistently displayed on all customer-facing material. This includes business cards, letterhead, envelopes, brochures, website, invoices, fax cover sheets, and signs. Color communicates the brand's feel so it must be consistent. Fonts need to be consistent across all your marketing communications.

Since your brand image is crucial to the success of your company you should think about keeping a brand handbook. A brand handbook captures and archives all of your branding elements including website colors, fonts, tag line, logo, stationery design, graphics, background music, dress code, etc. It can include instructions on how to answer the phone or anything else that is important to maintaining your brand. All these things communicate your brand and it is imperative that everyone join in to maintain a consistent brand.

A brand handbook can be helpful for communicating your brand's essentials to new employees, while emphasizing its importance to the existing staff. It should be reviewed and updated as brand elements are updated or revised. Finally, this handbook must be distributed and read by all employees.

Brands must be consistent if they are be valued by your customer.

*Get started today: Collect the individual elements of your brand. Start your brand handbook.*

# 42. Unique Value Proposition

"In order to be irreplaceable one must always be different."

**Coco Chanel (1883 – 1971) French Fashion Designer**

Every successful firm or product needs a Unique Value Proposition (UVP) which is fancy marketing talk for the reason a customer will choose to buy your offering. If you don't have a UVP it means that your offering is a pure commodity and you should not be reading this book—I cannot help you.

A UVP states your product's differences that are valued by the customer. These differences can be almost anything. For example, they can include:

- Superior service
- Greater product availability
- Higher quality
- Better performance
- Greater durability
- Respected image or prestige
- Technology leadership
- Satisfaction guarantee
- Lower cost
- Faster delivery
- More customer support

Think of a UVP as that special ingredient your business uses to prevent itself from becoming a "commodity." It should leap off the page and demand attention from your buyers since this is why they will buy now and will continue to buy from you. The challenge is to find that one thing that makes your offering different—that is all that you need to be chosen by your target market.

You could analyze the competition; generally this is wasted time since they probably don't have the answer. Your customers know the answer or will help you find it. Determine their pains or unfulfilled needs. Start focusing on what they cannot get but need.

If you have no differentiator, create one. Think about it, when you go to the super market to buy milk, you still have to make a choice whether it is price, packaging, low fat versus whole milk, or soy product. Pick the most unique aspect or benefit of your product and focus your marketing messaging there.

People buy because of your offering's uniqueness not because it is the same as others. Be different.

*Exercise: Describe your brands unique qualities using just three words.*

# 43. I See Colors

"The soul becomes dyed with the color of its thoughts."

**Marcus Aurelius (121 – 180) Roman Emperor**

No, this is not a flashback to the psychedelic sixties. Instead, this is a serious discussion about color and how it can be used in marketing.

While perceptions of color are somewhat subjective, there are some color effects that have universal meaning. Colors in the red area of the color spectrum are known as warm colors and include red, orange, and yellow. These warm colors evoke emotions ranging from feelings of warmth and comfort to feelings of anger and hostility.

Colors on the blue side of the spectrum are known as cool colors and include blue, purple, and green. These colors are often described as calm, but can also call to mind feelings of sadness or indifference. But, let's first have a history lesson.

Ancient cultures, including the Egyptians and Chinese, practiced chromotherapy, or using colors to heal. Red was used to stimulate the body and mind and to increase circulation. Yellow was thought to stimulate the nerves and purify the body. Orange was used to heal the lungs and to increase energy levels. Blue was believed to soothe illnesses and treat pain. Indigo shades were thought to alleviate skin problems.

Today, most psychologists view color therapy with skepticism and point out that the supposed effects of color have been exaggerated. Colors also have different meanings in different cultures. Research has demonstrated in many cases that the mood-altering effects of color may only be temporary.

Yet, when it comes to web design and creative work, colors define a business and a brand. When designing printed materials, logos, and websites, many factors come into play. One factor of great importance is color since your brand is expressed through your choice of color. Color evokes a mood or feeling and must be chosen carefully. It must be consistent with the image that you want to communicate to your target audience.

Red is a call to action since it is viewed as being aggressive and can be exciting. It is a great color for logos and for accents when it is used with other more neutral background colors. It can clash with green, blue, and purple. It is best used with other warm colors like yellow, brown, or orange. Red demands attention because it says stop and come look at me. It is too strong for a background color since it would be irritating or overwhelming.

Black can be a depressing, if not a mournful color. It feels heavy. Yet, it can also be sophisticated and alluring with luxurious and prestigious feelings. It functions well as a backdrop for an artist's work or with photographic images. It seems to go well with technical images or presentations. Black can be a great color for text on the website.

White is an excellent background for a professional business on a website. It denotes cleanliness, purity, and youth. It feels simple and innocent. Many of the best consumer websites choose white as the background of choice. Note that Google's homepage is white and very simple. Google uses primary colors to spell out its name in order to give their brand a youthful and fun vibe.

Green is the color of nature and the environment. Light green is a great background for professional service firms like a law firm or a CPA firm. Green communicates safety and encourages you to go forward. Bright green is trendy right now for high tech firms; it has a retro feel that reminds us of the sixties.

Blue can create an image of tranquility and peacefulness. Light blue is a common background for service-based businesses such as consulting or market research firms; it communicates a calm solution. Blue can be authoritative while dark blue is heavy and morose; think police officer. Medium or bright blue can also be perceived as over-the-top and goofy.

Beige is a great neutral color, which speaks of conservatism. By itself it is boring or plain. Paired up with accent colors like green or brown or blue, beige is very readable. Beige can make a super background, if complemented with the right accent colors.

Brown is a great color for text in print and on a website. Generally, brown is viewed as earthy or natural, while to others it might be dirty or dingy. Brown works well with green. It can also communicate a natural, rural or primitive look. Brown is warm and comfortable.

Yellow is the most irritating color out there and is great for getting your attention, but use it sparingly. Many great logos use yellow (often paired with red). Yellow is the color of cowardice or caution.

When choosing a color, you should consider the 216 colors supported by web browsers. It is generally recommended that you start with color choices compatible with the web palette and then consider color on paper. Go to Google and enter the words "web palette" and you will find all 216 vibrant colors. If you start with color on paper, it might not be found in the web palette. Consistency is a huge factor in building brand awareness with logos.

*Website color schemes: Three to four colors work best.*

# 44. Branding Power

"If you do things well, do them better, be daring,
be first, be different, be just."

**Anita Roddick (1942 – 2007) Businesswoman and Philanthropist**

Once significant brand equity is established then products can be successful in spite of themselves. Just look at McDonald's.

Author Selena Maranjian wrote in the Motley Fool recently about a research study that described a new way to get your kids to eat their broccoli: "Wrap it in the golden arches packaging of McDonald's. Sounds funny? Researchers presented several dozen children with a taste test, offering them various foods such as carrots, milk, and apple juice in both unmarked and McDonald's-branded wrappers. As you might expect, the McDonald's branded foods received uniformly higher marks," she concludes.

"Think about what this means. It shows how powerful brands can be in our minds. A mere brand label can affect how we perceive something. According to the study, the children's perception of taste was physically altered by the branding," says Maranjian.

This brand power is the reward that McDonald's gets for decades of messaging about their products. The parents of today's children drank Ronald McDonald's "Kool-Aid" for years themselves and are still drawn to the Golden Arches even when they would rather have a latte or some sushi. Like a powerful mating call, they bring their kids to McDonald's and teach them the burger and fries ritual. And so it is handed down from one generation to another.

The McDonald's brand is authentic—they know that they sell just burgers and fries and so does everyone else. And they are very consistent—their food never gets any better. Differentiated? Well, they have Ronald and they have those tasty nuggets made of chicken parts. Yet, no one can argue about the power of the McDonald's brand.

*Authenticity: Being faithful or devoted to internal rather than external ideas.*

# 45. Messaging Tells Your Story

"Everything you can imagine is real."

**Pablo Picasso (1881 – 1973) Painter**

Messaging is a fancy marketing term for the story that you tell about your company or your offering; most importantly, your message must be heard and understood by your customers, friends, and employees. This message must clear, concise, backed with evidence, and tell the right story.

Starting with the basics, it all starts with your company name. Your company name must be memorable, easy to say and spell, and must be associated with what you do. Sounds simple, but if your company's name is Mike's Mufflers and you are offering ballet lessons, you have a big problem right out of the starting gate. People won't hear your message if they are confused about what you do.

Presuming your company name makes sense, a message tells your customer, the media, and your other contacts a story that you want to be understood. It can be about a new product announcement, an event, or your competitive advantage.

For an advertising campaign, your ad agency will spend a great deal of time helping you craft the right message. Your message must be clear, concise, memorable, and meaningful. They will test the message with focus groups made up of your customers and friends. No matter how proud you are of the message you have written, the real test is how others respond to it. Often, these tests confirm the message is correct but, sometimes, the feedback sends you back to the drawing board.

Taglines tell a story or message. It may be the most powerful message that you will ever write since it appears on your website banner, letterhead, business cards, etc. Taglines need the same type of testing, so be sure to slow down and do it right.

For a message to be believed, you need to submit evidence. On a website this could be a page devoted to testimonials. Nothing is more believable than a customer reference or testimonial. Other types of evidence could include product specifications, customer lists, or press quotes. All help back up your message and the implied claims.

Messages are best understood when introduced one at a time. A marketing brochure needs a focus to its messaging because, if you try to deliver multiple messages in the same piece, you will likely miss your target. Think about the TV advertisements that you have watched. They almost always tell one story.

Finally, for messages to be remembered they must be delivered to the right people with frequency. A great message delivered to the wrong people will be ignored. A great message delivered once to the right people will be forgotten. There is no substitute for frequency of contact when delivering your message.

*Optimum Frequency: Sufficient contacts or touches for your customer to remember you without being irritated.*

# 46. Changing Your Company Name

"Change always comes bearing gifts."

**Price Pritchett (1941 – present) Businessman**

I got a call from a friend who had just joined a small company as the Marketing Director. After auditing the firm's marketing practices, he determined that the old company name had to go. The old name too closely resembled another firm's moniker and it was causing confusion in the marketplace. With new ownership at the firm, a change seemed to make sense.

He called me looking for some ideas for a new name and I gladly helped. In fact, we came up with a new company name that could be used as his URL with a dotcom suffix. All it took was 15 minutes. I was very pleased since it took me nearly six months to come up with my first book's name: First, Best, or Different; it was agonizing.

After we hung up I started to think about how a name change will impact his firm. I wrote a list of all the things, little or big, that a name change might impact. The list was frightening. It started with letting all the existing customers know about the change. And that was the easy part!

What about the website, the Yellow Pages, the trucks, the invoices, the letterhead, the signage, the business cards, the fax cover page, the voice-mail message, the company uniforms, the brochures, the product packaging, the shipping boxes, and the product labels? It is easy to forget how much time and money it takes to build brand awareness for a company name. The cost of such a change is immense.

Also, how about the old URL? Think of all the links that lead to that old URL. I was reading the other day about how large firms sometimes need to change names, if not get an "extreme makeover." The one that comes to mind is Andersen Consulting. Now known as Accenture, they used to be known as Andersen Consulting until a little problem happened with a client named Enron.

You know the story. The old URL became a dead link in a matter of months. For most firms changing a name, keeping the old URL would be critical; in fact, you would probably want to keep it for years so that your old customers could find you. Often this is done with a "redirect" from the old URL to the new one. In Accenture's case, they desperately wanted Andersen Consulting to not exist.

Additionally, don't forget about the lawyers. They need to help you with all your contracts both new and old that will need to be changed, amended, and rewritten. You will also need to verify that the new name is not used by another business.

Even with all this done, you will still need to co-brand the new and old name for a long time (probably for a year) to make sure that the old customers will remember the transition. It usually reads something like "ACCENTURE" (in big letters) "formerly known as Andersen Consulting" (in small letters). What this means is that you actually have two name changes to make: the transition name and then the final name.

*Name that tune: Always test new names with your target market. Once you pick a name it is hard to change it.*

# 47. The Name Game

"What's in a name? That which we call a rose by any
other name would smell as sweet."

**William Shakespeare (1564 – 1616) Playwright**

Naming your business or offering is a huge decision and one that you should research thoroughly, choose carefully, and test with your target market.

Here are a few ideas on what to consider:

- The shorter, the better. Shorter names are more memorable, easier to type into Google or Yahoo!, and more flexible since longer names tend to be more specific, if not more limiting.
- Include a solution or image in your name. For example, the Ford "Mustang" infers that it will be a fast or exciting car. It communicates reckless abandon, which appeals to the risk taker in some of us. The image of the Mustang also means beauty to some and power to others. It is timeless.
- Make sure that you can extend the title to other products, geographies, and services. Like a shorter name, a more generic name allows you to offer new solutions, which might have not been in your original marketing plan. The name "Google" seems to have no limitations, although I doubt that I would name my firm Google. A better example would be the name for an automobile repair shop; it might be better to name it "Mike's Garage" instead of "Mike's Tune Ups." The word garage allows you to do auto bodywork and transmissions if you decide to expand your line of services. "Mike's Tune Ups" is very limiting.
- Avoid trends or fads since your business or product might have a long life. The Mustang is timeless; the image is just as effective today as it was in 1964 when Ford introduced this moniker. A bad example from a few years back might be a music store named "Janet's Laser Disc Store." Who would have guessed that laser discs would have such a short product life? "Janet's Music" would have been a safer, albeit more boring choice.
- Use an original expression, which is unique to the product or firm. Avoid the use of clichés since we have all heard them

before. Instead, choose a name that stands out and demands attention. "Dunkin' Donuts" is a far better name than "Tom's Donuts."

- Include benefits of the solution in the name, if possible. This can be achieved by an image created by the choice of words used or an invented name. For example, combining the Latin word for truth, "veritas," with the word "horizon," created "Verizon Wireless." Combined they create an image of constancy, integrity, and no limits (at least, that is what their ad agency told them).
- Your name can be outrageous or daring, since your objective is to get noticed, while informing your customer about what you do. "DreamWorks," the brainchild of Steven Spielberg, develops, produces, and distributes films, video games, and television programming. Unique names are easier to find on an Internet search.
- Don't offend by accidentally referencing race, gender, ethnicity, heritage, etc. Marketplace diversity requires you to think about how the name will be interpreted by people different from yourself.
- Business names need to tie to an Internet domain name. This is getting harder and harder to do with the proliferation of existing domain names. In particular, if you want a domain name that ends in ".com," the preferred choice for businesses, you will be challenged to create something new or you will have to use multiple words.

*Google preferences: Google's mysterious ranking algorithm prefers real searchable names in the URL—that sounds odd since they chose www.google.com.*

# 48. Brand Strategy

"A goal without a plan is just a wish."

**Antoine de Saint-Exupery (1900 – 1944) French writer**

Companies have four basic options for an overall brand strategy: multi-product branding, sub-branding, multi-branding, and private branding. Each has its merits, so let's review them.

1. Multi-product branding employs a branding strategy that allows for one name for all products; this may also be called family branding or corporate branding. IBM generally employs this approach because of the significant brand equity that the IBM name offers and the lower advertising and promotion costs that come with that built-in awareness. A disadvantage to this approach could include customer confusion about what products are actually provided by the corporate entity. In IBM's case, they seem to make everything in the computer business; in reality, IBM has exited from a number of consumer product businesses such as PCs and consumer printers. Yet, I still think of IBM as a consumer product maker. Also, another negative is the possible dilution of the brand if products don't meet customer expectations.

2. A similar strategy is called sub-branding which utilizes the parent or corporate brand name with a unique product name. This is common in the automobile industry. For example, Ford Motors make the Mustang while Chevrolet offers the Corvette. Both products have been prestige product brands for both auto firms and have helped create brand equity for the parents. A downside to this approach might be the injury that an inferior product could have on the corporate brand. Ford is still trying to forget the Pinto and their exploding gas tanks.

3. Multi-branding is the domain of the giant consumer product firms with Procter and Gamble as the most famous example. In this case the product brands are uniquely marketed and have an identity all to their own. For example, most P&G products are seldom directly associated with the corporate brand. Scope, Crest, and Tide are P&G brands, but the average consumer does not know it. This obviously creates higher costs for advertising

and promotion. Yet, if a product bombs, the P&G brand chugs along unharmed.

4. <u>Private branding</u> is a strategy for the manufacturer that has limited or no distribution channels. In this case, a firm makes the product and sells it to another firm which gives it their own brand name. Many large retailers do this such as Sears and Wal-Mart; this allows the reseller to create a unique brand while receiving the branding rewards. The original manufacturer does what it does best: make the product.

*Origin of strategy: A Greek word for army.*

# 49. Strategies for Brand Growth

"The difficulty in life is the choice."

**George A. Moore (1852 – 1933) Irish Writer**

Creating a successful brand in the marketplace is very hard work and costs a lot of money. This is particularly true for consumer products where it takes millions of contacts to sell thousands of products. This is also true for the crowded B2B space where building brand awareness is getting tougher with global competitors coming out of the woodwork.

Once the brand is established the obvious question is what now? How do you keep the brand growing? The answer is that marketers have five different strategies for brand growth.

The first is called "line extension" which is when you offer a new product with the same brand name to the same market. An example of this would be the recent announcement by McDonald's to offer a super-sized version of the Big Mac, which is 40 percent larger than the regular Big Mac. This new burger leverages the success of the Big Mac while sticking with the tried and true formula that has made McDonald's so successful.

A second brand growth strategy is called "brand extension" which is the use of an existing brand name in a completely different product class. Harley Davidson has a powerful brand, which describes the benefits of rebellion and machismo for weekend riders (who actually are accountants and attorneys during the week). Harley's brand extension includes non-motorcycle items such as clothing and collectibles.

A third growth strategy for a brand could include "co-branding" which is the use of two brands for one product. Ford Motors partnered with Eddie Bauer to create special edition trucks that utilized the rugged outdoors appeal of the Eddie Bauer clothing line. Another example is the ice cream retailer Baskin-Robbins which sells ice cream with Hershey's Reese's Pieces.

A fourth strategy is a "new brand" strategy which leverages the existing brand's marketing clout. A classic example of a disastrous new brand strategy was Budweiser's introduction of Eagle Brand snacks. The thinking was that beer drinkers who eat salty snacks will drink more beer. True as that may be, Budweiser did not understand how to market snacks and the effort failed miserably.

Finally, a defensive strategy for brand growth is called a "fighting brand" or "flanker" strategy. This typically is used by firms that have successful brands with large market share to protect. Coca-Cola has a commanding market share, but has had to release numerous flanker brands in response to movement by competitors and to increased segmentation within the cola market. Recent flanker brands include Cherry Coke and Diet Cherry Coke. Of course, cannibalization of the Classic Coke market share is possible in this scenario, but the overall market share for Coca-Cola is protected and has grown.

*Game theory: In game theory, strategy is one of the options that a player may choose.*

# 50. Managing the Marketing Mix

"When choosing between two evils, I always like to try the one
I've never tried before."

**Mae West (1893 – 1980) Actress and Playwright**

The marketing mix (better known as the "4 Ps") is a term coined by author E. Jerome McCarthy in the 1950s and they are marketing gospel today: product, place, price, and promotion:

- <u>Product</u> is the goods, services, or solutions that the provider delivers. This is really the endgame for the entrepreneur since it is all about the customer and not the product, but more to come on that later.
- <u>Place</u> is the way or the method that you get your product, service, or solution to the customer. This could be a retail store, a website, or a sales representative.
- <u>Price</u> is the financial exchange for the value that the provider delivers to the customer. The customer deems that the price is right or fair and that your product is worth it. Implicit in this transaction is the fact the customer chooses your product instead of the competitor's offering.
- <u>Promotion</u> is how you get the message to the customer. In the broadest sense, this includes publicity, advertising, and public relations.

For the entrepreneur, the challenge is to adjust this mix of marketing tools to accommodate the changing needs of the competitive environment. For example, pricing might need to be reduced in response to competitive pressures. Alternatively, more advertising might be required to create awareness of the product.

Candidly, the 4 Ps are a bit out of date. The 4 Ps are derived from the provider's point of view rather than from the customer perspective. In the new millennium, the customer is in charge and demands to be served their way, when they want it, and where they want. Got it?

Dr. Bob Lauterborn, a professor at the University of North Carolina, gets it. He thinks that we need to toss out the 4 Ps. He contends that there are actually 4 Cs:

- <u>Consumer Wants and Needs</u>: Instead of products first, you need to find what the customer wants and then create the product, service, or solution. This makes too much sense. It is all about the customer, not the solution.
- <u>Cost to Satisfy</u>: Instead of price, think like the customer does. Customers ask the question, "What will it cost me to be satisfied and get what I need." The customer will pay a fair price for a fair deal.
- <u>Convenience to Buy</u>: Instead of place, the more pertinent question is how and where does the customer want to purchase? This question is getting tougher to answer with increasingly segmented consumer markets, the worldwide web, and the global economy.
- <u>Communication</u>: Instead of promotion, which stinks of manipulation or greed, you need to ask the customer questions and listen. Blasting the airwaves with a repetitive advertisement does not work anymore, since the customer is numb from too much advertising, while being more sophisticated than past generations. Customers have access to nearly as much information as providers, much to the consternation of the providers.

The 4 Cs make more sense to me.

*More Ps: Various academicians after McCarthy created more Ps including public opinion, political power, physical evidence, people, and process. There is no shortage of Ps.*

# 51. Marketing Innovative Products

"The man who has no imagination has no wings."

**Muhammad Ali (1942 – present) Legendary Boxer**

Innovative products need to be marketed and sold differently than other offerings since they require a special customer who is receptive to innovation. Most customers are skeptical and will wait until innovative products are mass marketed.

Here are a few suggestions on how to market innovative products:

- Not everyone will understand the need for the innovation. They will need to be educated about the problem. Think of it from their perspective—why should they care? Help them understand the problem that needs to be solved and how your product addresses that problem.
- Explain how your product is different. People buy things because of the differences not because it is the same. If your offering is truly innovative, this won't be a problem.
- Be authentic. Customers are drawn to sellers who believe in the offerings. Your enthusiasm will be contagious and appealing. If you fake it, they will see right through you.
- Position your product as a high-quality alternative. Innovation and quality make great companion benefits. Take the high road.
- Consider the impact of premium pricing. People are aware that innovative solutions cost more. Price the offering based on value.
- Innovative products need a customer who appreciates the value of the new product. Don't waste your time on the late adopters or laggards—they will only buy when they have no other alternative.
- Look for the innovative buyer or early adopter. Truly innovative buyers leave tracks. They buy other innovative products and visit leading edge websites. The good news is that they will seek you out since they are always on the hunt for the next new thing—so make a lot of noise so that they can find you.

*How to market Innovative Products: First, create an innovative product. Second, sell it to an innovative customer. Third, repeat.*

# 52. Price Strategically

"Hug the shore; let others try the deep."

**Virgil (70 B.C. – 19 B.C.) Roman Poet**

Undoubtedly, pricing an offering is one of the more important deci-sions that an entrepreneur makes, yet it is my observation that it seldom gets much thought. Pricing decisions are often emotionally based and made quickly even though they have a lasting impact.

The market can dictate a price point or price range for a commodity product when it is offered by many competitors. If that is the case, you are kind of stuck with market prices unless your offering has unique charac-teristics or benefits.

Otherwise, there are some basic questions that you need to ask your-self about your product, the customer, and the selling environment before you establish the price:

- Who is the customer for the offering? What is the region or geog-raphy served? How many potential customers can be served? These simple questions will determine your channel of distribu-tion costs.
- How will you market the offering? Over the web? By mail? In person? What are the costs of promotion and advertising? Simi-larly, your promotion mix will make a huge impact on your cost of sales.
- Is price elasticity a factor? Does product demand change if you move prices up or down? OK, this sounds simple, but it can actu-ally be vexing to many entrepreneurs. Lowering prices does not always increase sales volume; it can be a hard lesson learned once you lower a price and get stuck with it.
- What does your product really cost? This can be a really hard one for small firms since true cost accounting does not normally exist. Most small firms "estimate" cost and then apply a multiple of 3 or 4 to get a sales price. The problem exists in the word "esti-mate," since it generally means "underestimate." Most firms don't capture or know all the true costs. This is a red flag waving, so don't ignore it.

- Look outside the box. Are there any environmental factors that may impact pricing that are out of your control such as weather, legal or regulatory changes, or competitor misbehavior? They may be hard to forecast, but you need to be cognizant of the impact of these external factors.
- Pricing goals. What do you hope to achieve with this offering and its price? Maybe you want to open a new market or drive out a competitor? Or, is the offering supposed to drive big profits? If so, your product margins will need to be high and pricing defended.
- Can you make money by selling this product/service? If no, look elsewhere.

With these issues researched or decided, you can begin to address the pricing options. It still is a choice, but hopefully it is a more informed one.

*Price theory: Consider the forces that influence your price—costs, competitors, suppliers, availability of substitutes, and customers' preferences.*

# 53. *Pricing Below the Market*

"A billion here and a billion there, and pretty soon
you're talking real money."

**Everett Dirksen (1896 – 1969) Statesman**

Pricing below the market is a technique used by giant mass market firms to take market share. Also known as "penetration" pricing, this is a strategy where a provider sells products below market price to break into a market and/or to take market share. When enough competitors are scared out of the market, the giant firm will raise prices and recoup lost profits.

This is what the Japanese semiconductor makers did in the 1980's; buoyed by a lower cost of capital and a government-sponsored long-term objective, taking market share from the U.S. semiconductor firms was worth the short-term losses. You may recall that the U.S. manufacturers called foul on this practice and referred to it as "dumping."

Nonetheless, Japan emerged as a major player in the semiconductor memory chip business and pushed many U.S. suppliers out of the business. The risk paid off for the Japanese semiconductor industry.

This is a very interesting tactic, but hardly a tool for niche marketers like you and me. My advice is to price on value and keep the focus on customer needs.

*Loss leader: Loss leader pricing is when you sell at or below cost in order to attract more customers—the hope is that they will also buy other higher margin products now or in the future.*

# 54. Mark-up Pricing

"No great discovery was ever made without a bold guess."

**Sir Isaac Newton (1643 – 1727) Physicist, Mathematician, Theologian**

Many businesses use mark-up pricing. Mark-up pricing uses some multiple of cost, such as three or four times the "estimated cost" of the offering. The entrepreneur says, "If it costs a dollar to make the widget, I need to sell it for three or four dollars. At that price we are living large!"

Whoops! Look back a few words and you will see the word "estimated"; most entrepreneurs don't know what their actual costs truly are. Often they under-price their products since cost accounting at small firms is only the guessed sum of direct materials, direct labor, and some overhead (if they track it).

Another common pricing technique is to price like the competitor or maybe a little below. Some call this market or street pricing. Since when is the guy down the street a pricing genius? This is a really dumb tactic. I guess this approach presumes that the competitor is the price leader and has educated all customers to this price. My guess is that the competitor may have used a crystal ball or had his cousin Vinny price his product. Fallible? You bet. This pricing method is used at large and small firms.

*Mark-up pricing: Can be effective if cost accounting is accurate. Most small firms have lousy cost accounting.*

# 55. Skimming: A Pricing Strategy for New Products

"Never spend your money before you have it."

**Thomas Jefferson (1743-1826) Founding Father, President**

Price skimming is a pricing strategy which utilizes a high price for a brief period of time. This type of pricing is generally used with the introduction of a new product. The purpose of this pricing strategy is to "skim" the profits before the competition enters the market.

This type of pricing is often deployed for a product which has a competitive advantage that is not sustainable. This happens a great deal with new technology when an innovative product first captures the customer's attention and the competition later follows.

When TiVo launched its early DVR products they commanded a substantial pricing premium in the market with the early adopters. This premium helped pay back TiVo for the R&D costs associated with the creation of the new product and the new market. Where a highly innovative product is launched, research and development costs are likely to be high. This includes the costs of introducing the product to the market via promotion, advertising etc.

Yet, there are other reasons for establishing a high price. A company can build a high-quality image for its product by charging high prices initially. This is especially true for luxury products which can benefit from skimming since the buyer tends to be more 'prestige' conscious than price conscious. To this buyer the high price denotes quality.

Another reason to set a high price initially is to establish the new product as a prestige or a high quality product. Buyers have been taught that quality comes at a higher price, so, in a weird way, buyers are comforted by the higher pricing. Where the quality differences between competing brands is perceived to be large, or for offerings where such differences are not easily judged, the skimming strategy can work well. An example of the latter would be for the manufacturers of "designer" watches. Buyers of Rolex watches expect to pay more for the brand; it is almost as if they demand it.

The beauty of skimming is that the price can be lowered later if necessary. For example, when you begin with a high price, you have room to move down in price with the anticipated entrance of competition. The converse is seldom, if ever, true. Once you educate the market about your price, raising the price is damn near impossible. To generalize, most prices go down when competition joins the fray. This logic suggests that you should anchor with a price high and prepare to negotiate.

However, skimming is not the preferred pricing method for a niche market player. Niche marketers create value based on a sustainable competitive advantage and a partnership with the customer. The customer values the offering above other alternatives and considers the pricing fair.

Pricing on value is a better approach for niche players.

*Price elasticity: Price elasticity refers to the way prices change in relationship to the demand or the way demand changes in relationship to pricing. Essentially, price and demand are thus interrelated.*

# 56. Perceived Value Pricing

"Money will buy you a fine dog, but only love can make it wag its tail."

**Anonymous**

Niche marketers should price their products and services based on the value received by the customer: it is the customer's perception of value that counts. If you calculate price based on cost and/or the competition, you are not in a niche market or you are pricing incorrectly.

Niche market customers buy your product or service because it is different from the other options available. That difference is your value and it can be worth a premium price. Value is subjective and not every customer will need your product's unique benefits, but this is how niche marketing works. As a niche marketer, you focus on serving a market segment that has been overlooked or underserved; the value or difference you add is your special knowledge of their unique needs.

The value can come in the form of unique product or service features that you add. That value could come in many forms, even prestige. For example, Tiffany's is a "prestige" brand for jewelry; people buy jewelry at Tiffany's because of the brand. Yet, diamonds are diamonds. You can buy the same quality diamonds at Costco, but you don't get the prestige buying experience. For the Tiffany's customer, it is worth the price premium to walk out the store with the Tiffany's bag or box.

You can add value to your product by doing any of the following:

- Special payment terms
- After purchase service agreements
- Special packaging
- Fast delivery
- Concierge service
- Special product features
- Guarantees

Value based pricing is determined as the highest amount that a customer will pay for your product or service given the unique value that you offer when compared to the other alternatives. By giving the niche customer exactly what they want, there are no other real alternatives. If that is the case, price it accordingly.

Value based pricing is pricing for a product or service at a level that reflects the potential savings, the highest satisfaction level, or the maximum use that a client will receive from the purchase and the use of the product or service. Overall, a perceived value based price is set at the highest level that your target market is willing to pay, given these benefits. This type of pricing reflects a sustainable competitive advantage where there is little or no competition. This is niche market heaven.

However, be sure that your competitive advantage is real and defensible, or you have got trouble on the way. When utilizing perceived value based pricing how much is too much to charge? Look for tear stains on the checks you receive from customers. It also does not hurt to ask some of your better customers what they think about your pricing. If it hurts them to write you a check, then you are charging too much. If that is the case, you won't keep them as customers for long, unless you make changes.

An indicator that your pricing is accurate would be referrals because if you are getting referrals, you are priced fairly or you have an opportunity to increase prices. If your customers complain about pricing and leave, you have priced too high or you are not delivering the promised value proposition.

Pricing should be fair for both buyer and seller.

*Value: Provide a benefit that helps business stand out in the marketplace. The most useful/valuable business in the category or segment wins.*

# 57. Life is a Cabernet

"There is a devil in every berry of the grape."

**The Koran**

There is something special about a fine bottle of wine. For many, a fine wine is worth a hefty price premium. Yet, that price premium is how many wine lovers actually determine a fine wine's merit thinking that the higher the price the better the wine.

Scientists at California Institute of Technology studied premium pricing and its impact on drinkers of Cabernet Sauvignon. They asked 20 ordinary people to sample wine while undergoing functional MRIs of their brain activity. The subjects were told that they were going to taste five different Cabernet Sauvignons sold at different prices.

However, there were actually only three wines sampled, two being offered twice, marked with different prices. A $90 wine was provided marked with its real price and again marked $10, while another was presented at its real price of $5 and also marked $45.

The results were astonishing. The brains of the test group showed more pleasure at the higher price than the lower one, even for the same wine. In other words, changes in the price of the wine changed the actual pleasure experienced by the drinkers. On the other hand, when tasters didn't know any price comparisons, they rated the $5 wine as better than any of the others sampled.

What this means to you and me is that premium products "need" premium pricing. If you are marketing a high-end or luxury product, discounting or lowering the price is not consistent with the potential buyer's perception of value. The Cal Tech study tells us that part of the thrill of buying and enjoying a luxury item is its exclusivity, as determined by the price.

If quality is your competitive advantage, a higher price is the best match. Even during tough economic times the pricing for a high end product should be higher than for inferior products/services. If you discount too severely during these periods you will do irreparable harm to your brand image.

As for me, I think I will stick with Bud Light.

*Luxury products need: Luxury product buyers.*

# 58. Discounts Cut Deep

"The art is not in making money, but in keeping it."

**Anonymous**

To discount or not to discount, that is the question that many sales professionals must answer. At first view, it seems that discounting prices should stimulate new sales and be a good thing. But that is not always the case.

The best advice may to be to hesitate and think first. Let's examine the potential consequences of offering a discount:

- Profits are reduced. Is the extra sale worth the decrease in profits?
- With the pricing precedent set, customers will know to always ask for a lower price since they got one before.
- If your product is a commodity, you may risk the customers buying extra stock at the lower price and keeping inventory. Thus, you lose future sales at a higher price.
- Once discounted, raising prices is very difficult, if not altogether impossible. Customers will presume that this is the new normal.
- Depending on the commission plan, fewer sales dollars will equal less commission and this can de-motivate the sales force.
- Cash flow will slow down. Without cash how will your business stay afloat?

Alternatively, discounting may preserve the relationship and defend the customer relationship from the competitors. But, is it worth it?

*Deep discounts: Prices were artificially high or you are now losing money.*

# 59. Is Advertising Dead?

"Whatever begins also ends."

**Seneca (4 B.C. – 65 A.D.) Roman Statesman and Philosopher**

This may be somewhat of a sensational title but advertising as we know it is changing in a very big way because of new advances in technology. If you have read my first book "First, Best, or Different," you know that I am very critical of the traditional advertising model. Traditional marketing techniques, like advertising in a newspaper, are largely ineffective and grossly overpriced.

The current, outmoded advertising model is mass media based and delivers messages through print ads, television and radio commercials, and recently the Internet. The ads presume that all customers will want what the sponsor has, will understand the ad, and will respond to the call for action. These ads use a "spray and pray" methodology that is based on the assumption that, if you spend enough money and contact the customer a gazillion times, the prospective buyer will eventually get the message and buy the product.

This is, of course, absurd. The customer today has grown totally numb to all of these messages and does not want one-size-fits-all products anyway. Instead, the customer wants the product in a special size, color, configuration, and shape; it must be unique, if not custom. It must be delivered at a special time with special packaging. Mass marketing is on the way out.

Now enters IPTV (Internet Protocol Television). Perhaps the simplest definition of IPTV is that it is TV delivered through existing computer networks. You will get this new content through cable, the telephone line, and satellite. Coming to your plasma TV soon, this new content will allow you to watch exactly want you want when you want to watch it (remember, 99% of the current TV content is prerecorded anyway).

This new delivery mechanism will create a new industry of "mini-producers" who will create very specific content for special people like you. You will be able to get content as specific as a golf talk show for left handed duffers living in Orange County, California who want to hook up with opposite sex golfers for fun and frolic. No smokers please. I am not kidding; this is how TV is going to work in the not-too-distant future.

Since all of this new content will use the newest technologies, the viewer will leave tracks or digital fingerprints allowing the advertisers to perfectly pinpoint their messages to exactly the right customer: you.

Alas, the advertising industry will be saved!

*IPTV: Visit www.mrgco.com to learn more about IPTV.*

# 60. *Traditional Retail Advertising is Ineffective*

"Difficulties increase the nearer we get to the goal."

**Goethe (1749 – 1832) German Writer**

A recent online study by Deloitte and Touche uncovered that two-thirds of store visits during the holiday season were not influenced by holiday advertising. It turns out that most consumers picked stores because of their pre-existing familiarity with the stores and the stores locations. Additionally, the products purchased were researched on the Internet.

This means that all the money spent during holiday season for print, radio, and TV advertising was largely wasted. As I read the Los Angeles Times one Sunday morning, I was again reminded how much money is wasted on print advertising; I think I threw away about ten pounds of unread advertising.

So, why do the retail giants waste all this money? I think mostly it is because they have been well-trained by the giant advertising firms. The retailers are budgeted to spend this money and the spending is institutionalized. They do it because they have been told that it is the right thing to do.

Consumer shopping behavior is less and less impacted by traditional advertising methods. A cataclysmic shift occurred with consumers in the last year or so with use of search marketing on the Internet. More and more buyers are "pre-shopping" with search engines making them the most informed shopper ever. After doing exhaustive research on the web they visit stores to kick the tires. After viewing the products in-person, it is then a matter of price and delivery. The retail store is played against the Internet retailer: lowest price and availability wins.

Returning to the ineffectiveness of traditional advertising, the fix seems simple. Retailers need to increase their Internet marketing budgets for search engine optimization, Internet advertising, and viral marketing. To quote the giant retailer Sears, "where America shops" is now on the Internet.

*Oh yeah, one more thing: cut the budget for traditional advertising. It does not work any more.*

# 61. Web Advertising Comes of Age

"Small opportunities are often the beginning of great enterprises."

**Demosthenes (384 B.C. – 322 B.C.) Greek Statesman**

Market researcher IDC estimates that between 2008 and 2012 web advertising will grow at eight times the rate as traditional advertising; this growth rate effectively doubles web advertising revenues to $51.1 billion. Remarkably, Internet advertising revenues were effectively zero in 2000!

While Internet advertising is still relatively new, companies can successfully implement an Internet marketing strategy with dramatic results. The options include rich content, paid search campaigns, blogging, and article writing and social media.

A 2007 search study by Enquiro found that 65.3% of business buyers said they would start their research with a search engine. The study found a heavy reliance on online research in all aspects of the purchase cycle.

What really matters to the search engines? First of all, don't think of your home page as a static brochure—home page, product page, services page, about us, and maybe a news center. Rather, think of it as a resource for people to solve problems. Searchers will use a keyword or phrase that describes their problem, their pain or a general category of solution. Thus, be sure to populate your site with relevant terms that people will use.

Pay per click advertising is hot right now since it can pinpoint your messaging to people searching for your offering. Pay per click is a form of advertising found on search engines, advertising networks, websites and blogs. The advertiser pays when a visitor actually clicks on an "ad" to visit the advertiser's website. Advertisers bid on keywords or terms that they believe that their target customers use to find information on products or services.

Frequent content is important and this is why blogs help so much. Blogging is viewed as new content by the Search engine spiders each time you release a blog. If you don't have a blog consider creating one. Once loaded on your website, no maintenance is required from your web designer.

Article marketing is another high impact tool which is low cost and is a type of online advertising. Article marketing consists of short articles on topics of interest to your target audience or industry. Once written, you make these articles freely available for distribution and publication in the marketplace. Each article contains a 'bio box' and 'by-line' which include references and contact information for the author's business. Well written content articles released for free distribution have the potential of gaining the author business credibility within his or her market, as well as new clients.

Yet, even with this fabulous growth, Internet advertising still represents only 10 percent of the $495 billion spent on advertising worldwide in 2007 and lags behind advertising spent on newspapers, magazines, and TV. Yet, it is clear that these advertising dollars will continue to shift to the Internet from TV, radio, and print over the next five years.

This movement from the traditional advertisers to the web may actually happen sooner than forecasted.

*Advertising agencies: Create, plan, and handle advertising and other forms of promotion for its clients.*

# 62. Pay Per Click Advertising

"The more elaborate our means of communication,
he less we communicate."

**Joseph Priestley (1733 – 1804) Theologian and Scientist**

Pay per click is a form of advertising found on search engines, advertising networks, websites and blogs. The advertiser pays when a visitor actually clicks on an "ad" to visit the advertiser's website. Advertisers bid on keywords or terms that they believe that their target customers use to find information on products or services.

When a searcher enters a keyword or term in a search engine that matches the advertiser's keywords, the advertiser's ad is displayed. These ads are called "Sponsored links" or "sponsored ads" and appear next to or above the "natural" or organic results on the search engine text listings or results. You will typically see these ads displayed to the right of the text search results.

Pay per click ads may also appear on websites. In this case, Google AdSense and Yahoo! provide ads that are relevant to the content of the page where they appear, and no search function is involved.

The major players in the pay per click industry include Google AdWords, Yahoo! Search Marketing, and Microsoft; there also are many small players. Prices for per click can be as low at $0.10 per click. Popular search terms can cost as much as $10.00 per click or even more.

Sophisticated buyers of pay per click advertising learn to pick multiple keywords that better target their customer, but cost less. For example, "car dealers" is a common but expensive term that frequently gets bid high and may not be affordable. Yet, "Orange County California Car Dealers," which is a much more specific term, is much more affordable. The prices for keywords are determined by an auction process and thus can change.

Pay per click advertising has taken the web by storm and for good reason. You have seen thousands of these ads on the right side of a Google or Yahoo! search; the ads scream for you to click on them for more information. It may seem like you ignore them, but statistically they are one of the best and cheapest ways to advertise on the web.

These Internet ads help you deliver a short promotional message to your target market. As the name says, they click on your ad and you pay. Sometimes you pay a lot. The key is setting up a good ad that drives the right traffic to your site. Here are a few thoughts on doing pay per click advertising the right way, which maximizes the hits and minimizes the expenses.

Write simple ads that attract the web surfer while telling them what you promoting. The big three (Google, Yahoo! and MSN) have different rules for the ad creation, but the mission is the same. Write clear, simple copy that compels your reader to click for more information. Use of key words is critical, so be sure to include them in your ad copy. Remember that your ad readers are doing web searches and have keywords on the brain. Also, these keywords are what match your ad with their search. Don't try to trick the reader into clicking; likely they won't buy what you are selling and all this does is cost you money.

When a web visitor clicks on your ad, they want to go where they can get more information, or they just want to buy. Your website may not be the best destination. If you sell many products or if your website is complex, you may want to consider a simple landing page that gives the visitor what they want. Visitors are very impatient and won't waste time searching though your site for what they need. It is a two or three click world.

Not all ads work the first time, so be sure to test and tweak them. I recommend short duration ads to start, which is the beauty of the Internet and pay per click advertising. Ads are easy to create. It can take just a few minutes to create them, if your ad copy is ready to go. Once the ad is approved, which is generally in three to four days with Google and Yahoo!, your ads will get immediate feedback.

The ads cost real money and it pays to have your ad in a prominent place at the top of the listed ads. A general rule of thumb is to stay in the top 25% of the listed ads since most clicks occur in this quartile. Below the top 25% is no man's land and the ads are not worth the money. Note that the ad prices are set in an auction environment and are quite variable. Experiment with key words and descriptive phrases. Avoid lengthy or complex descriptions since they will just be overlooked.

Paid inclusion is another variation of online advertising that is related to pay per click. So what is the difference between paid inclusion and pay per click advertising? First, let's agree to a few definitions.

Paid inclusion is a search engine marketing product where the search engine company charges fees related to the inclusion of websites in their search index. Let's now say you launch a new website and you want to get the word out about your site. Paid inclusion is one way to get noticed. Specifically, you can contact the search engines directly and register your site for a fee. For example, Alta Vista offers such a service for a fee.

Paid inclusion products are provided by many search engine companies, the most notable exception being Google. Inktomi, Alta Vista, and many other specialized search engine firms charge to list your website. The fee covers an annual subscription for one web page, which will automatically be cataloged on a regular basis.

Paid inclusion and pay per click both hope to drive traffic to the website. Paid inclusion positions itself as a registration process for "legitimate" websites which basically means those websites that can afford the fees. It could be argued that paid inclusion is simply advertising. Yet, paid inclusion really works; in fact, many SEO (search engine optimization) companies rely on paid inclusion as a part of their "secret sauce" to help improve site rankings.

Paid inclusion is like being a member of a special club which advertises its members. Pay per click is like the Yellow Pages. The end game is the same.

*Pay per click: Invest in PPC after your website is truly optimized. Be sure to manage it carefully since it can be expensive.*

# 63. Beware of Click Fraud

"The liar and the thief rejoice in their first year only"

**Greek proverb**

Online advertising has been hailed as one of the most effective and economical ways to reach customers in the new millennium. Google AdWords, Google Ad Sense, and Yahoo! Pay per click are three of the more common publishers of online advertisements. Recently, Click Forensics, a web market researcher, determined that 13.7% of clicks are fraudulent.

Google and Yahoo! both offer online advertising programs that allow website owners and even bloggers the money-making opportunity to show "contextual ads" on their own pages. A contextual ad is advertising on a website that is targeted to the specific individual who is visiting the website; they use a system that scans the text of a website for keywords and returns ads to the web page based on what the user is viewing, either through ads placed on the page or pop-up ads. The search engines then pay the publisher most of the generated revenue.

Click fraud is easy. You place an ad and watch the clicks build up and this looks great, at least for a while. Your competitor finds your ad and camps out at the keyboard repeatedly clicking your ad. The dollars add up in a hurry. This malicious mischief can also be automated with software robots pushing the clicks through to your website. You get stuck with click fees. The motivation is to make the competitor waste money on online advertising. This is an obvious source of fraud.

But it turns out the publishers (the firms selling the ads) also commit fraud. They know best that volume of clicks is the prevalent indicator of success. Pushing the numbers helps the publishers sell more online programs. The Click Forensics report indicated that the fraud is actually greater (up to 30%) at the smaller publishers of which there are hundreds of firms too numerous to name.

What this means to folks like us (I use Google AdWords) is that we need to carefully monitor our online advertising. Truthfully, clicks are just clicks. Focus on the real measures of online marketing success which could include sales leads, website registrations, online purchases, and sample requests—these are the metrics that really count.

*Fraud: Intentional deception for personal gain.*

# 64. What is Advergaming?

"Half the game is 90% mental."

**Yogi Berra (1925 – present) Baseball Hall of Famer**

Picture this. You are a 17-year-old kid who got a free download for a cool new video game. You open the game, bypass the instructions (since you never read them anyway) and start playing the game. The game seems a little funky but you play it anyway. Some dumb advertisement keeps on popping up and getting in the way. You ignore it. The game is easy. Game over. You move on, but you remember the dumb ad.

Welcome to advergaming which is the insertion of a paid advertisement into a video game. The game itself can be found online via a download or a streaming video or offline in a software-based game. Some advertisements have the sponsor's name and logo on the banner of the game. Other ads are hidden in the game itself in a subliminal fashion.

The video game industry (also known as interactive entertainment) is huge. DFC Intelligence has forecasted worldwide videogame and interactive entertainment industry revenue to reach $57 billion in 2009. Gamers play a game for an average of 25 minutes while 42% of gamers play online video games one or more hours per week. This makes for a captive audience for advertisers.

Look a little more deeply: Consider these statistics from the Entertainment Software Association:

- The average game player is 35 years old and has been playing games for 13 years.
- The average age of the most frequent game purchaser is 40 years old.
- Forty percent of all game players are women. In fact, women over the age of 18 represent a significantly greater portion of the game-playing population (33 percent) than boys age 17 or younger (18 percent).
- In 2008, 26 percent of Americans over the age of 50 played video games, an increase from nine percent in 1999.

- Thirty-six percent of heads of households play games on a wireless device, such as a cell phone or PDA, up from 20 percent in 2002.

Advertisers have set up special websites just for gamers where different online games can be played along with the advertising messages. Games have also proven to be a great tool to drive traffic to traditional websites; in this case, there is advertising to get people to play the game that has the sponsor's advertising in the game. The US Army created a video game which doubles as a recruiting tool. All is fair in the advergaming world.

Product placement is a common technique in the video game industry. Examples include a soft drink such as Coca-Cola, which could be consumed by the hero in a video game. A BMX bike race video game might feature a Kawasaki BMX bike. A skateboarding game could include the hero Tony Hawk using a certain brand of skateboard as well as wearing clothes from a specific manufacturer.

Game players are hooked. This demographic spends more time playing games than watching television or doing most anything. This is a very sought after demographic that has high discretionary income and lots of free time.

Game on!

*Gamers unite: Advergaming is a perfect way to connect with this audience.*

# 65. *Why Not Advertise Outdoors?*

"Camping—nature's way of promoting the motel industry."

**Dave Barry (1947 – present) Writer**

While Internet advertising is the "new thing," outdoor or out-of-home advertising can be a very effective and affordable method to get your message out to your target market. With people spending more and more time in their vehicles (it is estimated that 150 million commute to work daily), you have a captive audience and the message is hard to miss.

A common example of outdoor advertising is the use of billboards along the highway. It is interesting to note that the use of billboards originated in the 19th century with printed signs posted on wooden boards. Flashing to the present, billboards can now be electronic and customizable; in fact, they can be rented by the hour and deliver multiple messages. And billboards are hard to miss.

A newer form of outdoor advertising includes car, bus, and train "wrapping." As it sounds, a car is wrapped bumper to bumper with digitally-printed adhesive material. City buses can be rented on a monthly basis and plastered with over 90 feet of printed vinyl graphics. Amtrak offers space on the sides of their rail cars; you can deliver your message when your customers are stopped at the railroad crossing. Private autos can be transformed into mobile advertisements, while the car owner is commissioned $400-500 per month; this method is especially good at targeting college students, since no one else would be crazy enough to do this to their car.

If you have the budget, hot air balloons have proven to be incredibly effective for reaching a mass audience. Still a rarity that makes people gasp and point, the Goodyear blimp is the biggest mobile outdoor advertisement on the planet. Smaller scale hot air balloons include replicas of beer cans, football helmets, cartoon characters, autos, and bumblebees. Attend an outdoor professional football game and you will be entertained all game long with floating advertisements. On a smaller scale, car dealerships know the value of balloons for weekend sales; they get attention and they are dirt cheap.

Maybe more accessible and affordable is the use of "wild posting" which includes "rock band" stickers that are plastered on street signs, or flyers posted in public restrooms for an upcoming concert. Another form of wild posting is the use of elaborate signs drawn in colored chalk on sidewalks in public areas. This method targets the younger demographic and has a short life, but can be amazingly effective.

The use of professional street teams can be very effective in high-traffic urban areas. Street teams consist of a group of choreographed dancers or marchers who often carry signs or props to promote something. They ambush their audience unexpectedly with dancing, noise, music, yelling, and energy. These teams quickly deliver the message and move on to another street corner. The audience is typically left stunned wondering what just happened to them.

You need to be careful about this type of advertising though. Comedy Central got into trouble a couple of years ago because their guerilla marketing attempt, which put robot-looking advertisements out in public. Some people thought that those objects were bombs and called the police. Unless you want bad press and even some fines you should clear your advertising campaign with the authorities if there is the slightest chance that someone might think you are planting a bomb.

Outdoor advertising works because it is so visible and it targets the customer precisely. Other outdoor methods include bus stop benches, kiosks, store windows, sandwich signs, and sign twirlers. Outdoor advertising can deliver repetitive 24/7 exposure and it can target a specific geography such as an intersection or a Zip Code. It's larger-than-life proportions and endless creativity demands to be noticed. Finally, the cost per customer contact is amazingly inexpensive.

*Outdoor Advertising: Depends on the mobility of the customer to find it repeatedly.*

# 66. If You Advertise, Be Sure to Measure It

"How many legs does a dog have if you call the tail a leg?
Four—calling a tail a leg doesn't make it a leg."

**Abraham Lincoln (1809 – 1865) President**

Advertising is tough for most small-to-medium size businesses since it is expensive, difficult to connect with your target customer, and hard to measure for effectiveness. However, there are some tricks when setting up your advertising campaign to ensure that the campaign's effectiveness can be measured. The simplest method for tracking advertising is to ask the customer how they heard about your business or product. Most of the time, your customers will tell you exactly how they found you; this could be because of advertising or not.

If your campaign requires or allows them to call in on the phone, set up a separate phone number. When that new line rings, you obviously know that the advertisement created the opportunity. If this is a large-scale campaign that has different customer segments or different advertising mediums involved, you can create multiple phone numbers for tracking purposes. For example, if the scale of your campaign is large enough and you are using multiple magazines as your advertising vehicle, you could set up separate phone numbers for each magazine. This tracking data could prove powerful when choosing which magazine to use for your next campaign.

Another trick for tracking incoming phone calls is to have your customer call requesting different names or aliases; in this case, the customer calls asking for a specific individual to hear more about the special offer. When the phone rings and the customers ask to speak with "Bob," you know that the caller saw your ad in Rolling Stone Magazine and not Wired Magazine.

Coupons or special pricing can also be keyed to separate advertising methods. On a postcard mailing that has a mail-in tear off, the tear off can be color coded or marked to indicate which magazine worked. Separate mail addresses can be effective for advertising campaign tracking efforts;

add a P.O. Box for the campaign. The same technique works on the web; set up separate sites for each campaign. Or, on your website, have them indicate how they found your website when they fill out the permission documents.

Most of these suggestions are inexpensive and simple to implement for tracking advertising. The data should be helpful when making choices about your next advertising.

*Coupons work: Advertising Age reports that 87% of all shoppers use coupons. I guess I am in the 13%.*

# 67. *Show Me a Sign*

"The problem with communication ... is the illusion that it has been accomplished."

**George Bernard Shaw (1856 – 1950) Irish Playwright**

For you "bricks and mortar types," the sign on the front of your building or store is the first impression you make with your customers. Make sure that is a positive one by adhering to the following rules:

- Make sure that the name on your sign is the name of your business. I went into a restaurant the other day called "Luigi's" for some pasta; it turned out to be a British Pub. They had just opened and had not change the sign yet. Go figure.
- Your sign needs to be consistent with your brand image including font, color, and design; it should match your stationary, brochures, and business cards.
- It should be readable from the street; if the letters are too small or if the sign is too intricate to read, what good is it?
- If you include a tagline on the sign that says open 24 hours, make sure that you stay open 24 hours. I stopped at a 24 hour coffee shop recently to discover that it was closed. I won't be going back there.
- For the highest impact, your sign should be lighted at night. Routinely check the light bulbs, since burned out light bulbs will reflect poorly on your business (no pun intended).
- The best colors for a sign are red and yellow, since they attract your eye better than other colors.
- Clean your sign periodically so it shines.

*Sign up now: Read your lease agreement carefully since signage can be severely restricted on some buildings.*

# 68. *Advertising on Social Networks*

"Remember, no man is a failure who has friends."

**From the movie "It's a Wonderful Life"**

Unless you have been living in a cave, you probably have heard about MySpace. MySpace is one of the best examples of "social networking" with over 100 million members. Membership is mostly teenagers and "twenty-somethings," but the membership spans five-year-olds to grandparents. You may be next.

In a nutshell, MySpace provides the member a personal webpage for the user's photos, blog, and personal profile that is customized for the likes, dislikes, favorite bands, movies, and books of the member. There's also MySpace mail, instant message, chat, and discussion groups. Many MySpace users have abandoned "old fashioned" email systems like AOL or Hotmail in favor of user-friendly email on MySpace.

Webpage members invite their friends to sign up, who in turn invite their friends to sign up. You are allowed search through all the members to find like-minded people who are between certain ages, are looking for relationships, and who live within a few miles of your zip code. See a photo you like? Leave a message for the person and ask to be made a "friend." You can mark your information as public or private, although a quick tour shows that most pages are public. Parental controls are available for the kiddies, but the content can get risqué by Time Magazine standards.

So what's the big deal? Advertising is now coming to age on MySpace. In addition to MySpace, Facebook now accepts advertising. Other social networks are also getting in the game.

*If you are interested: I recommend that you visit MySpace or Facebook so you can familiarize yourself with social networking. Be sure to check out their terms of use for advertisers.*

# 69. *Try Advertising in Unusual Places*

"The world is but a canvas to the imagination."

**Henry David Thoreau (1817 – 1862) Author and Transcendentalist**

One way to build awareness with your customer is to advertise in unusual places, especially places where you don't expect to see advertisements.

For example, I was traveling the other day and went through security at LAX airport. As I placed my PC in the plastic tray, I was surprised to see an advertisement for a major office supply chain. I think that's very clever since many people are traveling on business and are always in the market for office supplies.

Not long ago I heard a knock at the front door of my home. When I opened it, no one was there, but there was a container of salt on my doorstep. Unique to this salt container was a label with the smiling face of my local realtor, along with his contact information. I promptly put the salt in my cupboard. Of course, I see it every single day and I suppose that I will continue to see his smiling face for many months to come.

This morning I picked up the newspaper and found a sample of Starbucks coffee stuffed inside in the paper's protective plastic bag so I made myself a cup of coffee. The coffee tasted great and I liked the price: free. Those Starbucks folks are pretty darn smart.

The novel placement of these ads got my attention. And that is what it is all about.

*Homework: Look for advertising in unusual places. Where do your customers regularly congregate?*

# 70. *Goodbye Yellow Pages*

"Why does it take a minute to say hello and forever to say goodbye?"

**Anonymous**

If you are still devoting significant dollars to the Yellow Pages, you might want to reconsider your budget. The printed yellow page books are definitely on the way out.

The younger buyer first looks to Google, Yahoo!, or MSN search engines on the Internet even when looking to buy local services. Having grown up with laptops, this is just second nature to them since they are "native PC users." The Internet allows buyers to comparison shop easily and faster. The advent of the Internet on cell phones and smart phones is opening up a whole new arena for search.

The older buyer may still go to the Yellow Pages as will other demographic groups that are slow to do business on the Internet. Lower income and minority groups may also lag behind the younger buyer; the printed Yellow Pages may be fine for them now, but not for long.

A good use of your advertising dollar would be to make sure that your business is included in search engine databases. Even if you don't have a website, make sure you are listed on the appropriate web directories; list your business name, services offered, 800 number, address, etc.

I do recommend that you have a website, since most people doing a search will want to visit your website after they have identified your firm in a search. You might want to do a search on yourself or your company. See if you can find yourself. If you don't turn up in the first two pages of text search data, you are in trouble; most web searches don't go to the third page.

If you want to use the Yellow Pages most effectively, plan on spending significant money. Research studies have shown that bigger ads get more calls. Check and see what size ad your direct competitors use and then jump up to the next size or larger. Also, like in all print advertising, color demands attention and will help your ad response rate.

If you are a local business, be sure to emphasize your location. Many buyers prefer to work with a local business. I am personally drawn to an advertisement that portrays the business as "owner operated"; I like doing business with small firms that have a pride of ownership. Be sure to include your website address in the advertisement.

Things are changing. The decades-long tradition of the printed Yellow Pages is changing. Decrease your spending in this category now and move the budget dollars to other advertising and promotional categories such as your website.

*The Yellow Pages industry is still gigantic: U.S. Yellow Pages revenue is expected to decline 0.5% to $16.54 billion in 2009.*

*Source (2009 Simba Information report).*

# 71. Say Hello to Online Classifieds

"You had me at hello."

**Jerry Maguire (1996) Fictional Character in "Jerry Maguire"**

Craigslist was founded in 1995 as a hobby by founder Craig Newmark as an e-mail list of local events in San Francisco. Today the online classified giant has more than 12 billion page views per month and more than 50 million visitors each month. Craigslist has estimated revenues in 2009 of over $80 million. Not bad when you consider most of their classified ads are free. Their job board ads cost $25 in most markets which is a fraction of the cost of most of the other online classified advertisers.

Newspaper classified ads are dying. The newspaper industry has been caught in a tailspin the last few years which is a trend blamed on plummeting ad revenues, declining readership, growing competition from the Internet and a deepening national recession. The outlook for double digit declines in print based classified advertising will likely continue as people embrace Craigslist. Yet, Craigslist is not alone. There is a virtual stampede to this new advertising format. Other entrants include Kijiji, Oodle, and MySpace.

I find Kijiji particularly interesting. They describe themselves as "a free local classifieds website for your community with a goal at Kijiji is to create a clean and easy-to-use marketplace that allows you to browse and post listings in areas such as Pets, Motors, For Sale, Housing, Jobs, and Services." The word "Kijiji" (pronounced key-gee-gee) means "village" in Swahili. This word captures the essence of what we are creating—a community where members can connect with one another to exchange goods, ideas, and services. Kijiji sites are currently available in more than 1,000 cities and countries around the world. In the US, Kijiji was launched in 220 cities on June 29, 2007.

Per the Kijiji website:

- As of July 2008, Kijiji attracted nearly 5 million monthly unique visitors and more than 300,000 organic live listings.
- Kijiji has generated more than 400 million page views since launch – more than one for every person living in the United States.

- You'll find over 40,000 listings for dogs and puppies ready for adoption on Kijiji.
- Over 70,000 items are For Sale on Kijiji – more than enough to fill each seat in Chicago's Soldier Field.
- There are over 40,000 cars and vehicles listed on Kijiji – twelve for every county in the US.

While many think of these sites as a good place to buy or sell discarded consumer goods, small businesses to medium sized businesses need to embrace this new advertising format. Online publishers have reached into local, regional, national, and global markets gaining access to special niche markets. If you want to connect with the buyers of sports memorabilia in Miami or find a web designer in Los Angeles, online publishers can do it quickly with little or no cost.

Online advertising is perfect for business. It is clearly an efficient and inexpensive way to reach your customers and prospects.

*It's not classified: Craigslist gets more than 20 billion page views per month! Think of ways for you to advertise on Craigslist.*

*Source www.craigslist.org.*

P.S.    Online marketing giant eBay agrees with me. They bought Kijiji and have rebranded it as eBay Classifieds.

# 72. *Speak To Me in Plain English*

"I guess I should warn you, if I turn out to be particularly clear, you've probably misunderstood what I've said."

**Alan Greenspan (1926 – present) Economist and former Federal Reserve Chairman**

Every day we are bombarded by overly complex, jargon-rich messages from every media source: radio, TV, Internet, and print. Most of these messages are not even understandable. It is clear that there is an epidemic of business "double talk" out there and it has got to stop. The English language is under assault by smarmy business executives, confused sales representatives, and overzealous advertising agencies. This practice is lazy and cheap. The buzzwords and business clichés don't work anymore. I am sick of it. How about you?

Read this one: "Our value proposition is leveraged on our legacy-system-enabled protocols which provide strategic global connectivity. It is our goal to maximize shareholder value while being proactive, cost efficient, customer-centric, and quality driven."

Huh? What did he say? When I hear words like this my eyes glaze over and I don't listen. I bet that I am not alone. How about you? Marketers (and, seemingly, everyone else) seem to have forgotten how to write and speak in plain English. Instead, they pepper the customer with business communications that drip with meaningless business jargon such as "leading edge value proposition" or "extensible brand legacy." What does this stuff really mean?

This is even truer in a business plan. Guy Kawasaki, author of "The Art of the Start" says, "Keep it simple. If you can't describe your business model in 10 words or less, you don't have a business model. Avoid whatever business language is currently hip (strategic, mission-critical, world-class, synergistic, first-mover, scalable, enterprise-class, etc.). Business language does not make a business model."

Fight back by asking salespeople what they mean by these absurd phrases; beware that it might stop them dead in their tracks. Note the nervous laughter as they try to define "committed to excellence." Edit your own words by reading it back to yourself aloud; if it sounds confusing to you, you can bet that it will be confusing to your customer.

And it is not just business communications. Recently, the USDA did a study that showed that 35 Million Americans were "food insecure." It turns out that what they meant to say was that these people were hungry (I.E. they did not have enough food to eat!). I rest my case.

Combat this insult on the English language with simple, plain communication. This plain talk is especially important in brochures when your objective is to sell something or, at least, communicate. Simplify your message instead of making it more complex. Delete the data, the superfluous information, and buzzwords. Try saying what you mean, rather than trying to sound smart.

As far as those others who might destroy the English language, I recommend that you have a little fun. Next time someone tells you that they are "committed to excellence," ask them what they mean by that? Expect an awkward pause followed by tap dancing.

*A simple solution: Say and write what you mean. Look over your marketing material and take out all the meaningless business jargon.*

# 73. Don't Look a Gift Horse in the Mouth

"Metaphors have a way of holding the most truth in the least space."

**Orson Scott Card (1951 – present) Science Fiction Author**

Ever wonder what the expression "Don't look a gift horse in the mouth" really means? A current interpretation might be that it is impolite to receive a gift and then question the value of that gift. Long ago when we all rode horses it had something to do with a horse's age and its teeth, or "So a wise man told me."

The above equine expression is a metaphor. Metaphors are used as a way to better describe something. More specifically, metaphors are comparisons that show how two things that are not alike in most ways are similar in one important way. Secondly, this particular metaphor about the gift horse is a dead metaphor, since it has lost its original meaning or context. When metaphors are overused they become clichés and they can have little or no meaning at all and might actually confuse the listener.

Salespeople use metaphors all the time to better communicate what they mean. In particular, salespeople use metaphors to help customers understand an offering's benefits and they also help the salespeople to be remembered, "For better or for worse." While it is true that metaphors can help salespeople communicate better, poorly chosen metaphors can have the opposite effect much like "Pissing in the wind" or "Never squat with your spurs on."

Here are a few tips on metaphor usage:

- Use as few words as possible. Long metaphors can put customers to sleep or confuse them.
- Avoid clichés. It can be like "The blind leading the blind."
- Selling is not Shakespeare. He said, "All the world's a stage, and all the men and women merely players: They have their exits and their entrances…" I still don't know what that means and neither will your customers.

- Don't overdo them; say what you mean. Too many metaphors will make you look like you are "Not the sharpest knife in the drawer" or "The light's on and nobody is home" or "One card short of a full deck" (you might look stupid).
- Use appropriate metaphors for your audience. "Let dead dogs lie" may be offensive to someone who just lost their favorite dog.
- Avoid mixing metaphors such "As much fun as shooting monkeys in a barrel."
- Finally, make an effort to either use more original metaphors, or simply choose a straightforward description.

*As they say back home: "If you can't run with the big dogs, stay on the porch."*

# 74. A Personal Touch with Note Cards

"Writing comes more easily if you have something to say."

**Sholem Asch (1880 – 1957) Novelist**

The Internet age is one that has lost its personal touch, if not its humanity. Little personalization is done. Everything is digitized, automated, and delivered but is done without compassion or style.

Letters are addressed to "Dear Occupant" or "Please insert your name here." Seemingly, every letter received has a label created from a database by printer. Often misspelled and with wrong annotations, they are dispassionate and rude. Therefore, we toss them in the trash without opening them. Worse yet, e-mails bombard us daily to such an extent that we filter them for spam such as mail from strangers, salespeople, and lost relatives. But even with this editing, we still pound away at the delete key. Who wants all this junk mail?

Note cards are mail that always gets opened. The "retro power" of the handwritten note card is now truly amazing. When an envelope comes to your name and address written in cursive, don't you open it first? This is the appeal of the handwritten note card, arguably a relic from the past, but an effective tool in our sterile Internet age nonetheless.

I recommend that you go to the local printer and get stationery made on good paper with professionally printed letterhead. Note cards give a personal touch in our depersonalized world. Always handwrite the address on the envelope. Don't use labels or printed envelopes and always use a real stamp. Make it look like a party invitation or, better yet, a love letter.

Say thanks or give congratulations. Don't qualify or demean these acts of kindness and generosity with limiting words or thoughts. If you like someone or something, say it. For example, if you want to congratulate someone on a job well done, write that. Then back it up with evidence by citing an example. Avoid using qualifying or demeaning words like "This is just a note to say thanks." What do you mean "just a note?" Instead, say thanks and give a reason why.

Give compliments and avoid flattery. When you compliment someone or something, explain why and give an example. A compliment without evidence is just flattery. Flattery is not remembered and is not as believable. Compliments are remembered, if not cherished. Say it with a handwritten note card today.

*Action Item: Go to the printer and order personalized note cards with envelopes that match your business card (I.E. paper, color, ink, typeface, etc.).*

# 75. A Few Words on Business Cards

"Empty heads are very fond of long titles."

**Old German Proverb**

The ubiquitous business card is a critical tool for communicating your brand. Make sure it reflects your image and that you maximize its usefulness.

Here are 12 hints for better business cards:

1. Print the card using color. Study after study shows that color printing significantly impacts the readers' ability to notice and remember.
2. Don't cram too much printing or too many images on the card; leave white space for an easy-to-read look.
3. If you have your photo on your card, have a professional photographer take your photo; look your best. The photo card is a common practice in some industries such as real estate.
4. Include your tag line and logo. Beware that some logos look great when full-sized but lose detail when shrunk down for a business card. This is a design issue to avoid. In addition, some businesses or industries don't put logos on cards; beware of protocol.
5. Make sure that the information on the card is typo free and accurate. If the information changes, buy new cards. Handwritten corrections look amateurish.
6. Use a standard-size card, since business card storage systems presume a standard size and shape.
7. Get your cards printed professionally on quality paper; although the do-it-yourself business cards for the laser printer are getting better, they still look homemade to me.
8. Include all pertinent information such as phone, fax, website, e-mail address, mail address, cell phone, etc. Duh!
9. The back of the card is a great place for a mission statement, product information, or something that you want to communicate to everyone.
10. Don't put pricing on the back since business cards are evergreen and prices are not.

11. It is OK to list services or products on the card, but remember that plans change and your cards could quickly be obsolete if you make changes to your product line.
12. Your business cards should reflect the theme, color, and logo used in all your marketing communications including your website. Send a consistent message.

May I have your business card?

*Business cards: Date back to 17th century England and were used for maps, promissory notes, and simple contracts. Does your business card have all twelve elements I just covered?*

# 76. *The Beta Buzz*

"We all live life in beta now."

**Bruce Nussbaum, BusinessWeek Contributing Editor**

Take a quick tour of the new and trendy websites on the Internet and you will find the frequent and liberal use of the word "Beta." In most cases, the word Beta is used almost like a tagline under the company or product name to signify that this offering is new, cool, or different. The purpose is to create a "buzz" or the perception of leadership for an offering.

The term Beta, the second letter of the Greek alphabet (β), is frequently used in the software industry where they give different monikers to different software versions. Before a software product is declared Beta, it is called an "Alpha" version; this is a version that is yet to be tested and has features or functions that are still being developed. While bugs may remain, the product is ready for use in the field.

After the Beta version is tested and used by the customer, corrections are often made. The final version is then "released"; this means that it is approved for manufacturing and customer use.

Returning to the Internet, a quick search for the word Beta and you will find thousands of websites all marked Beta, even when they have been in production for years. For example, Google Video and Google Mail both are labeled as Beta versions despite the fact that they have been around for a while. In some cases, the term Beta infers that this is the turf for sophisticated users only. In most cases, we are to believe that these website offerings are just plain cool.

You will also see the word Beta used as a description of something quirky or different. A quick visit to MySpace will confirm that it is the rage with the 13- 25 year olds. That is "so Beta," or so they say.

There can be negative connotations to the word Beta. In a dog pack, the Beta animal is a distant second in order of importance and has little authority. In politics, it is a derogatory term used to describe a male candidate: a "beta male" is perceived to be unable to lead his party to victory. Betamax is a 1975 trademarked term for Sony Corporation which describes the notoriously failed Betamax video tape recording format that was trumped by VHS.

So, choose your words carefully. I Beta go now.

*It's Greek to me: The Greek alphabet has twenty-four letters and has been used to write the Greek language since the late 9th century BC.*

# 77. Public Speaking Made Easy

"If I am to speak ten minutes, I need a week for preparation;
if fifteen minutes, three days; if half an hour, two days; if an hour,
I am ready now."

**Woodrow Wilson (1856 – 1924) President**

I recently attended a workshop on public speaking moderated by consultant Brian Collins; the workshop was designed to help business executives become better speakers. This session reminded me about how important it is for entrepreneurs to speak with confidence in front of groups.

Here are a few tips that I picked up from Brian:

- Smile. This radiates confidence.
- Pause before you begin. This will help you and the audience to relax.
- Eye contact is critical to communication. Look at people directly for two seconds.
- Show up early and check out the venue. This gives you time to adjust things.
- Avoid cold drinks before a speech; they constrict the vocal cords.
- Drink hot herbal tea to sooth the vocal cords.
- Eat breakfast. Avoid dairy. Limit caffeine.
- Avoid flashy accessories that may reflect light. That means no "bling" for the ladies such as earrings.
- Rehearse in front of a mirror or use a video camera; this will help you monitor your use of gestures.
- Avoid filler words or expressions such as "and," "you know," etc.
- Speak conversationally. Avoid "business-speak" or words that you are uncomfortable using. Speak as if you are having coffee with friends.
- Open with a compelling introduction. Try asking the audience a question.
- Slow down and tell your story clearly.
- Repeat yourself. This helps people remember your message.
- Remember that you know more about your subject than 98% of your audience, so speak with authority.

- Always write your own introduction for the introducer to read. This avoids any false expectations.
- Conclude by repeating your message. People typically remember only one or two things from a speech, so make sure that they remember the most important points.
- Bask in the applause!

*Be sure to visit: Brian Collins at http://www.ovation.tv.*

# 78. Great Logos Communicate Your Brand

"Simplicity is the ultimate sophistication."

**Leonardo da Vinci (1452 – 1519) Renaissance Genius**

I accidentally insulted a friend of mine who asked for my opinion about a logo design that he had worked on for months. I candidly told him to start over since his logo violated many of the principles of good logo design. It was not what he wanted to hear.

You know a good logo when you see one. It somehow gets your attention and makes you think or pause. It communicates a message or an essence—it describes the brand and your firm's identity. Or, at least it should.

Potential customers look for a logo to tell them about the value your business will deliver. More than a first impression, a logo describes what might be. For the repeat customer, a logo talks about your firm's consistency and commitment, while reassuring the customer that buying your product again is a smart decision.

A good logo is easily understood and memorable. A logo should comfortably fit on a business card and also work on a billboard. Always test the appeal of your logo with your target audience; make sure it tells the story you want told.

A great logo incorporates five basic elements: shape, color, contrast, differentiation, and functionality.

As far as shape is concerned, know that smooth lines or rounded edges can convey serene or passive messages, while jagged edges or sharp corners communicate urgency or aggression. The Nike swoosh is both graceful and powerful while a lightning bolt is aggressive and full of action. A logo with ragged edges communicates excitement or daring.

Colors evoke mood and can be provocative or benign. When choosing a color, you should consider the colors supported by web browsers; it turns out there are 216 colors on the web palette.

Ever notice that many of most memorable logos are invariably red and/or yellow? Think of the most successful companies and look at the logos: Coca Cola, Nike, and McDonald's. It is no accident, since red and yellow are attention grabbing and sometimes irritating colors. When these two loud colors are overdone, they can actually scream "look at me" to the customer. Orange has recently gained popularity as a logo color; it has a "retro" feel that is very stylish today.

So should your firm have a red or yellow logo? Yes, if that color reflects the image of your firm and if you need a logo that screams, "Look at me." Otherwise, there are many other colors on the color wheel to choose. Orange is a hot color for technology companies as is bright green; I am told these are very "retro."

Contrast is achieved when the logo communicates well in black and white in addition to color. If the logo uses colors too close to each other on the color wheel, it may not communicate well and instead might confuse the viewer.

You can differentiate your logo by using templates to get ideas flowing. Avoid a logo that looks like your competitor's logo. Expresses your uniqueness—otherwise why do one?

As for functionality, consider how a logo will look on a business card; if it works on small scale, it will likely look OK when blown up on the web or on a brochure. Also, make sure the logo can be faxed clearly; overly ornate logos lose detail when faxed, while some are not even readable.

An important objective for a good logo is for it to be legible and understood. If you have ever examined a logo and not really understood what it was or what the image was trying to say, then you have seen a bad logo.

Logos must very quickly communicate and be understood. Intricate or arcane logos will fail to meet this objective. Also, when testing prospective logos, make sure that you don't offend your potential audience due to accidental ethnic or racial slurs, gender bias, or other such blunders.

Finally, test your logo with your customers—how they feel about your logo is most important.

*Recommendation: Keep your tag line off your logo since you might want to change your tag line later.*

# 79. *Marketing Mantras Make Money*

"Let him think I am more than I am and I will be so."

**Ernest Hemingway (1899 – 1961) Author**

A mantra is a religious prayer or mystical phrase or poem that instills concentration when repeated and is used for meditation and prayer. The key is to focus on the mantra and to block out everything else.

A marketing mantra is three to five words that describe how your business or offering is different. It must be easy to say and remember while being easily understood. If it is in writing, it should leap off the page with authenticity and integrity. It can be used internally or externally. It should say how you are different instead of how you are the same.

Your marketing mantra should be positive. Study after study shows that positive messages sell better than negative messages and so it is with mantras. Many marketing messages are negative. Who can forget "American Express: Don't Leave Home without it?" I always feared what might happen if I chose to leave without it, so I switched to MasterCard.

Mantras help focus your employees and your customers on what makes your offering different. This focus is critical since customers buy because of your differences, not because you are like the competition or have similar benefits. An example of a marketing mantra is "Diamonds Are Forever" by DeBeers Corporation. It accentuates the point that unlike other gifts, diamonds will outlast them all and they will never go out of style.

Another example of a mantra is Burger King's "Have it Your Way"; this mantra told us that fast food could be customized at Burger King, unlike the food at McDonald's. During its time, this was a very powerful message about how Burger King was different from Mickey D's.

You can write a mantra by first writing down a list of your distinctive competencies, which are the unique benefits of your offering that your customers value. Try to boil it down to a few words while experimenting with the order of the words. Reduce it to three to five unique words that say how your firm is different. Alliteration can help and shorter is always better.

Next, test it with friends, employees, and customers. See if they react positively and if they agree that it says how your offering is different. Change it if necessary and try it again. When you get the message right, blanket the earth with your mantra. For this is the most important message you will ever tell your customers and prospects.

By the way, the difference between a tag line and a marketing mantra is mostly intention. Tag lines can deliver any type of message while a marketing mantra focuses on how your offering is different.

Be first, best, or different. Be first, best, or different. Be first, best, or different. Be first, best, or different. Be first, best, or different....

*P. S. Thanks to Guy Kawasaki for his work with mantras. Check out his book "Art of the Start."*

# 80. Elevator Pitches Move Investors

"Nobody cares if you can't dance well.  Just get up and dance."

**Dave Barry (1941 – present) Musician**

You are in the proverbial elevator and, low and behold, Bill Gates is standing right next to you. Gulp! He turns your way and says, "So, tell me about your business." You have 60 seconds to describe your business. Maybe he can invest in your business.

Investors are not your customers, so don't try to sell them product features or benefits. Investors are people that may want to "own" part of your company, so tell them how your business will deliver a strong return on their investment. Help them understand why they should invest in your firm.

The elevator pitch is meant to be started and finished during a long elevator ride in a tall building. Thus, if you can't deliver your message in that length of time, your pitch is too long. Entrepreneurs are notorious for loving their idea too much while investors may easily bore; keep it short and to the point.

Your elevator pitch must have the following elements:

• What is your offering?
• Describe your customer and their special needs.
• How will you make money?
• Describe the competition.
• How is your offering different?
• Why will the customer buy?
• Describe the management team or founders.

Use plain English and avoid "business-speak." Speak clearly and concisely while saving the big words for the lawyers. Keep the pitch below a minute with no more than 200 words. Practice it until it is memorized and natural. Deliver it with lots of eye contact. Investors respond to passion but beware of going over the top. This is just business to the investor so you better not joke around since investors are a serious lot.

The objective is to create interest and get a next meeting with the investor or to send them an executive summary. Here is a sample pitch for my first book:

"First, Best, or Different: What Every Entrepreneur Needs to Know About Niche Marketing" is a new book dedicated to helping entrepreneurs target, sell, and serve customer segments who have been underserved or overlooked. Using short, easy-to-read chapters written in plain English, the book demystifies the art of niche marketing. If you apply the book's simple techniques and methods, your business will be rewarded with increased sales, higher profits, and happy customers."

Let's get real. Sixty seconds goes by quickly, so you need to wordsmith this statement carefully and practice it dozens of times. Also, be prepared for Type-A people to interrupt you with questions. That's OK since that is a buying signal.

Ready, set, go!

*Fast Pitch: A business plan competition that consists of a group of entrepreneurs who have 90 second to tell a panel of investors about their business concept.*

# 81. Writing Better

"The difference between the almost right word & the right word is really a large matter—it's the difference between the lightning bug and the lightning."

**Mark Twain (1835 – 1910) Author**

Writing better copy for websites, brochures, and business letters is hard work, but the impact is remarkable. Here are a few best practices to consider:

- Hire a professional copywriter if you can afford it. Be advised that the good ones are very busy and always booked.
- Write concisely and get to the point. People are busy and don't have the time to find your message in the copy.
- Remember people don't read anymore, they scan. Use bullets and white space to help the reader find your important points.
- Avoid business-speak by not using meaningless phrases such as "committed to excellence."
- Shorter words are best. Leave the big words for the lawyers and doctors.
- Avoid dead metaphors. A dead metaphor is an expression that has lost its true meaning. For example, consider the expression "son of a gun," what does it mean? According to Wikipedia, it is a British naval slang term that refers to a child of questionable parentage conceived on the gun deck. Now that is meaningful!
- Write like Hemingway not like Shakespeare. Cut out the heavy or overly ornate language and use short sentences with real words.
- Edit your copy by reading it aloud to yourself since this will help you find dropped words or awkward phrasing.
- Have a third party read your copy. I guarantee that they will find mistakes that you missed.
- Use spell check. Duh.

Better writing helps you communicate better and sell more.

*The secret to good writing: Proofreading.*

# 82. Your E-mail Signature

"A signature always reveals a man's character—
and sometimes even his name"

**Evan Esar (1899 – 1995) Humorist**

Much is written about subject lines for e-mail marketing communication. An effective e-mail campaign starts with a snappy subject line that motivates the recipient to open the e-mail. Without that first step the e-mail gets the delete key and it is all over. Yet, the way your e-mail signature looks may be equally important since it assists the reader with the call to action, whether it is to call you directly, to e-mail you back, or to visit your website.

Your e-mail signature says a lot about your brand. Of course, the basics should be there including your full name, title, company name, mail address, office phone, fax, and website. Consider this list as the minimum requirements.

Adding your cell phone is a personal choice that needs to be considered. Adding your cell phone to your signature sends a message that you are available and ready to do business. This is an important and not so subtle message that a salesperson might want to communicate. On the other hand, do you really want to receive cell phone calls from your clients as you are boarding a plane or when you are having lunch with another client?

Caller ID may allow you to screen your calls, but if you answer the cell phone call, you had better give the caller your full attention or this could backfire on you. Nothing is ruder than a preoccupied caller on the other end of the line. It is for this reason that I believe that the cell phone number in the e-mail signature is not appropriate for everyone.

Other contact information could include the trendy alternatives such as your Skype phone number or your blog URL. These trendy addresses and phone numbers send a message that you are technologically savvy and hip. But, if you advertise them as contact information, be sure to check them.

One way to make your e-mail signature unique and memorable is to include a personal tagline or marketing mantra. I fully support the use of a tagline or mantra that tells the reader why you are different. It should be no more than three to five words and it should tell your customers why you are special. My mantra is "Be First, Best, or Different" and it appears at the top of my e-mail signature.

Famous quotations can be powerful, funny, inspiring, or thoughtful. Choose the quote carefully since it will communicate a lot about you and your brand. A former sales rep of mine carefully selected a quotation each week for his e-mail signature; frankly, I enjoyed this addition to his e-mails and I looked forward to the new quote each week. It made the rep memorable and different which is a good thing. A word of caution needs to be said since the wrong quote could make you look silly or could offend the reader. Beware of sarcasm or double meanings or any kind of sexual innuendo.

For some businesspeople a short bio can be an appropriate addition to the e-mail signature. I recommend no more than 50 carefully chosen words that communicate what you are all about. For example, I use a bio that reads "John Bradley Jackson has over twenty-five years of sales and marketing experience from Silicon Valley and Wall Street. He is the author of the new book "First, Best, or Different: What Every Entrepreneur Needs to Know About Niche Marketing" and has written over 100 Internet articles on sales, marketing, and negotiation." (Note to self: mine is actually 52 words and is a mouthful; maybe I should work on this a bit).

In closing (pun intended), be sure to choose your e-mail signature carefully since this is a statement about you and your brand. And, it helps people contact you.

*John Hancock: Slang for a signature and named after the first signer of the United States Declaration of Independence.*

# *83. Text-Speak*

"To be great is to be misunderstood."

**Ralph Waldo Emerson (1803 – 1882) Transcendentalist Author**

Text messaging has created a new "language" of sorts that is destroying the written word and has infected all aspects of our society. Driven by young cell phone users who would rather text than talk, these abbreviations are appearing in advertising, new media, and college term papers.

SMS (Short Message Service) technology is a communications protocol allowing for short text messages to be sent between mobile telephone devices. Text messaging has become the most widely used data application in the world with 2.4 billion users—74% of all mobile phones send or receive text messages.

What SMS has done is to create a new language based on the use of fewer key strokes. For example, consider the following:

- "how r u?" means "How are you?"
- "lol" means "Laugh out loud."
- "brb" means "Be right back."
- "ttyl" means "Talk to you later."
- "pcb" means "Please Call Back."

My concern is that I don't think this destruction of the English language is going away. In fact, I think it will only become more common. While at first it may seem to be no big deal, when you dig deeper into text-speak, you will see that many discrepancies or exceptions exist. For example:

- "because" can be written as "cuz," "bcuz," "bcz," "bcos," "bc," "coz," and "bcoz."
- "lol" may mean "Laugh out loud" or "Lots of love" or "Lots Of Laughter."
- "Got to go" can be written as "g2g" or "gtg."
- "Tomorrow" can be written as "tom," "2moz," "2moro," "2mrw," or "2mara."

Honestly, English is hard enough without all this new slang. Yet, this phenomenon is real. The Associated Press is reporting that New Zealand is going to let high school students use text-speaking or texting acronyms in national exams. The move has been extremely controversial.

Advertisers seem to be greeting this trend. AT&T /Cingular recently ran a highly successful commercial which featured a mother and daughter having a conversation talking in cell phone text-speak. You actually had to understand text-speak to be able to understand the advertisement's message.

IMHO (in my humble opinion), text-speak does not belong in business communications, but I may be drowned out by the thundering herd of text message users. So, to you who are text-speak illiterate, I recommend that you "rtfm" (read the flippin' manual) and get on board.

The reason for my flip-flop on this issue is cuz (because) hcb! (Holy Cow Batman!), this text-speak is real.

*Hand:  Have a nice day.*

# 84. Humor, Funny Stuff, and Sarcasm in Marketing

"I am thankful for laughter, except when milk comes out of my nose."

**Woody Allen (1935 – present) Director, Actor, Screenwriter**

In the ancient Greek poem "The Odyssey," the story's hero, Odysseus, tells the Cyclops that his name is "Nobody." When Odysseus instructs his men to drive a fiery iron spit into the monster's single eye, the Cyclops yells out in vain, "Friends, Nobody is killing me now," so no one comes to help. This action-adventure humor, dating to around 800 B.C., is one of the first recorded jokes, according to the classics scholar Owen Ewald, who recently presented his findings on "Humor in the Ancient World" at Seattle Pacific University.

But, seriously, does humor belong in your advertisements, websites, brochures, sales pitches, or in your blogs? My answer is maybe but you need to proceed with caution! The decision depends in large part on your audience.

B2B markets are made up of businesspeople and they are a serious lot—just ask them. No time for jokes or funny business. When I was naming my book "First, Best, or Different," I tested my prospective titles with business book readers. All of my funny titles bombed. My prospective readers were offended by funny titles such as "When Pigs Fly"; I was told with indignation that their businesses were not pigs. I think it was Bob Dole (1996 Republican nominee and World War II veteran) who said, "You don't want to get into a wrestling match with a pig. You both will get dirty, and the pig will like it."

While I agree humor can increase the effectiveness of many marketing activities, there are pitfalls or areas of risk when adding humor to your marketing effort. For example, how many times have you laughed at the Super Bowl commercials, but can't remember what they were advertising? The joke gets attention but does not necessarily communicate the value proposition.

Also, what is funny to you can be offensive to others. While ethnic jokes are understood to be potentially offensive to some, people can get offended seemingly by the most benign things. Even jokes about hair color can prove offensive. For example, "Why do blond nurses bring red magic markers to work? They bring red markers to work in case, they have to draw blood." Now that is funny... or is it?

Humor is also regional and cultural. What works in New York may not work in Kentucky. For example, "Kentucky: Five Million People; Fifteen Last Names" may be offensive to Kentuckians. Please send my apologies to the state of Kentucky and the fifteen families who live there. Is that funny? Not to my Kentucky relatives.

I find humor to be particularly misplaced in e-mail communication because it is a two dimensional medium and can be easily misconstrued. Simple sarcasm can be interpreted as mean spirited. Have you ever had someone react angrily to an email you wrote when you truly meant no ill will? I know I have. Because of this I have all my blogs read by a professional proofreader and morals expert (my wife Janet).

When in doubt, be discriminating about your use of humor in your marketing. If you feel your funny idea might be offensive, it probably is. It is just safer to keep the jokes for the country club or dinner table.

*Dumb question: What do you call cheese that isn't yours? Answer: Nacho Cheese.*

# 85. How to Write Great
# E-mail Sales Letters

"Writing is easy. All you have to do is cross out the wrong words."

**Mark Twain (1835 – 1910) Humorist and Author**

It was not that long ago when formal business letters were the primary selling tool for B2B selling. The customer would say, "Send me a proposal" and salespeople would willingly oblige with a multiple page letter, stamped, sealed, and delivered by the U.S. Postal Service. E-mail has changed the landscape and the formal business letter is almost a thing of the past.

Letters were long and full of details along with glittering business generalities about value propositions, features, and benefits. Letters were read and distributed for others to read and comment upon. They were filed away for future reference.

E-mails are very different from letters. Most e-mails don't even get opened because of poor subject lines, spam filters, and sheer volume. Busy executives receive hundreds of e-mails a week (sometimes daily) and look for reasons to delete them. It is important to recognize that e-mails can be deleted at anytime and for any reason, even if they are important.

E-mails dominate B2B communication. E-mail volume dwarfs that of the telephone, fax, and direct mailer. If you are like me, you are getting dozens if not hundreds of e-mail messages a day; most are spam and get deleted. The rest are scanned or put aside to be read later. The truth is most e-mails don't get read. Given this low survival rate of an e-mail, the writer must resolve to communicate efficiently with the hope to engage the reader.

Here are a few thoughts about how to write better e-mails:

- Use simple subject lines. Use a subject line that accurately describes the purpose of the e-mail. Don't tease or fib. Clever subject lines reek of spam. Write honest subject lines that say what is in the e-mail.

- Don't tease or mislead the reader since they will just delete it if you do. Avoid the use of any spam like words such as "free," "discount," "Viagra," etc in your subject line, since your e-mail won't get through the spam filters.
- Use short subject lines with no more than 3-5 words. Some e-mail formats truncate long subject lines.
- Always personalize the e-mail with the reader's name. It is cliché, but no word is more important than the reader's name. Limit your CCs to people who really need to read your e-mail.
- Limit your email to one subject only; this allows the reader to pass the e-mail on if necessary. Got another subject? Send another e-mail.
- Use the "rule of thirds" and divide the email into three parts: the opening, the body, and the call to action. The opening should say who you are and what you want.
- Give context. If the reader does not know you by name, tell them how you came to contact them or where you met. Give them a reason to continue reading.
- The body of the letter should deliver the meat of your message. I recommend using only three bullets. If it cannot be said with three bullets, you are making the subject too complicated.
- Avoid attachments. Attachments are the domain of viruses, spam, and eye fatigue. Ever fearful of hackers, readers more and more are choosing not to open attachments.
- Tell the truth. If you are selling something say so. A good value proposition tells the reader why to buy. Don't beat around the bush with language. Just say what you have to say and be done with it.
- Choose your words carefully since you want your e-mails to be remembered; it is OK to break out the thesaurus and choose a new clever word.
- Benefits sell while features tell. Speeds and feeds will be ignored. Focus on how your offering helps the reader.
- Key points need white space. Present your key points with lists, dashes, asterisks, or bullets surrounded by white space. This says read me.
- Call to action. Close with the next step, the call to action, or what is needed. Have a clear call to action. Tell your recipient what they need to do and how to do it such as "visit my website to order my book First, Best, or Different."
- Contact information. Include your signature with all your contact information.

- Consider a Postscript. Postscripts are a great place for a reminder about the call to action or for an incentive.
- Finally, rather than pressing the send key, how about you save the message. Go back to the message later and check for typos and proper grammar. The key to good writing is good editing.
- E-mail is best for messages that are positive or neutral. If the message is negative, it is best to call them on the phone.
- Never send an e-mail when you are angry; put it aside and review it later.
- Read your e-mails aloud before sending to insure that they read the way that you intended.
- Don't write anything in an e-mail that you wouldn't put on a billboard; e-mails can be easily forwarded without your knowledge.
- Beware of e-mail strings that get forwarded; some people will go back and read everything (you may not want them to do that).
- Don't be sarcastic or joke around since the humor could get lost in translation.
- Always say thank you and be friendly in your e-mails; it is easy for e-mails to seem curt or angry or rude.
- At the end of every e-mail, include your contact information.
- Don't assume that they kept your last e-mail.

Know and comply with your company e-mail policies; more and more employers are writing e-mail policies that are increasingly restrictive. According to a survey by Proofpoint, 40% of large companies staff employees to read other people's e-mails in a search for violations to their e-mail policies. Big brother is watching.

*E-mail tip: Save all your e-mails; don't delete them. E-mails should be saved for seven years just like tax records.*

# 86. Nobody Answers My E-Mail Letters!

"If I am a legend, then why am I so lonely?"

**Judy Garland (1922 – 1969) Actress**

You send carefully worded e-mails to your customers and prospects every day, but you seldom hear back from them. When you talk with them on the phone, they almost never remember seeing your e-mail. Frequently, they will ask you to resend the original e-mail so that they can read it. What the heck is going on?

The answer is a simple one. There is a glut of e-mails flooding your customers' inboxes and they are numb from it all. I know executives who receive hundreds of e-mails a day, but who only read a handful of them. E-mail volume itself is the first problem.

Guess what? Most of the time, your customers don't even open your e-mails. Worse yet, they often don't even receive them in their inboxes. The reason is spam. Spam is a big business. According to BusinessWeek, up to 90% of the e-mails traversing the Internet are spam. According to the ePrivacy Group, the volume of spam has been growing by 18% per month this last year. Your customers have no choice but shield themselves with spam filters and this creates the accidental blocking of legitimate e-mail messages from you. Even the most sophisticated spam filters will still capture legitimate e-mails.

Spam is a big business which favors doing more of it. If a spammer selling low cost drugs gets only 1 in 1,000 people to respond, it can be economically satisfying to the spammer. These folks are not going away in the short run.

In fact, it is easy to visualize a future world with opt-in invitation only e-mail. But for now, you need to rethink your communication strategies. If you depend on e-mail for customer communication, you must make every effort to not look like spam. Avoid forwarding messages or having a forward abbreviation in the subject line (FW.). Avoid sending unnecessary attachments; instead send links. Keep your e-mails short. Avoid large distribution lists.

Consider alternate channels of communication including direct mail and phone calls. It may seem old fashioned but the telephone works pretty well and your voice mails don't get caught by spam filters. If someone does not listen to your whole voice mail, then you have a different issue at play.

Postcards have a 100% open rate and are relatively inexpensive. Three dimensional mailers such as small packages can also be amazingly effective since everyone likes presents. FedEx packages will almost always get opened. Faxes have a retro feel to them and can be very effective and low cost.

Finally, be forgiving about your customers' lack of e-mail response. Their in-box may be full.

*Increase your response rate: Try writing clear, easy to understand subject lines. It is said that you have about two seconds and 50 characters to get your message across. Or you will be deleted or marked as spam.*

# 87. *Choose Your Words Wisely*

"Action speaks louder than words but not nearly as often."

**Mark Twain (1835 – 1910) Humorist and Author**

Words change. Words that we used long ago may have new meanings today. Words can also have different meanings in different cultures. Be careful to choose yours wisely or you might not get your point across.

Words change meaning over time. I was talking with my daughter about the movie "Pirates of the Caribbean" and pirates' "booty" when she got embarrassed because of my ignorance. To her booty meant buttocks or bottom (thanks to rap music). A similar thing happened when I was looking for my sandals. I asked my son if he had seen my "thongs" when he reminded me that thongs are underwear these days. These faux pas were unintentional on my part but are examples of how language can be transient, short-lived and can cause discomfort or can even completely sabotage a business deal by inadvertently offending someone.

Technology has changed the meaning of words. Remember when a firewall delayed or stopped the spread of fire? Or when a virus was something that caused a cold? Or, when the web was something that only a spider could make? To me spam is canned meat and best served with fried eggs and rye toast while to others spam is unwanted emails about Viagra or low cost mortgages. A hub was the center of a wheel not long ago; today it has something to do with a computer network.

Culture gives words and phrases different meaning even when the language is the same. In England they might promise to "knock you up" in the morning which means that they will call you on the phone. Another UK phrase is "totally pissed," which means you are drunk. Of course, this would mean that you are angry in the United States. In the U.S. Barbie is a doll, while in Australia a "barbie" it is an outdoor barbeque.

Words are formed all the time. Some are faddish or temporary and will quickly fade away while other words become permanent. Some words are created by the manipulation of suffixes and prefixes. For example, the noun plane when added with a prefix "de" creates the verb "deplane" which is something that the little guy on Fantasy Island used to repeat when he saw airplanes landing. It also means to get off the plane.

Technology is big on using and creating compound words, which is the pairing of two common words to create one new word that sounds cool or innovative. "Middleware" (a type of software) combines two common words to make a new one. Or, how about "guesstimate" which is a blended word that uses guess and estimate as root words. The technology crowd loves acronyms and initials. I bet you didn't know that "JPEG" actually means Joint Photographic Experts Group (I sure didn't).

Sometimes proper nouns become a part of our everyday language such as to "Google" something on the web. My good friend Greg who works at Yahoo! questions why I would use such a limiting and offensive phrase. Watergate is a now a word that means corruption or deceit instead of a hotel near Washington D.C.

Words change and so do their meanings. Think carefully before you speak and write or use them in an e-mail.

*Words: Words can have dictionary meanings which are called denotations. Words can have emotional meanings which are connotations. Choose your words carefully.*

# 88. *Think Twice Before You Send That E-mail Letter*

"A man who does not think for himself does not think at all."

**Oscar Wilde (1854 – 1900) Irish Playwright**

When communicating with a customer, which is the best method or channel of communication: face-to-face, phone, or e-mail?

Face-to-face meetings provide an opportunity to create rapport and expand relationships far better than phone or e-mail. Meetings in-person can be rich with social cues such as body language, which can help you understand the other party's emotions or reactions. I have seen studies that suggest that as much as three times the information is communicated in-person when compared to e-mail communication. Thus, nothing beats face-to-face meetings when you are creating relationships.

If the relationship already exists, then phone and or e-mail can be efficient choices. Phone communication is effective when problems exist with an existing relationship and when emotions may be involved. These emotions can get lost or distorted in an e-mail. The phone is a great way to maintain a relationship (I.E. let's catch up).

Yet, in the new millennium, e-mail communication reigns supreme. Many selling situations are relegated to e-mail; this includes the first meeting with a prospective customer. E-mail is different in that it can give all parties a chance to think about their responses and to be more exact. Oddly enough, some studies have shown e-mail communication to be more blunt or aggressive. E-mail can be heaven for passive-aggressive types. These are the folks that can't say it to your face, but will gladly "flame you" in an e-mail with multiple other parties copied.

E-mail is convenient and quick, but it can also be misunderstood and cause significant problems when communicating with customers. Missing from e-mails are all the social cues of a face-to-face meeting including eye contact, body language, facial expressions, tone of voice, and smell (remember, we are still mammals). Without these cues it is difficult to discern the true meaning of the e-mail.

E-mails are easily misunderstood because of the lack of social cues and because the authors often will only think about themselves (and not about the reader). Also, e-mail can be prone to impulsivity and errors, which is somewhat like face-to-face communication, but without the feedback from the other party.

When in doubt, call the customer instead of sending an e-mail. Better yet, go see the see them in-person.

*Flame: To "flame" someone on the web means to send an insulting or offensive message.*

# 89. P.S. Everyone Reads the Postscript

"When he wrote a letter, he would put that which was most material in the postscript, as if it had been a by-matter."

**Francis Bacon Sr. (1561 – 1626) Philosopher, Statesman, Scientist**

Postscripts have been a very effective tool in direct mail marketing industry for many years. More often than not, the call to action is repeated in the postscript along with a special incentive.

A postscript (from post scriptum, a Latin expression meaning "after writing" and abbreviated P.S. or p.s.) is a sentence, paragraph, or occasionally many paragraphs added, often hastily and incidentally, after the signature of a letter or (sometimes) the main body of an essay or book.

After the headline, the "P.S." is the second most frequently read part of the letter. A P.S. always gets read and it encourages the customer to act now.

While a postscript isn't mandatory, it grabs attention in commercial e-mails, too. Often, readers will read the subject line and the hook, scan the key elements and go directly to the P.S. The P.S. should restate your hook and highlight your offer.

Postscripts have all the fun.

*Postscript: The term comes from the Latin phrase "post scriptum" which is an expression which means "after writing." Do you use postscripts in your marketing material?*

# 90. *Writing Great E-mail Marketing Copy*

"We humans are social beings. Whether we like it or not, there is hardly a moment of our lives when we do not benefit from others' activities. For this reason it is hardly surprising that most of our happiness arises in the context of our relationships with others."

**The Dalai Lama (1935 – present) Tibetan Buddhism Leader**

Writing great e-mail marketing copy is hard work. You can always outsource it to a professional copywriter, but you will discover that the good ones are already booked and that they are very expensive. If your budget dictates doing this writing in-house, here are a few ideas, in no particular order.

Great writing requires great proofreading, which is extremely hard work (you can trust me on this one since it is very hard for me). One tip on proofreading your own writing is to read it aloud. This helps you catch dropped words and mistakes. Another method is to have someone else proof your copy.

Remember to run a "spell check." Run it a second time since errors don't always get caught in the first pass with spell check (believe it or not).

Timeliness is critical to effective e-mail marketing messages. Current events or news references can add timeliness to a campaign. For example, a reference to the rising cost of gasoline or the price of oil might add timeliness to an e-mail from an auto parts retailer.

Keep the e-mail short. While there is considerable debate in the e-mail community about short form versus long form, you must remember that the e-mail's purpose is to get the reader to take the next step and click to the website or landing page. From the subject line to the postscript, the e-mail should offer the reader the most relevant information in as few words as possible. Customers are busy and many feel overwhelmed by too much e-mail. Messages that are short and to the point are more likely to be read. When writing e-mail text, try to state the ideas in as few words as possible.

The long form argument is that an engaged reader will want more information now rather than later and if you insist on making them click for more information, they might disengage. Generally speaking, short form is preferred over long form. When in doubt, test both and see what your readers think.

Writing better e-mails is all about good writing for a busy reader. Unlike a novel or a letter to your mom from summer camp, readers of commercial marketing e-mails are very impatient; you probably have less than five seconds to get the reader's attention. If you don't get the reader's attention, he or she might delete the e-mail or, worse, hit the spam button.

It starts with the first sentence of the lead paragraph. That first sentence needs to arouse the curiosity of the reader and make them want to read more. Often this means that the first sentence needs to be slightly controversial. Starting with a question is a good way to get things going for the reader. For example, another way to start this chapter might have been "Ever read an e-mail that made you mad?" Did I get your attention? If so, read on.

With your curiosity now piqued, the first paragraph must deliver the goods: the four "Ws and an H." The lead paragraph must say who, what, when, where, why, and how. This is extremely critical to e-mail marketing since the reader may read no further than that first paragraph. Yet, the ultimate goal is to explain to the reader the benefits of your offering which are placed in the middle of the e-mail or the next paragraph.

These benefits may be best presented as bullets:

- Three to five bullets will suffice.
- Benefits must crisp, clear, and tangible.
- They must be written in the reader's language.

Finally, the e-mail must have a call to action which is the next step for the reader to take. It can be a "buy now" link, an 800 number to dial, or a landing page to visit. This call to action must be direct and easy to do.

Customers will start reading an e-mail from the beginning and read the introduction to see if it's worth spending more of their time. Readers tend to pay less and less attention to what is written as they scan more quickly through the rest of the e-mail.

Another must for writing better e-mail marketing campaigns is to speak the readers' language; this includes jargon, tone, and content. If you are addressing CEOs, be sure to write like a CEO. This might mean using to-the-point (almost blunt) language with bullets and a clear call to action since CEOs are busy and direct.

Include value in the e-mail copy itself. Give the reader a tip or advice that they can use right away. Don't make them fill out a form to get it. Relationships are based on reciprocity so start it off with a digital gift such as a free e-book.

To make sure customers read the most relevant information, put the most important information (often referred to as the hook) at the top, followed by the most important supporting information. Each successive paragraph will receive less and less of the reader's attention and should contain less and less important information. Bullets and images will help the reader scan and focus on your key points.

E-mail marketing is more than just getting past the spam filters. In fact, writing better e-mail copy only begins once the customer opens the e-mail.

*Guam and Spam: The average Guamanian consumes 16 cans of Spam per year which is the highest Spam consumption in the world.*

*Source (http://en.wikipedia.org/wiki/Spam).*

# 91. Risky Business: E-mail Marketing and Children

"It takes a village to raise a child."

**African Proverb**

For many e-mail and web marketers the youth market represents a major financial opportunity. But beware, the legal risks are high. The web-site "Xanga" was recently fined $1 Million for COPPA violations, for repeatedly allowing children under 13 to sign up for the service without getting their parent's consent.

The Children's Online Privacy Protection Act of 1998 (COPPA) is a United States federal law effective April 21, 2000, that applies to the online collection of personal information by persons or entities under U.S. jurisdiction from children under 13 years of age.

It states that a website operator must include in a privacy policy that states how to seek verifiable consent from a parent or guardian, and what responsibilities an operator has to protect children's privacy and safety online including restrictions on the marketing to those under 13.

The act applies to websites and online services operated for commercial purposes that are either directed to children under age 13 or have actual knowledge that children under 13 are providing information online. What this means to the website owner is that you must beware of the under-age visitor or registrant. The negative consequences are enormous.

For more information, consult your attorney.

*Kids and Advertising: Advertising is a pervasive influence on children and adolescents. Young people view more than 40,000 ads per year on television alone and increasingly are being exposed to advertising on the Internet, in magazines, and in schools. This exposure may contribute significantly to childhood and adolescent obesity, poor nutrition, and cigarette and alcohol use.*

*Source
(http://pediatrics.aappublications.org/cgi/content/full/118/6/2563).*

# 92. *When Opt-in E-mail Becomes SPAM*

"Wife: Have you got anything without SPAM?
Waitress: Well, there's SPAM egg sausage and SPAM,
that's not got much SPAM in it.
Wife: I don't want any SPAM!
Man: Why can't she have egg bacon SPAM and sausage?
Wife: That's got SPAM in it!
Man: Hasn't got as much SPAM in it as
SPAM egg sausage and SPAM, has it?
Vikings: SPAM! SPAM! SPAM! SPAM! Lovely SPAM!
Wonderful SPAM!"

**Monty Python**

The quote above is the infamous SPAM sketch which was the inspiration for use of the word SPAM for junk advertising on the Internet. SPAM is now ubiquitous on the web to the chagrin of Hormel, the maker of the canned meat product "Spam."

On the web, e-mail marketers figure that once a list member has opted-in that this means that their readers will read and value their e-mail marketing letters. Well, this is not always the case.

According to blogger Stefan Eyram, "BACN" is a marketing e-mail that many readers agreed to receive, but is not immediately read, if at all. It's not spam, exactly, because they agreed to it. These messages are only mildly interesting and are not urgent. They idle in the in-box or in a file folder like a magazine stack on the coffee table.

The reader might have opted-in to a list on an auto parts supplier's site and agreed to accept e-mails about sales and promotions. In practice, virtually all the mailings have been for promotions for auto parts that the reader did not need or desire. Yet, there is a chance something relevant might come along, so the reader does not immediately delete the e-mail.

Thus, there is a fine line between BACN and SPAM. The danger is that the sender will keep sending the less than relevant messages until the reader opts-out. The risk is that the reader will one day declare this a nuisance and hit the spam button. Too many spam complaints and the sender will be black-listed and develop a reputation as a spammer.

For example, six months ago I bought a used red Corvette and I was quite excited. I immediately purchased a new set of fancy floor mats from an Internet auto parts store. Since that purchase, I have received weekly e-mails about auto parts that are totally irrelevant to me such as monster tires for off-road trucks. Initially I hesitated to delete theses messages since my purchase experience was good, but I now have little hope that any of the future messages will be relevant.

What this means to the sender is that they must continue to ask their list for additional or new preferences. Just because someone opted-in one year ago does not mean that they have the same interest today. Also, a periodic campaign to ask members to opt-in again might help improve your list quality and help the sender avoid the spam button.

Beware of assuming that your messages are relevant since BACN can quickly change into SPAM.

*Spam: The ingredients of SPAM are chopped pork shoulder meat with ham meat added. Salt, water, sugar, and sodium nitrite are added for flavor.*

*Source (Ask Yahoo!).*

# 93. *Personalize Your E-mail Marketing Letters*

"Fate chooses your relations, you choose your friends."

**Jacques Deville (1738 - 1813) French Poet**

A highly effective marketing technique used by successful e-mail marketers is to personalize the e-mail letter. This personalization can be accomplished in many ways.

One way to personalize an e-mail letter is to use the recipient's organization logo or web site. The purpose of a personalized image is to provide a familiar frame of reference in the most compelling way possible, resulting in the recipient feeling better understood and more comfortable, leading toward better acceptance of the offer.

Personalization can also include personalized subject lines by including information that refers to the stated preferences of the customer segment that you are marketing to. For example, you can also personalize your e-mail offer by adding a comment that recognizes a customer's five straight years of patronage. Or, you can refer to recent customer transactions by recommending complimentary products for purchase.

Or, you can incorporate maps or directions to the nearest store or facility. You can reference important dates such as an expiration date. Personalization works because your subscribers feel like they already have a relationship and the dialog is a one-to-one conversation. The goal is for it to feel real and not faked.

The more you personalize your e-mail marketing campaign with information from your database, the more important it becomes to have the correct data. Errors in your data can damage your campaign by showing how poorly you know the recipient instead of how well. Always have default information to substitute in case you are missing data.

You can write your copy so that substituting this default text maintains the flow of the copy. Also, respect the privacy of the recipient and avoid the use of any sensitive information such as financial or health status.

*E-mail Buddy list: A buddy list is a list of people a user maintains and hopes to stay in contact with via email.*

# 94. Smaller E-mail Marketing Lists Are Better

"Small is the number of people who see with their eyes
and think with their minds"

**Albert Einstein (1879 – 1955) Nobel Laureate for Physics**

Contrary to popular opinion, large e-mail databases are typically not better. Often large databases will include "dead" e-mail addresses which exaggerate the "monetary value" of the list.

It makes good business sense to cull your list regularly. This includes a prompt management of "opt-out requests" which are people who are not receiving value from the relationship with you. Move fast on these requests or the recipients will report you as spam. Additionally, a periodic revisit to all opt-in recipients with the request to opt-in again can significantly improve your list quality. Of course, it can make your list smaller.

Here are some additional reasons why it makes sense to cull your list:

- A better list provides better statistics about your list since the dead or unresponsive e-mails are removed. For example, your open rates will be higher. In truth, the number of total opened e-mails does not change, but now the open rate statistic is more in tune with reality.
- It makes economic sense that fewer e-mails sent costs less money.
- Your spam complaints will go down since you are not sending e-mails to uninterested readers.
- Improved deliverability should keep you off blacklists.
- Your reputation score should improve.

Smaller lists make good business sense.

*The best email list: A list of one.*

# 95. Staying in Touch with E-mail Newsletters

"My friends are my estate."

**Emily Dickinson (1830 – 1886) Poet**

Newsletters are a great way to stay in touch with your customers and prospects; they can create a new relationship or maintain an existing one.

When sending a regular newsletter to your subscribers, always make sure that it's sent on the same day, at the same time. Your punctuality and your consistency speak volumes about your brand and about your commitment to your subscribers. Your subscribers will come to "expect" your e-mail to arrive in their inbox on the same day at the same time.

As for frequency, I recommend at least a quarterly mailing since e-mail address turnover is so high these days. I saw a statistic from Google that said e-mail addresses turnover at an annual rate of 31%! So if you don't mail to your list once a quarter, your list will start to decay.

Frequency is a function of how important or relevant the content is for the reader. To be sent weekly means that the reader is making almost daily decisions about your content. For example, a stock picking newsletter might fit a weekly distribution but this also means that it ages quickly and has a short shelf life. In my opinion, a monthly distribution is fine for most businesses.

The big debate in the e-mail marketing community is HTML or plain text better? HTML is colorful and eye catching but oddly enough spam filters for many e-mail readers like MS Outlook, Gmail, etc will disable the images. This means that all your readers see is the text unless they go to the trouble to open the images.

Keep your fonts simple and readable. There is nothing more frustrating than having to decipher an overly ornate font. Be kind to the readers with "over forty eyes" by giving them a font that is big enough that they don't have to run to get their reading glasses. Also, single columns are best since eye tracking studies show that a single column is easier to scan.

Finally, people don't read much these days. Most people prefer to scan newsletter headlines and seldom finish articles. So remember not to beat around the bush and be sure to make your point right away before they hit the delete key.

*Recommendation: Constant Contact is a great starter e-mail marketing software tool. Visit http://www.constantcontact.com/index.jsp.*

# 96. Are You a Spammer?

"Oh, what a tangled web we weave when first we practice to deceive!"

**Sir Walter Scott (1771 - 1832) Scottish Author & Novelist**

My money says that there is about a 50% chance that you are a spammer and don't know it. Why do I think so? It is my observation that although the CAN-SPAM Act of 2003 is old news, half of the commercial e-mail marketers either ignore the law or simply don't understand it.

I monitored my incoming e-mails for seven days and guess what I found? About 50% of the e-mails that I received were not in compliance. Most of these e-mails came from sources that I had opted-in to. By the way, these were mostly legitimate firms that sent e-mails that did not get caught by my spam filter.

The CAN-SPAM Act of 2003 (which was updated on May 12, 2008) very specifically identifies the following:

- Bans false or misleading "from" lines.
- Prohibits deceptive subject lines.
- Requires an opt-out method.
- Requires that e-mail be identified as an advertisement.
- Requires the sender's valid physical postal address or P.O. Box.
- States that an e-mail recipient cannot be required to pay a fee, provide information other than his or her e-mail address and opt-out preferences.

Further, each violation is subject to fines of up to $11,000 and other fines could be applied. While it is true that prosecution has been modest to date, it is increasing. The courts are getting progressively tougher while consumers and businesses have grown weary of the constant bombardment by spammers whether they are opt-in or not. The law is quite specific, yet companies are largely ignoring it. Why? Ignorance of the law is a factor, but the lack of enforcement is the root cause.

With the consequences of spamming potentially so dire, here are a few things you can do to avoid that problem:

- Maintain and use your own e-mail list. The best lists are built by you one name at a time. Never share your list; this destroys your list's integrity. Never buy your lists from list providers since you never know how they really got the names and if they truly opt-in.
- Always request your list members to opt-in and always verify a second time with a verification e-mail. This is referred to as double opt-in. Most importantly, if someone opts-out, remove them from your list immediately.
- E-mail your list members only when it is important or when you can bring value to the reader.
- Always send e-mails from a person with a real name instead of a company; recipients are far more likely to welcome mail from a real person.
- Avoid spam words or phrases in the subject line; this is the kiss of death. Google "common spam words" and you will be blown away at the list.
- Don't use attachments since readers are increasingly afraid of attachments carrying viruses. Use links instead.
- Good subject lines are seldom over five words and always include the reader. The purpose of the subject is to get the reader to open the e-mail. Never put your company or yourself in the subject line.
- Spam filters are becoming increasingly sophisticated. Beware of including complex images in the body of your e-mail.
- Shorter e-mails are more likely to get opened since readers will look at file size before opening and may delete a large file.
- Be sure to include a snail mail address on every e-mail; this makes you compliant with the Federal CAN-SPAM law.

My recommendation is to obey the law today and avoid the wrath of the court system tomorrow. There may be reckoning and it won't be pretty.

*Check this out: Visit the McAfee (virus software maker) website at (http://www.mcafee.com/us/threat_center/anti_spam/spam_top10.html) and you can see the top ten spam subject lines from the last 24 hours. Also, go read the CAN-Spam Act for Commercial E-mailers at http://www.ftc. gov/bcp/edu/pubs/business/ecommerce/bus61.shtm.*

# 97. Mobile Devices and E-mail Marketing

"None are so hopelessly enslaved as those who falsely believe they are free."

**Goethe (1749 – 1832) German Writer**

Mobile devices have changed the face of e-mail marketing. A recent survey by American Online uncovered the following about the users of PDAs:

- 59% of people e-mailing from portable devices are checking e-mail in bed while in their pajamas.
- 53% are checking e-mail while in the bathroom.
- 37% are checking e-mail while they drive.
- 12% are checking e-mail while they are in church (heaven help us!).

What this means to e-mail marketers is that their messages are being scanned, not read, very quickly. Most often the goal of the PDA user is to figure out what to delete and what to save for later when they view their messages on their PC. The challenge for the e-mail marketer is get their message across quickly on the small screen of the PDA or else they are trashed.

This means no images, no graphics, and few links (most people don't use them anyway). Oh, by the way, did I mention that there are no standards for PDA displays (fonts, screen size, formats, etc)?

This means that simple messages work best. Mostly what you need is some well written text. E-mail on a PDA is like a very long subject line.

*PDA: PDA means personal digital assistant, but is also text messaging speak for public display of affection.*

# 98. Trust Is Everything in E-mail Marketing

"Trust everybody, but cut the cards."

**Finley Peter Dunne (1867 – 1936) Humorist and Author**

Trust is hard to define, but we know it when we see it or feel it. And this is particularly true with e-mail marketing. The truest measure of trust in commercial e-mail marketing may be the "reputation score" which is calculated by all the individual ISPs.

A reputation score is a complex algorithm used by the ISPs to calculate a score that reflects the sender's deliverability. This reputation score can determine whether your e-mails will be delivered to the inbox, the bulk email folder, or not delivered at all. The reputation score criteria can include the frequency or history of email campaigns, bounce back percentages, opt-in abuse, spam complaints, sender authentication, accreditation services, and many others.

The major ISP spam filters care less and less about how your subject line reads or the words used. Instead they focus on the sender's reputation. This applies to Hotmail, Gmail, EarthLink, Yahoo!, and AOL. I have read that subject line words may account for less than 80% of sender reputation score.

And this applies to unsolicited e-mails and to e-mails from trusted senders which were opted-in. Instead of hitting the unsubscribe key to opt-out of a newsletter, as many as 20% of e-mail recipients hit the spam key. Why? It is an easy way to end the relationship. This finding is from a recent survey conducted by eMarketer in 2007.

This means that companies and individuals are increasingly growing less tolerant of unwanted and irrelevant e-mails. The key to maintaining a good reputation score may be keyed to relevancy. If your e-mail provides valuable or desirable information to the recipient you will be considered relevant. If not, you are just spam.

*Trusted Sender: A trusted sender is the author of an email that you choose to open more than once.*

# 99. *Subject Lines Enable E-mail Marketing*

"The most dangerous of all falsehoods is a slightly distorted truth."

**G. C. Lichtenberg (1742 – 1799) German Scientist and Satirist**

Subject lines are a critical element of e-mail marketing since they are a key determinant in getting your e-mails opened. No matter how terrific your message or offer is if your e-mail does not get opened you have accomplished nothing. The subject line's job is to get the reader to open the e-mail, no more and no less.

A surprisingly large percentage of e-mail messages don't make it to your target recipient when you conduct a large e-mail campaign. Most are snared by spam filters, firewalls, and some are eliminated by the delete key without being opened. The reasons for this high e-mail mortality rate are many, but the deadly reason is a poor subject line. If the subject line looks like spam or a sales pitch, the message is history.

You don't have to be Shakespeare to write effective subject lines; instead it takes some common sense along with an understanding of what the spam filters look for and what your recipients view as relevant, tantalizing, or interesting. Avoid the use of "spam-like" words or phrases such as "free," "make $10,000 in day," "Viagra," etc. Don't use exclamation points. Questions marks are fine.

Your subject needs to be short. A good rule of thumb it to keep it less than 50 characters and I personally prefer them shorter than that—write five to seven well chosen words and leave it at that. Be a drinking fountain and not a fire hose. Also, be advised that long subject lines can get automatically truncated by the Internet service providers, so shorter is always better. For instance, AOL 9.0 auto-truncates at 51 characters. Long messages will get cut off and won't communicate.

The words written must include the reader or must be about the reader. Remember it is all about them and not about you or your offering. Whenever possible personalize the e-mail by including the recipient in it. Use of the word "you" is powerful or titles like "9 out of 10 Lawyers

Recommend" which identifies the target recipient as a lawyer. Conversely, never put your name or product name in the e-mail unless you know the recipient personally. Otherwise, this is just another reason to hit the delete key. The subject line must be compelling, about the recipient or the recipient's issues, and must have a call to action to open the e-mail.

Normally you want to include the benefits of your offering. For example, the subject line "Learn Spanish in Just Six Weeks" delivers a powerful benefit about how you can master Spanish quickly and easily. How will they do this? They have to open the e-mail to find out.

Consider writing the subject line after you have written the body of your e-mail. Finish the body copy and then brainstorm subject lines that are compelling and relevant. It could be argued that you should spend more time writing the subject line than the body since the subject line is so important. Narrow down your subject line candidates to two of your favorites.

If this is a large campaign, consider testing the subject lines with a sample. You could do an internal test at your company or with friends to determine which is better. Always test your e-mails first with a small distribution or test the subject line words with Google AdWords. Another simple test might be to split your list in half to see which works best. Track your success and learn from your failures.

A subject line is just like a headline; it hooks the reader into reading more. Make it compelling, interesting, and maybe a little sensational (just like a newspaper headline or a headline on People Magazine). Important words go first in the subject line. People are impatient and may not finish reading the entire subject line.

It is better to be specific and not generalize in subject lines. For example, use "file folders" instead of "office supplies." Numbers are powerful as well; for example, "10 Easy Ways to Store Your Photos" is compelling when compared to "Ways to Store Your Photos."

Finally, always tell the truth. Never tease or mislead the recipient. The subject line should always be specific, direct, and honest. Lies, fibs, and exaggerations will just be deleted or, worse, the recipient will report the email as spam.

*Test it: Always test your subject lines. If you have two good ones, try them both. Remember, it is not what you think—it is what the recipient thinks.*

# 100. E-mail Marketing Sender Lines

"If you stand straight, do not fear a crooked shadow."

**Chinese proverb**

Even though e-mail marketing sender lines may not sound like a difficult concept to master there are a few things that you need to keep in mind.

Most of the information written is common sense, but still the world of Internet marketing is relatively new and fluid. What worked 18 months ago is now less effective given the increased sophistication and decreased patience of e-mail recipients. Forrester Research says that the average person gets 110 unsolicited e-mail offers a week; no wonder the delete key is used so often.

With that said, here is a sampling of the right and wrong things to do when it comes to composing sender lines for e-mail:

- The sender line determines if the e-mail should be deleted or not, so make sure it does not look like spam.
- E-mails should come from people and not from companies or from odd looking names. For example, the sender should read johnbradleyjackson@gmail.com and not from firstbestordifferent@gmail.com.
- If a sender name works, continue to use it. Brand it.
- Remember the sender name triggers the decision to delete without opening if it looks odd.

*Send it to me: Code your direct mail with unique send names to track campaign success.*

# 101. Webinars Work Wonders

"We met—'twas a crowd."

**Thomas Haynes Bayly (1797 – 1839) English Poet and Dramatist**

Webinars are a terrific way to market, sell, and service customers; the good news is that they are increasingly becoming comfortable with this method of communication. While webinars don't offer all the benefits of a face-to-face meeting, they are far better than phone calls and e-mails.

You can use webinars to roll out a new product or to hold a sales meeting. Most webinar systems allow for multiple, if not many, participants to join a conference call with a web based presentation using in the form of a PowerPoint. Compared to the cost of traditional meetings, which can include travel, hotels, facility rentals and catering, webinars are low-cost events for the host and the attendees. The host pays for the webinar software and sometimes for a presenter, while the attendees join in for free.

The webinar software allows presenters and attendees to interact and collaborate through live polls, question and answer periods, and document sharing, making it easy for attendees to participate in and learn from the event. Webinars also allow geographically dispersed customers and colleagues to join. Video is also an option and you can record and archive meetings or presentations. These features make webinars a compelling method of communication.

Admittedly, it takes some practice with the software to manage a webinar, although the major webinar software providers have made them fairly easy to master. I recommend that you try a few dry runs to get yourself acquainted with the features. Like any other presentation, preparation will help the webinars run smoothly.

Here are a few recommendations for successfully conducting a webinar:

- Have a hard start and stop time for the meeting. People are busy so don't waste their time.
- Get down to business. Don't use the meeting for idle chit chat.
- Do a roll call on the front end. While the attendees may be visible to the presenter, depending on the settings for the software,

your attendees may not know who else is on the call. This may not be practical for webinars with many attendees.

- Create an agenda and have supporting materials that you can easily incorporate into your presentation and share with attendees if needed.
- Being ready to share a video, spreadsheet, or Web site will keep your webinar interactive and help you better answer questions.
- As you go through the PowerPoint, be sure to announce the page number.
- Use color to divide each slide into thirds: beginning, middle, and end–each a different color.
- Slides should be even simpler than normal. Overly complex slides slow down the pace of the meeting. Six bullets per slide is a good standard to keep. Visuals such as simple graphs and charts will also help.
- Maintain a high energy level. Think of webinars like a performance on TV or radio. A dull presenter makes for a bad webinar.
- Live polls offer a great way for a large group to give you feedback.
- Online chat is an interesting feature which allows remote staff to collaborate while the presentation is being made.
- Consider using two or more speakers to create a "ham and egg" effect—this makes for a more interesting presentation.
- Depending on the size of the group, leaving the mute button in the off position will allow for interaction. Large groups will need to be muted until the end of the call; be sure to offer a question and answer period at the end.
- Large groups can intimidate listeners during the question and answer period. Prepare questions just in case nobody has a question. It is also possible to plant questions with staff members.
- Have a specific call to action. Make it clear what is the next step for your listeners.

Webinars have limitations. Hostile attendees are hard to manage in a large group; this favors the use of the mute switch with canned questions at the end. Also, webinars can be a little impersonal when compared to face-to-face communication. Beware of coming off as too slick or prepared. Interaction with the audience should help avoid this pitfall.

*Two Options: I recommend "GoToWebinar" at www.Webinar.GoTo Meeting.com/ and "WebEx" at www.webex.com. Both are easy to use and surprisingly affordable.*

# 102. Save Time with Direct Mail

"Everywhere is walking distance if you have the time."

**Steven Wright (1955 – present) Comedian and Actor**

It is sales legend that it costs far less money to keep an existing customer than it does to find a new one. Customers that have bought from you in the past are likely to buy again and represent your best leads. Thus, staying in touch with these folks is a must do for any business and direct mail is one of the most efficient ways to stay in contact.

Here are a few tips on maintaining relationships with direct mail:

- Direct mail to your customers frequently. Monthly may be too often, but a quarterly mailing is reasonable. Update them on new products, price changes, service reminders, and special events. Treat them as "insiders" who deserve to know about these things first (I.E. ahead of your prospects).
- Keep their addresses updated. This information changes frequently and direct mail is a great way to "ferret out" this new information. Always ask for email addresses and phone numbers.
- Refresh your direct mailer design. Customers know what your mailers look like, so beware of sending the same message or same look too often. A new look for your direct mailer can complement a new message.
- Personalize the mailer whenever possible. Handwrite a note on the mailer or include a Post-it with a few words. Make the customer feel special.
- Always include your website address on the mailer along with your other contact info.

Research shows that direct mail remains a cost effective way to connect with clients. Email is terrific, but a multi-media strategy works better. This can include direct mail, email, telephone, in-person meetings, public relations, and advertising.

When all is said and done, there is no substitute for frequency of contact with your customers.

*United States Postal Service: In business for 200 years and they still won't guarantee delivery.*

# 103. Send Thanksgiving Cards

"I awoke this morning with devout thanksgiving for my friends,
the old and the new."

**Ralph Waldo Emerson (1803 – 1882) Poet**

Be different this holiday season. Don't be like everyone else and send holiday cards and gifts for Christmas, Hanukah, and New Years. Instead, send Thanksgiving cards or gifts.

Your well-intentioned best wishes during the year-end holidays will only get watered down by the crush of others doing the same thing. Additionally, sending a Christmas card to someone of another faith is inconsiderate, if not dumb.

But, let me digress and tell you a little about Thanksgiving. Thanksgiving is a uniquely North American holiday and universal in its appeal. Thanksgiving is celebrated on the fourth Thursday of November in the United States and on the second Monday of October in Canada. The four day weekend and some sympathetic marketing have made the holiday a bigger deal in the United States.

According to Wikipedia, the early settlers of Plymouth Colony in Massachusetts were particularly grateful to Squanto, the Native American who taught them how to both catch eel and grow corn and also served as their native interpreter (as Squanto had converted to Christianity and learned English as a slave in Europe). Without Squanto's assistance, the settlers might not have survived in the New World.

The Plymouth settlers (who came to be called "Pilgrims") set apart a holiday immediately after their first harvest in 1621. They held an autumn celebration of food, feasting, and praising God. The Pilgrims invited the Native Americans for a feast that lasted three days.

Historical revisionists tend to take a harsher view and tell a story that includes lots of ale, abuse of the Native Americans, and land grabbing by the whites, but I prefer to dwell on the traditional message of Thanksgiving which modern marketers describe as a time of thanks and fellowship with family and friends.

Therefore, be like the Pilgrims and invite your neighbors over for Thanksgiving dinner. Send your customers and colleagues cards expressing your gratitude.

Do this and you will be remembered for being different from the crowd.

*Other cards: How about cards for Independence Day, Cinco de Mayo, or even Groundhog's Day?*

# 104. Product Promotion is a Call to Action

"Without promotion something terrible happens—nothing!"

**P.T. Barnum (1810 – 1891) Circus Magnate**

Unlike advertising and public relations which create publicity and awareness, product promotion delivers a call to action. Typically, the call to action is for the customer to buy now; often there is an incentive offered to encourage the customer to do so.

The goal of product promotion is get the product in front of the customer or channel of distribution. While customer knows the product promotion is overtly sponsored by the offering firm, the call to action can be compelling. Or, at least, that is what the sponsoring firm hopes.

Here are some common product promotion techniques:

- Give it away: If the lifetime value of the customer purchases is greater than the cost of the giveaway, then it can make economic sense to give the product away. For example, in the pharmaceutical industry free drug samples are given to physicians to dispense to patients to demonstrate their benefits. If successful, the patient may be prescribed the drugs.
- Trial: Similar to giving it away, a trial gives the customer a chance to use the product for a short duration of time. If satisfied the customer can keep the product and continue usage. A good example would be trial software; this a common approach for anti-virus software makers.
- Event marketing: Everybody loves a party. Event marketing uses the power of the crowd to entice people to buy now. This could be a sidewalk sale in the retail store or a grand opening for a business.
- Discounting: Offering a special price which is only available for a limited time is a time proven product promotion technique. This discount is frequently offered via a coupon. Delay and the price will go up (I.E. you snooze, you lose).

- Bundling: This means offering a second complimentary product as a part of a package. Buy the PC and the printer is free. Or, it could be two for the price of one.
- Contests: Try your luck and you might be a winner. Contests are another tried and true method to get the customer to take action. This is commonly used by the retail giants.
- White paper: The technology crowd loves the soft sell of the third party authored white paper which tells all about their product versus the competition. Everybody knows that this research is bought and paid for, but it works.
- Tchotchke: Yiddish for a small gift, these branded items demand attention and are the gold standard of trade shows. The best giveaways are evergreen and remain on the customer's desk or shelf as memorabilia of past shows.

Product promotion works because customers need a reason to buy now. It is up to you to give them that reason.

*Tchotchke: There are many ways to spell this word. According to Wikipedia, there are a variety of spellings for the English usage of the term including chotchkas, tshotshke, tshatshke, tchatchke, chachke, or chochke because there is no standardized translation.*

# 105. Experiential Marketing

"Who are you going to believe, me or your own eyes?"

**Groucho Marx (1890 – 1977) Comedian and Actor**

Experiential Marketing, sometimes called "XM," is a trendy term used in the business press to describe a category of marketing activities that requires a direct encounter with a customer. This direct encounter is different from the majority of marketing activities which are mostly passive in nature.

For example, advertising is a very passive medium that bombards the customer with messages that need to be listened to or read. Print advertising requests the reader to stop and read the message but, in most cases, we skim over the ad or just ignore it. In fact, most ads never get noticed. Luckily, modern day Homo sapiens have developed an "internal TiVo" that automatically deletes most advertisements (this is a basic survival characteristic for the species).

Experiential marketing describes an encounter with a customer that makes them feel something. Walking through a department store recently, an attractive woman salesperson sprayed me with perfume as I walked by the cosmetics counter. It was an aggressive act, but it was a powerful encounter. I will never go to that store again.

You encounter XM almost everyday. At a fine restaurant, the waiter brings a sampling of desserts to your table which looks and smells great. This approach is far more stimulating to your senses than the traditional question, "Saved room for dessert?"

Another common example is a Sunday morning newspaper advertisement for a new brand of shampoo that includes a sample for you to use. The personal contact with the brand is very powerful, albeit an expensive advertising technique. This is how I get most of my toiletries.

During the holidays, you are approached by the Salvation Army bell-ringers who look you in the eye while ringing that clanging bell. Somehow the whole experience reminds you of Christmas or Hanukkah past. It tugs at your heart, so you toss a quarter in the bucket (yes, I am kind of cheap).

A trendy XM tactic is the use of street teams that perform skits on street corners in urban areas; they sing and dance and cavort while delivering a message about an event or offering. You feel compelled to stop and watch these idiots prance around. Secretly, you guess that the performers all must have graduate degrees in dance or philosophy. You give a big sigh of relief that you changed your major to business from Theater Arts, or else this would be you dancing for minimum wage.

The use of "street teams" is becoming a common promotion technique used in urban environments or at crowded venues. In a nutshell, street teams attempt to promote or advertise something, they create a buzz about an offering or an event.

Some say that the music industry started it all when attempting to promote concerts. Using mostly volunteers and devoted fans, the teams were sponsored by the music label or the band itself to generate a buzz for an upcoming show. The rewards for the street team participants generally consisted of free concert tickets, t-shirts, and bragging rights that they worked for the "band."

The street team did whatever was necessary to promote the band or event; this could include telephone blitzes, parading in costume, posting flyers, text messaging friends, and handing out coupons on the street corner. Anything goes that will promote the band. This method was precise in targeting the customer since it used social networks like buddy lists on cell phones. Location also played a big role since they focused on the night clubs where the fans hung out.

These grassroots organizations have now gone mainstream with companies specializing in this type of promotion. You may recall political organizations using this technique to get voters to register to vote. Or, you may even remember PETA (People for the Ethical Treatment of Animals) for using this marketing technique. In fact, street teams are a key component of PETA's marketing strategy. Does this seem a bit on the lunatic fringe for you?

Apple Computer has used street teams extensively at trade shows to sell iPods, while Hispanic media giant Univision has used street teams to create buzz about its Spanish language programming. The corporate list of street team sponsors now includes FedEx, Verizon, and Warner Brothers, to name a few.

Thus, experiential marketing elicits a feeling based on a direct contact with a customer.

*Touch them: Experiential marketing works because of personal contact—people feel actively involved in the promotion.*

# 106. Wild Posting

"All good things are wild and free"

**Henry David Thoreau (1817 – 1862) Author and Philosopher**

Although it has been around for many centuries, "wild posting" is the current rage for product offerings and events that have a need for an "in-your-face" style of promotion. You have no doubt seen wild postings as you walked through an urban area where construction site barricades are plastered with the dozens or even hundreds of posters for a rock concert. Or, you might have seen hundreds of posters for the movie "Spiderman" displayed on the side of a building. Yes, that is wild posting.

For hundreds of years posting signs along highways or on the side of buildings was a common way to advertise. Sometimes people opposed it; the expression "post no bills" was often seen on the side of buildings begging wild posters not to stick stuff on their buildings. I guess these posted signs were considered an early version of graffiti.

Recently, this technique has been used for technology products such as cell phones and high speed Internet services. AT&T posted banners for the "fastest Internet in town for $14.99 a month" on an overpass in downtown Los Angeles. Microsoft used wild posting for its MSN "butterfly" by using a "static-cling" style poster, which was easily removed and did not harm the surface where it was posted.

Mainstream companies are turning to wild posting because it is inexpensive; all it requires is printing and minimum wage labor. Also, it is demographic-specific since you can pinpoint the exact city block where you want the posting to go. For instance, you can post near a football stadium or an amphitheater where people walk by after a major sporting or music event. Wild posting works 24/7 or, at least, until someone takes it down or posts something on top of it.

Could it work for your business? If your customer walks a certain route or drives by a certain location frequently, it just might.

*Wild things: What is mild to you may be wild to others. Proceed with caution.*

# 107. Jumbo Squid Invade California!

"If you believe everything you read, you better not read."

**Japanese proverb**

Run for the hills! We are being invaded by monstrous sea creatures! All is lost! This is an actual headline from the Associated Press on 7/25/2007, which describes the increased sightings of seven foot squid off the coast of California. Yet, if you take the headline literally, Armageddon has come. This is the power of a provocative headline.

The editor at the Associated Press decided to spice up this dull fishing story and pique the interest of the readership. Nothing works better than a sensational headline. It got my attention, but I felt that the headline misled or teased me too much.

When writing press releases or copy for brochures, good headlines are essential. The purpose of the headline is first to get the attention of the reader by summarizing the copy or content below it. The headline must be interesting, but not mislead the reader.

Here are some recommendations for writing better headlines:

- Use strong verbs like "NY Yankees Spank the Boston Red Sox."
- Uses numbers such as "8.0 Earthquake Hits LA."
- More punctuation is better such commas and semi-colons: "Bush, Cheney Agree: Stay in Iraq."
- Beware of double meanings like "Sharks Attack LA"; is this a hockey or a fish story?
- Don't exaggerate, lie or mislead because it will just irritate the reader. "Jumbo Squid Invade California" seems a bit overdone to me. There are no jumbo squid in my driveway.
- Don't use a silly headline unless it is a silly story. "Hearts Ache for Help" is an inappropriate headline when the story is about heart disease.
- Don't start a headline with a verb; instead say who or what. For example, "Slaughtered in the Thousands" begs the question who or what was slaughtered? Mosquitoes? Rats? Bloggers?

- Beware of abbreviations. Your reader might misunderstand. "Flood Waters Rise in LA" could mean Los Angeles or Louisiana.

Well-written headlines are powerful. They are a call to action to read more. So be sure that you headline delivers the write message.

*P.S. You can read the actual Jumbo Squid article at: http://dsc. discovery.com/news/2007/07/25/jumbosquid_ani_02.html?category=animals &guid=20070725170000.*

# 108. Press Kits

"Harmony seldom makes a headline."

**Silas Bent (1882 – 1945) Journalist**

One important part of a public relations effort is the compilation of a press kit. A press kit provides summary information about the company for the media. That info could include recent press releases, a company backgrounder, bios of key executives, product specifications, and anything else the media might need to know about the company.

Traditionally, this material comes in a glossy folder for mailing or in-person delivery. Today, more often than not, the press kit comes as a soft copy via email or on a flash drive. Most companies have both printed and e-copy versions available.

In a nutshell, a press kit needs the following items:

- Company Backgrounder: This backgrounder can be written in essay form or can be a bulleted listing. It should describe the products and/or services your company provides, as well as the primary benefit you offer the customer. Be sure to include all the basics such as company name, address, phone, email, fax, website, key executives, and key contacts. Consider this an executive summary and presume that no one will read the other materials in the kit.
- Profiles: Biographies of key executives in your company will add a personal feel to the kit. Depending on the size of the company, resumes and photos may be appropriate. Otherwise, brief bio sheets may be appropriate.
- Recent Press Releases: This is a no brainer but you should include only newsworthy, recent releases. Old news will just be tossed or deleted. Be sure to print these press releases on letterhead.
- Testimonials or User Reviews: This inclusion may be or may not be appropriate depending on your industry. Your testimonials must be credible if not rock solid. Third party opinion will be worth far more than your own boasting, so consider using customer feedback to promote your offering.

- Brochures: Don't over do it, but a few up-to-date product brochures can be included.

Honestly, you don't want to include much more than this since the call to action is for the media to contact you for an interview or to ask questions. Public Relations are all about relationships with the media and not about shipping paper or data.

*Relationships count: Take a reporter to lunch.*

# 109. Public Relations is Vanity Gone to College

"The caterpillar does all the work and the butterfly gets all the publicity."

**George Carlin (1937 – 2008) Comedian**

Too many press releases beat the drum about new product releases, product features, and the daring follies of egomaniacal CEOs. Most of this bilge is just plain vanity and worthless to their audience. Can you hear the delete key tapping away? Good PR informs that reader about matters to them, not the authoring company.

Creating publicity with public relations is a lot of hard work but studies show that PR is 7-8 times more believable than advertising. Getting your name in the newspaper, in the trade press, on the Internet, on the radio, or on television helps build credibility and helps build your brand. Unlike advertising, which is paid for, publicity or "ink" is earned by building relationships and hard work.

A PR strategy has the following essential elements:

- Create the positioning message; what is the one thing that you want your target market to know about you or your firm?
- Write a two- to three-word mantra which describes the message. These will be the words used in your workplace and externally. They must be memorable and believable.
- Test your message with your staff, your vendors, and your customers. How does the target audience receive it? Adjust your message based on the feedback. Test it again.
- Create press releases so that you present your pitch in the form of news. More than a commercial, tie the launch of your press releases to a significant event to create timeliness. The press is always interested in what is timely, informative, and they like it to be a bit controversial.
- Create press kits; when they call, you need to send follow-up materials. They always ask for them. This is done by e-mail more and more. Some may ask for paper, so have both types ready.

- Create product evaluation kits; these are great selling tools for customers. Include a sample of your merchandise. This can be done virtually on the web or by mail.
- Create mailing lists for customers, prospects, and everyone else that needs to hear your story. This name development is critical and needs to be an ongoing process. The best lists are built by getting permission from visitors to your website. Lists can also be purchased and PR firms can help with this task.
- Introduce yourself to analysts, industry mavens, and people of influence. This may seem daunting on your own, but if you start asking around and watching for names in the industry periodicals, you will find them. This is also when a PR agency helps a lot. Your goal is to build a relationship with these movers and shakers; it is up to you to stay in touch since they won't call you.
- Make some noise! This would be press releases, interviews, and events. Be sure you contact PR Newswire, Business Wire, Market Wire etc. Throw a party! Frequency of contact is the number one criteria in a purchasing decision, so you cannot have enough publicity.
- Track your success by monitoring new leads, number of press quotes, and other indicators of awareness. This will help evaluate the effectiveness of your current PR efforts and help with future PR choices.
- Create a constituency with the readership by seeking feedback and involving them in the critique of your PR effort. Heed their advice and modify the plan. This will also help facilitate the creation of relationships with the press.

Build awareness, create a constituency, and solve problems; be more than noise. Be a source of knowledge on the problem that your product or solution solves.

*Constituency: A group of people who believe in you.*

# 110. Extreme Makeover: Marketing and PR Edition

"There is no such thing as bad publicity except your own obituary."

**Brendan Behan (1923 – 1964) Irish Poet and Writer**

It's time for an "extreme makeover" of your current thinking about what makes a great marketing and public relations strategy. The traditional methods of marketing and PR are quickly becoming ineffective and if you don't know what I mean, you will soon.

In his new book, "The New Rules of Marketing and PR: How to Use News Releases, Blogs, Podcasting, Viral Marketing, and Online Media to Reach Buyers Directly," David Meerman Scott bring us up-to-date on how to get your message out to your target market using Web 2.0 technology. Actually, his book is less about technology and is more about meeting your customer where they live and work and play on the Internet.

The old days of blasting the customer with repeated press releases through the business wires and relying solely on the relationships offered by PR Agencies has given way to communicating directly with the customer about what really matters to them. My blog is a good example of what Scott calls the "new rules." A blog, if properly done, focuses its energies on the needs, problems, and issues of the customer rather than that of the blogger. Thus, the whole orientation of marketing and PR has changed.

Don't get me wrong, PR agencies do a great service. As a third party, PR firms can be very effective in helping the entrepreneur craft the right message to take to the market. This is hard work and most entrepreneurs are lousy at this. Additionally, a PR firm can save the entrepreneur time by getting the message to the gurus, the press, and the analysts. But, relying on the PR agency to be the brute force of your marketing plan is flat out wrong nowadays.

Customers have increasingly grown cynical of traditional PR and all the spin that comes with it. Instead, customers respond to authentic messages about their problems. And, they rely heavily on the advice and experience of other customers who share these same problems. This is why wikis, forums, and blogs have taken the web by storm.

The web also offers you a way to track your buzz. Here are a couple ways to monitor your PR efforts on the web:

- Set up Google Alerts based on specific search terms such as your company or product names. This will allow you to keep current with your industry and see who is writing about you.
- Set up RSS alerts with Technorati.com. This will allow you to track bloggers who post things about your firm or products.

Remember, it is all about them (I.E. the customer) and not about you.

*Late Night Reading: David Meerman Scott gets it. Read "The New Rules of Marketing and PR: How to Use News Releases, Blogs, Podcasting, Viral Marketing, and Online Media to Reach Buyers Directly" now.*

# *111. Why Blog?*

"Why do writers write? Because it isn't there."

**Thomas Berger (1924 – present) Novelist**

Why do I Blog? I get asked this question a lot. Yes, it takes a lot of time and brain cells, both of which I have a very limited supply. To blog regularly requires tons of research, fact checking, writing, and editing. It is hard work.

I don't blog for the money since my blog is free. I don't measure my success by the number of visitors to my site, yet I have many. The answer is that I blog to help people. And I suppose that sounds a little high-minded. But, of all the things that I do, including teaching at a university, running my own company, consulting with entrepreneurs, writing books, and speaking at conferences, blogging has the biggest impact of all.

Blogging is my way to share with others who know me and with others who I will never speak with or meet. Some like to call this "thought leadership," which is a very uppity term. For me, it is the best way to communicate clearly with my target audience with my audience being people who want to learn more about marketing, sales, and negotiation.

Because I blog, I have been invited to speak at conferences, quoted in the national press, and have been interviewed on MSNBC. My motivation is not fame, rather it is the desire to teach and help others. Certainly a by-product of my success as a blogger includes book sales, paid speaking engagements, and consulting. This helps me pay the bills, which is important with two kids in college.

Seemingly every day my phone rings, or I get e-mails from people who I have never met before. They read my blog and want to share an idea or ask a question. That interchange is a thrill to me and is its own reward. This is why I blog.

When I wrote my first book, "First, Best, or Different," I included a chapter on the importance of blogging. Little did I know at the time that blogging would become the core of own book marketing effort. Indulge me as I tell you about my own blogging story.

Back in August of 2006 I wrote my first blog at the suggestion of my web designer Greg. He encouraged me by saying that it could help my website's page ranking and that blogs were becoming very popular. So, I gave it try. I carefully proofread my first article and hit the "publish now" key. Off it went and nothing happened. I wrote a second blog and then a third and got the same results. I told all my friends that I was now a blogger. They said, "That's great," and then they changed the subject. I encouraged them to read and subscribe to my blog. Almost no one did. I couldn't get my own family to read it.

Call me stubborn, but I kept on writing and blogging. I wrote on topics that I thought my book readers would like and I made sure that I was blogging five times a week. It felt like putting a message in a bottle and throwing it out to sea. I wasn't sure if anyone would ever read them.

In a few weeks (maybe five or six actually), I did a Google search for my website firstbestordifferent.com and I found it on the first page of the search results! Before the blog, my website was nowhere to be found since I had done no search engine optimization. I then did a search for John Bradley Jackson (I know this must sound vain) and I found myself! Hey, Mom, your son is an Internet celebrity, or almost.

This was all the positive reinforcement that I needed. I kept on blogging. Now it is some time later and the results are incredible. My little blog is now read by thousands of readers around the world and many are subscribers. I have created a brand for my book and for myself as a thought leader on the subjects of marketing, sales, and negotiation.

My website, my name, and my articles are linked to hundreds of other websites. I have been asked to speak at numerous corporate events and my book's first printing looks like a sell out. All this because I blogged.

Maybe you should consider a blog, too. Can you think of a better way to connect with your target audience?

*Some light reading: check out my blog at www.firstbestordifferent. com/blog.*

# 112. Blogging for Beginners

"Writing is the best way to talk without being interrupted."

**Jules Renard (1864 – 1910) French Author**

Blogging is easy. I am a big believer in this dynamic method of communication because it is a great way to create a personal dialog with your customers and prospects (and whoever else reads it). A side benefit of a blog is that it refreshes your website with new content with every entry and this pleases the major search engines. Your reward will include a higher search ranking and your site will be found with greater frequency.

But, before you launch your own blog please consider the following things:

- Make sure that your website is up-to-date with lots of content. This is important since the "call to action" for most blogs is to visit the author's website.
- Does your target audience read blogs? Certainly younger demographics do and so does the technology crowd. Grandma and Grandpa may not read blogs yet, but give them time.
- Is there a need for this type of forum in your industry? I think the answer would be yes for most industries, but there may be some commodity businesses when a discussion is not really needed. Truthfully, I am hard pressed to find an industry where a blog will not provide value.
- If your blog is public (and that is the only reason to do this anyway), will you be comfortable tackling tough issues in front of your customers, prospects, and competitors? This could earn you praise and criticism. I think a good blog calls it like it is and controversy may come with the territory.
- Make sure that you are up for the commitment of routinely writing or it will not be worth your time. A good rule of thumb is to blog three to five times a week (there are no hard and fast rules).
- Good blogs target a specific target audience and speak to the needs, issues, and problems of that audience. It is not about you and it is all about them.
- Blog software is free in most cases. I use WordPress and it works fine for me.

- I think blogs are best when written in the first person with an informal and direct style. Think 8th grade grammar and sentence structure.
- Do you like to write and are you good at it? I know that is a simple question, but if it hurts you to write, don't start a blog.
- The secret to good writing is good editing. It goes like this: write, edit, edit again, and be sure to edit again.
- Find a blog mentor who has a blog and has learned how to do it the hard way. Maybe she or he can save you some time.
- Be humble and expect a lot of feedback.
- Make sure that you are up for the commitment of routinely writing or it will not be worth your time. Blogs must be refreshed frequently to be useful.
- Keep your blogs short with no more than 500 words. Less than 250 words might even be better.
- Save the big words for the lawyers. Instead, say what you mean and stop there.
- Educate, inform, or offer opinion. Write about topics that will be interesting to your target audience.
- Offer links to other resources. This is helpful to your readers.
- Encourage readers to comment by asking their opinion.
- Don't expect a lot of comments since people are very busy.
- Clever headlines help get your blog read while keywords help get your blog found.
- End the blog on an up note or with a moral or with a suggestion or an incentive.
- Postscripts always get read.

*Blog software: Most blog software is free and easily set up. I recommend Wordpress.*

# 113. Flogs and Blogs Are Not the Same

"When in doubt, tell the truth."

**Mark Twain (1835 – 1910) Humorist and Author**

As you know, I am a big fan of blogging. Blogging is a terrific way to build your personal and corporate brand as a knowledge broker, which is my term for someone who writes or speaks on the interests, needs, or problems of a customer segment. Key to a successful blog is authenticity. This brings us to the subject of "flogs."

A flog is a fake blog. In effect, a flog is a joke or more likely a staged or paid for advertisement disguised as a blog. Flogs are sponsored by companies to create interest for their offerings, while positioning the interests of the audience as an afterthought.

An infamous example is described by Wikipedia: "Wal-Marting Across America was written by two Wal-Mart 'fans' who decided to travel across America in a RV and blog about the experience as they visited Wal-Mart's along the way. While the two people actually did travel across America for the purpose of this blog, it was revealed to be paid for by Wal-Mart." This flog actually backfired for Wal-Mart with readers becoming angry at the ruse. They protested openly on the web and it turned into a public relations disaster for Wal-Mart.

A credible blog must be authentic. I recommend that they be written in the first person, in plain English, and must address topics that the readers care about. The blog's purpose is to help, inform, or entertain the reader. Admittedly, the blogger hopes to build a constituency with the readers, but that is the blogger's reward rather than the purpose of the blog itself.

*Blogging for one: Start blogging by pleasing yourself. Make sure what you write is true to your personal convictions and beliefs.*

# 114. Are There Too Many Blogs?

"All that we are is the result of what we have thought."

**Buddha (563 B.C. – 483 B.C.) Spiritual Leader**

Earlier this year, blog tracker Technorati estimated that there were 112.8 million active English language blogs. They also believe that there already are 75 million Chinese language blogs. Of course, this begs a few questions. Are there too many blogs? Who really needs this much information? Who is reading this stuff? Why blog?

These questions hit pretty close to home for me since I have been an active blogger for two years. My quick but qualified answer is that blogging remains a very viable way to communicate to others, yet you need to speak to a highly targeted audience or nobody will read it.

Looking at blog readers it is clear that most people find blogs via a search engine like Yahoo! or Google with key words. Referrals remain a powerful source, too. Readers are looking to solve a problem, be entertained, or get information.

Readers are looking for very specific content. This means that the blog topics must be focused narrowly around a specific subject rather than miscellaneous ramblings about life or business or whatever. Of course, this is the essence of niche marketing for blogs: providing information on subjects that are overlooked or underserved.

Thus, blog content is everything. Readers want to read about themselves and their interests, not about the blogger. Vanity may be the biggest mistake by bloggers. Keep yourself out the of the blog content. Generally speaking, nobody cares about you and your last trip to the supermarket.

Few people choose to subscribe to blogs. Most visit a blog once and seldom go back. Sometimes readers are intrigued and will choose to bookmark the URL, but most of the time it does not happen.

Blog writers need to "fact check" and publish only accurate information. The web is chock full of inaccuracies, errors, and outright lies. Google any subject and you will find conflicting information from multiple bloggers. This insults the reader and assaults the medium.

Tell it like it is and explain how and why you feel the way you do about the subject. Shorter blogs are better. Long blogs just don't get read. In-depth conversations have their place but not on a blog.

Finally, monetized blogs turn me off. These are the blogs that are plastered with advertisements, Google AdSense, and live links embedded in the blog text. Yuck. If I want to be sold something, I can watch network TV.

Are there too many blogs? Yes, there may be too many blogs, but there is a shortage of relevant blogs that give readers what they really want. For the business blogger, this requires them to target a very specific audience while providing information about what matters to the reader.

*Blogs and authenticity: A good blog should be authentic. You will know it when you read it.*

# 115. Blogs, Forums, and the Competition

"The wise learn many things from their enemies."

**Aristophanes (446 B.C. – 386 B.C.) Athenian Comic**

You may not be a blogger yourself but reading blogs written by your competition and your customers may prove to be a great way to conduct market research. Increasingly, blogs, along with forums, are becoming honey pots for people to gather insight and information about products, companies, and industries.

Blogs and forums are creating communities for people to express themselves about their wants, needs, and desires. For example, discussion groups are common in the financial arena as investors share their insight about stocks and companies. Check out Yahoo! Finance and you will see what I mean.

Blogs are a great way to understand your competition and the messages that they send to their customers and partners. While it is common for a big company to use a Public Relations firm to assist with blog publishing, many smaller firms will freely tell the world how they feel about things.

Customer forums are cropping up every day in virtually all industries from consumer products to professional services. Many of these forums are highly specialized. For example, I read a forum for Corvette enthusiasts called the Corvette Forum (http://www.corvetteforum.com/), which allows people like me to share their thoughts about buying, selling, and maintaining Corvettes with other Corvette owners. This forum has no affiliation with Chevrolet, but you can bet that the folks at GM read this forum religiously.

Consider setting up a RSS feed to search for subjects of interest to you and your business. For the average web surfer, RSS provides a way to see at a glance if your favorite blogs have updated their content. Using a simple RSS feed reading program, you can subscribe to the feeds from any supporting site to get this information and link directly to the new articles that interest you. You can set up the RSS feed to find articles or blogs by keyword.

Let the research begin.

*Support your local blogger: Subscribe to blogs that you like or find helpful. Pass them on to your friends.*

# 116. Create Website Traffic with Article Marketing

"Writing is thinking on paper"

**William Zinsser (1922 – present) Writer and Teacher**

Article marketing is one of the best ways to optimize your website, create new sales leads, and to garner new publicity. The really good news is that it is free and relatively easy (OK, it does take some time and a few brain cells).

If you are not familiar with article marketing, it is the process of writing short (250-500 word) feature articles for the web that are posted on Internet magazines, commonly called e-zines. You may recall doing a search when you entered in some key words on a subject of interest and found these informative articles written by subject matter experts. At the end of the article was a byline with the author's name and an URL for you to click on for more information.

There are many benefits to on-line article marketing. Articles are sticky; once an article is accepted on an e-zine website, it can stay listed for months or years. When your articles are posted on numerous e-zine websites, the search engine spiders pick this up and send your website ranking sky high the organic way (I.E. no fees!). By writing the article you are positioned as a subject matter expert, which creates sales leads coming to you instead of you chasing them.

The articles themselves tend to be "all about" or "how to" summaries about a specific topic or, to put it another way, think niche and be specific. Article readers are looking for help with a problem or they want to learn more about a subject. Remember, the article is not an advertisement, although the author gets credit.

Articles can be submitted directly to e-zines that cover your topic, or you can submit to article submission websites that will route them for you. The submission websites have rules of engagement for the articles such as length, topic, and style, but they can be a very efficient way to distribute your article.

My own success with article marketing may be the best example that I can offer of how article marketing works. I have posted hundreds of articles on the web using this method over the past 36 months and the results are astounding. Just about every day I hear from people who have read my articles; they buy my book, ask me to speak at events, ask me to consult, or just want to get to know me. I owe this all to article marketing.

Give article marketing a try. It is a great way to get your message out to your target market.

*Write an article: Pick a subject that is important to your customers. Be objective and don't sell anything.*

# 117. Cause Marketing is for the Birds

"Those who can, do. Those who can do more, volunteer."

**Anonymous**

Procter and Gamble, manufacturer of Dawn Liquid Dishwashing Detergent, scored a public relations home run with an advertising campaign that described how the International Bird Rescue Research Center endorsed the use of Dawn to clean up birds that get "oiled" by oil spills.

Per P&G, "For 25 years, wildlife rescuers have used Dawn® dishwashing liquid to gently remove oil from aquatic animals. Animal rescue groups choose Dawn because it removes the greasy oil—while being gentle on delicate feathers and skin. Animal rescue organizations have used thousands of donated bottles of Dawn to save the lives of countless animals.

"Over the 25 years Dawn has been involved, the success rate for saving oiled wildlife has jumped from three percent to ninety percent. And now Dawn is increasing the support we give to these organizations by making a contribution to improve their facilities and spreading the word about the many things everyone can do to prevent oil from getting into the environment."

In this national television advertisement, Dawn did not even mention that Dawn was "good for dishes." Instead, they positioned Dawn as a concerned member of the environmental community. This is cause marketing (a marketing activity that supports a charitable event, a cause, or a non-profit organization) at its finest. The positive spin from this ad and the buzz that it has created is extraordinary. Do a Google search on "Dawn" and you will be amazed at the chatter and the positive publicity that this campaign has generated.

The lesson for entrepreneurs is that cause marketing pays. Giving time to a charitable event or organization can create a strong promotional event for yourself, build your network, and help build your brand. Cause marketing is a marketing activity that supports a charitable event, a cause, or a non-profit organization. Although philanthropy by corporations has been a common promotional tool for a long time, connecting this good work with a company's advertising and public relations campaign is relatively new.

This technique can be applied on a smaller scale in a local community or an industry. It could be driven by your affiliation with a favorite charity, a kid's soccer team, or a church. By getting involved and giving, you can receive free publicity for the good work. You can then tout this good work with your PR and advertising efforts. Research shows that this type of positive publicity can increase sales and brand loyalty.

Your action is to find a cause that you are passionate about and get involved. The payoff will come back in your improved image. And it will feel good too.

*Getting involved: Choose a charity or a cause that makes your heart race. Be a part of it. Make it yours.*

# 118. Sales Leadership: Who is Minding the Store?

> "It's hard to lead a cavalry charge if you think you look
> funny on a horse."
>
> **Adlai Stevenson (1900 – 1965) Statesman**

What makes a great sales leader? Is it a manager with confidence, an ego under control, and empathy for others? Or, is he or she an egocentric, power-mad narcissist?

A recent article by Live Science suggests that it is probably the latter. The article suggests that, "Narcissists are overconfident about their abilities and like to be in charge. They are most likely to step in as leaders, be they politicians or power brokers." Sadly, many narcissists are also selected as sales managers.

The article continued, "However, their initiative doesn't mean they are the best leaders. Narcissists don't outperform others in leadership roles. Narcissists tend to be egotistical types who exaggerate their talents and abilities, and lack empathy for others."

The researchers stress that, "Narcissism is not the same as high self-esteem. A person with high self-esteem is confident and charming, but they also have a caring component and they want to develop intimacy with others. Narcissists have an inflated view of their talents and abilities and are all about themselves. They don't care as much about others."

Unfortunately, narcissists become sales leaders since they love power, are egotistical, and are usually charming and extroverted. This profile doesn't make for better sales leaders. Narcissistic sales leaders make poor choices since their focus is about themselves rather than the team or company. They just don't care about others.

Organizations select the narcissists for leadership roles for the wrong reasons including the unending pleading by the narcissist to get the job, along with the personal charisma they exude. They fool management into giving them the job.

Need a strong sales leader? Look for someone with patience, analytical skills, quiet self confidence, and a desire to help others. Although every organization is different, hiring a sales manager is not as simple as it looks. In fact, the wrong sales manager can quickly damage morale, if not scare away the sales representatives and potentially injure the firm.

A common mistake is to promote a high achieving sales rep who wants to move up in management. Unfortunately, a highly successful sales rep may be exactly the wrong candidate for sales management. Often aggressive sales representatives are impatient, lack team-player characteristics, and tend to have huge egos; these can be exactly the wrong characteristics for a sales manager.

In my opinion, the following general characteristics or traits are needed for a good sales manager:

- Teaching skills: This includes the ability and interest to help others learn.
- Empathy: A good sales manager needs to understand how representatives feel and how to react accordingly. Sales teams can be highly emotional and fragile. Insensitive sales managers fail.
- Ego in check: A strong ego is required, but the needs of the team are greater than the manager's.
- Communication skills: This skill is an obvious requirement that includes the ability to lead the sales team and to work with the other departments.
- Relationship skills: This is the ability to create long-term relationships with internal and external customers. Sales managers must be likeable.
- Analytical skills: The best sales managers must be able to decide the strategic options in complex sales situations. They have to make the tough calls.
- Right "presence": Great sales managers exude confidence, professionalism, and competence.
- Works well with other departments: Needs to have a good rapport with finance, marketing, manufacturing, and all the other departments that have something to do with the creation and sale of the product.
- Wins through the victories of the team: Gets satisfaction by helping sales representatives win; this knocks out a lot of representatives who want to be managers.

- Ability to handle pressure: On a day-to-day basis, the sales manager is "under the gun" more than any employee in a typical firm.
- Continuous learner: I find that the best sales managers are always looking for new ways to get things done. They are naturally curious.
- Sales manager experience: I always favor gray hair when it comes to hiring a sales manager. Conversely, rookies will likely make mistakes and those mistakes could be costly.

Remember to do an extensive background check on external candidates. Look for a history of strong performances with good references. Life is short, so hire winners.

*Finding winners: Winners hang out with other winners. Go to where they meet. Read what they read. Do what they do. Eat what they eat. And, there they shall be.*

# 119. Internal Selling Can Be the Hardest Sale

"Organization is the enemy of improvisation."

**Anonymous**

You beat the competition. You secured commitment from the customer. And you got the order. Congratulations, but the selling is not over. The next step is to go back and sell to your own company and it may end up being the hardest sales call you make.

To fulfill your commitments to your customer will require that all departments at your firm understand their job and accept responsibility for the agreement that you just secured with the customer. Depending on the industry you are in and the nature of the product, this could mean manufacturing, customer service, legal, finance, customer support functions, operations, and others. For a successful customer relationship, each of these departments needs to understand what they need to do and how their work relates to customer satisfaction.

Here are a few basic tips for selling internally:

- Accept the fact that you need to sell internally and that it is your job to do it; no one else will do it for you.
- You need to communicate the big picture of what this customer relationship means to each individual. Why is this customer important?
- You need to explain the unique attributes of the new customer agreement. Don't expect people to seek out the details about the new agreement. Be specific.
- Expect resistance. People naturally resist change and increases in workload. Be patient with these initial reactions.
- Don't personalize initial errors or mistakes. Properly servicing a new customer is a learning experience which may take some trial and error.
- Bring the customer onsite to help the support staff understand the customer and commit to servicing them properly.

- Say thanks. Do this a lot. Be sincere, because without the internal staff the job won't get done.

Have you noticed anything here? The internal sales cycle almost directly mirrors the steps you needed to take to get the business in the first place. It's all about understanding your role in the process and communicating to everyone about everything.

Look at any internal resistance as they need more information about what needs to be done and why. Sometimes, your internal support people become inflexible (just like a prospect gets used to saying "no") and requires special handling to move things forward. Your goal is to make this a "win/win situation," which it will be if you take the time and effort to be courteous, professional and sincere to your "internal" customers.

*A simple thing to do: Forgive people who make a mistake for the first time.*

# 120. *Call Me on My Cell Phone*

"I don't answer the phone. I get the feeling whenever I do that there will be someone on the other end."

**Fred Couples (1959 – present) Golfer**

Cell phone usage has radically changed over the past five years. It was not that long ago that corporate usage of cell phones was considered a luxury and their usage was closely scrutinized for cost reasons since it was so expensive. It is an understatement to say that cell phone usage today is ubiquitous.

It is increasingly common for customers and sales representatives to share cell phone numbers. In fact, many people have land line phone messages that offer their cell phone number. Often the message is something like "please leave me a message, but if the matter is urgent please call me on my cell phone." It is then up to you to escalate the call to their cell phone. Additionally, many people list their cell phone numbers on their websites, business cards, and letterhead. Clearly some people prefer to use their cell phones over their land lines.

Yet, others feel differently. For some people, the cell phone is a link to their private lives and not appropriate for business use. Some people use cell phones for outgoing calls only and choose to share their cell phone numbers with only a few close friends and associates. Some companies list cell phone numbers on the company phone directory, while others consider cell phone numbers as confidential or for emergency use only.

The largest social study of mobile phones users ever conducted in July, 2006 by Mobile Life (www.mobilelife2006.co.uk) identified six cohorts or types of cell phone users. In a nutshell, here is what they found:

- Generation Mobile: Style conscious cell phone users. Typically singles, students, or first time employees (age 18-24). The brand of the phone and the features make it cool.
- Phonatics: Single, employed professionals who consider their cell phones to be their most prized electronic possession. You can text message them anytime (age 18-34).

- Practicals: Cost conscious cell phone users who don't care about style or function (age 18-34).
- Smart Connectors: Affluent cell phone users who use their phones to organize their lives (age 25-44). Can you say Blackberry?
- Fingers and Thumbs: Cell phone laggards who use the cell phone only when they have to (age 25-80).
- Silver Cynics: Hold outs or maybe on their first phone (age 55 plus).

So, returning to the subject of calling customers on cell phones, when is it appropriate to call the customer's cell phone and when is not? Here are a few thoughts:

- As the cell phone usage study indicates, not everyone thinks like you do about cell phones. Ask them ahead of time for permission to call their cell phone or when to call. Odds are if they have an issue with it, they will tell you.
- Avoid calling their cell phone after business hours. Instead call between nine and five (be respectful of time zones).
- Weekend cell phone calling may be inappropriate, although some people may say, "call me anytime."
- If they did not personally give you their cell phone number, it may not be appropriate to call them on their cell.
- It is always appropriate to call their cell phone in case of an emergency (use good judgment on that one).
- If you call them on their cell and they seem busy or irritated, ask them for an appointment later.
- It is the end of the quarter and you cannot get a hold of them at the office. Call them on their cell phone, but beware of looking like a stalker.
- Repeated cell phone calls leave digital trails. They may not want to speak with you and have been screening their calls to avoid you.
- If they won't answer their cell phone, try leaving a text message to explain why you need to speak with them.
- Consider a multi-pronged approach by calling land lines and cell phones, while also sending emails. Faxes might work too. If time allows, try the US Mail or FedEx. Try something different.

One more thought. I think that there is a new cohort of cell phone users which the study did not identify. I would call it "native users"; they have grown up with cell phones and know nothing else. My 16-year old daughter sleeps with her cell phone and sends text messages all night long (yes, we now make her put it away at bedtime).

*A riddle: Does the cell phone ring in the forest if you are not there?*

# 121. Why Top Sales Representatives Quit

"It's always too early to quit."

**Norman Vincent Peale (1898 – 1993) Preacher and Author**

Every sales manager's worst nightmare is the surprise resignation of a top sales rep. Sooner or later it happens. So, what went wrong?

When managing high performing sales representatives, it is a common practice to leave these people alone. They know what to do and are doing it so well that you don't want to interfere with their success. You may think they are happy until another company recruits them away.

The reality is that top performers can easily get restless without a steady stream of opportunities and kudos. By giving them too much "room," you may accidentally signal that you don't care about them. While top performers do not want you to "micromanage" them, they don't want to be ignored.

It is my estimation that top sales representatives leave for many reasons including the following:

- Desire for a new challenge, personal growth, and advancement; this is the "grass is greener elsewhere" syndrome.
- Increased expectations with declining rewards; the quotas just keep getting bigger and bigger. Success seems penalized.
- Poor management. This can be a "lousy" direct supervisor, "out of touch" top management, or just a lack of feedback from management. I could devote a whole chapter to this one.
- Feeling disconnected from the company vision, mission, and strategy (more lousy management).
- Broken promises (the kiss of death).
- Too many changes to their accounts, territory, and direct manager. They just get fed up with it all and move on.
- More money at another employer (this one is easily avoidable).
- Personal needs not being met. After all, top representatives are people, too.

The consequences of replacing lost sales representatives can be very dramatic. Lost sales are an obvious consequence when a salesperson leaves. To add insult to injury, this does not even take into consideration the departed representative's attempts to move his or her past customers over to the new employer. However, there are often unseen costs, like the reduced productivity from the departing rep that is inevitably distracted during his or her job search and therefore contributes less during this time period (I.E. "short-timer's blues").

When senior sales representatives leave, your customers often experience the following:

- An interruption in the relationship.
- A negative impact on their own productivity.
- Time wasted reorienting the new rep to their operation and the way they work.

The change in account managers can set customer relationships back months and give competitors an advantage. This is especially true if the transition to the new account manager is not well managed. At a certain point, repeated changes in your sales staff can send a message of organizational instability and create the impression that the organization does not care about the account relationship.

*Quit now: If you are working with unethical people, quit immediately.*

# 122. How to Retain Top Sales Representatives

"In hell there is no retention."

**Miguel de Cervantes Saavedra (1547 – 1616) Spanish Novelist**

Top sales representatives need special care and feeding. As mentioned in the last chapter, giving them too much space can be a prescription to lose them to the competition. Instead, create a strategy to keep them on your team.

Here are some strategies to retain your top representatives:

- Enrich their jobs: Additional responsibilities such as extra leadership opportunities and responsibilities can make their jobs more meaningful. Solicit their advice on important issues or invite them to be part of an advisory board where they can offer expertise on a formal basis and be recognized as valued leaders.
- Career Development: Top representatives tend to be strategic and this carries over to how they manage their career and their needs for development. The performance review process is a great time to explore the aspirations and goals of your best representatives. This process of listening to their goals is meaningful almost by itself, while the proactive follow-up throughout the year can help create a long-term employee.
- Give senior representatives a chance to mentor others: Mentoring offers them a stake in the company while they can benefit other sales representatives. Mentoring may also provide an opportunity for extra compensation. It is worth it.
- Additional and long-term compensation: Provide pay packages superior to the market for top representatives including special pay premiums, stock options, or bonuses. A few extra dollars could save you a lot of heartache.
- Hire and train mangers to speak the language of the senior representatives: Nothing is more frustrating to top sales representatives than when management "does not get it." This applies to first level sales management and to the managers above them.

The best way for management to learn the language is to get out of headquarters and visit the remote offices and clients.

- Provide challenging work: Top sales representatives want work that is interesting, challenging, and that has an impact. Involve them in the business.

- Work relationships: Top sales representatives stay when they have strong relationships with others they work with. Encourage team building and project assignments involving work with peers.

- Recognition: People tend to stay when they feel that their contributions are appreciated by others. Compensation provides recognition, but other forms of non-monetary recognition are also important such as praise, awards, and the words "thank you." This should be done at company meetings, in writing, and on the job. I have read that the ratio of praise to constructive criticism should optimally be in a five to one ratio.

- Work/life balance: For some people, personal priorities or circumstances make the difference between leaving and staying. Individuals will stay with a company that cares about their health, family, and personal needs. For example, many companies are providing flexible schedules, remote work locations, and are experimenting with other ways to help individuals manage their work and personal life issues. In a tight job market, flexibility and creativity is needed.

- Communications: Effective communications strengthen employee identification with the company and builds trust.

- Effective Management: Good managers actively listen, set clear performance expectations, support performance, and give feedback along with recognition. They take a personal interest in the needs and expectations of their representatives. Large spans of control can work to counter these goals, by the way.

- Treat retention as an on-going priority: This retention strategy challenges us to focus on retention as a daily task, rather than on reactive attempts to reverse surprise resignations.

- Make recruiting an on-going priority: Even when you are not hiring it is crucial to cultivate relationships with quality people within your industry.

*To stay or leave: If you are contemplating leaving a job or a relationship, the best question to ask yourself is "Why should you stay?" The answer should come easily; if not, just leave.*

# 123. How to Sense Impending Doom

"Negativity can only feed on negativity."

**Elisabeth Kubler-Ross (1926 – 2004) Author**

The chapter title above is an actual headline from BusinessWeek Online from a while ago. The story that followed described new technologies that helps monitor bridges and how experts who can analyze the results are in short supply. This article was written in the wake of a Minneapolis bridge collapse disaster. The message is simple: more bridges will collapse soon. All is lost.

My point, you ask? The media is overwhelmingly negative. The sad truth is that journalists are a miserable lot. They are pessimistic by nature and gravitate to the dark side of most issues: the macabre, the suffering, the dead and the dying, the failed, Armageddon, etc.

They just loved the trashing of Enron. Send the bums to prison. How about the collapse of the real estate market? How about Barry Bonds and his home runs? The man has no talent and his success is all due to steroids. How about George W. Bush and his low approval ratings?

All this misery is headline news. But why to do they write such depressing crud? The answer is quite simple: about 70% of their readers feel the same way. They, too, are pessimistic and miserable. How about terrorists? They are everywhere, so we must now take our shoes off at airports and we are not allowed to carry toothpaste on airplanes. Feel safer now?

The media is only reflecting the times and what a sorry state it is. Study after study reveals the current state of our culture as depressed, downtrodden, and pessimistic. For some reason, Western culture seems to have lost its "Mojo." Optimism is so last century. Or is it?

My friends, this is where salespeople enter the picture. Generally speaking, salespeople are optimistic. Given the choice between despair and a happy outlook, they go for happy. When something bad happens, the optimistic salesperson shrugs it off as bad luck and keeps on going. Optimists think that things will be OK. They believe that the future is bright.

Optimistic salespeople tend to make more money than the pessimistic buyers. I have heard estimates that optimistic people earn more than 50% more during their lifetime than their negative counterparts.

They live longer too. For example, the world's oldest person at one time, a Japanese woman, died at age 114. She attributed her long life to eating well, getting a good night's sleep, and a positive attitude. I bet she was in sales. That's just a guess on my part but I bet that I am right.

Selling requires a Zen-like trance where the salesperson must focus on a positive outcome despite the objections of negative buyers. These negative energies that emanate from the buyers are requests to make them happier. In fact, negative buyers seem to be attracted to the positive energy of the salesperson's sunny attitude.

*Your true purpose: The true purpose of the salesperson is to bring light to this dark little planet before it explodes.*

# 124. Common Characteristics of Excellent Salespeople

"Excellence is to do a common thing in an uncommon way."

**Booker T. Washington (1856 – 1915) Educator, Author, and African-American Leader**

Having managed salespeople for many years while being a peddler myself, I have observed how salespeople behave, both good and not so good. Salespeople that are truly excellent behave the same way, more or less. Said another way, successful salespeople tend to exhibit some common behavioral characteristics.

Here are a few things that I have observed about truly excellent salespeople:

- Always prepared, successful sales representatives spend a lot time preparing for sales calls. They gather information about their customers so they can better understand the key issues and needs.
- This "pre-flight" planning keeps them from wasting the customer's time at the meeting. This preparation gives the rep confidence along with an air of professionalism.
- Sales professionals become the industry experts or, as I like to call them, "knowledge brokers." They read trade journals and often attend networking/industry trade shows to learn even more. They set themselves apart by the knowledge they are able to bring to the customer that is over and above what any of their competitors can offer.
- They have only face-to-face meetings with qualified customers. Their time is valuable so they don't waste it on unqualified prospects. They ask the tough questions before the face-to-face meeting.
- Great salespeople show up early for meetings. This punctuality demonstrates their commitment and helps build trust.
- If the customer wants small talk at the beginning of the meeting then great representatives will comply. If the customer just wants to get down to business and avoid small talk, great representatives sense this and get down to business.

- They are never loud or overly talkative, instead they tend to be pleasant and sincere and maybe even a little reserved. Great salespeople allow the customer to set the tone of the meeting.
- They are comfortable with silence in the meeting and will allow the customer time to think.
- Excellent salespeople check their egos at the door. The focus of the meeting is on the customer and not on the solution.
- Great salespeople always deliver something valuable. This may be unique information about the industry, product, or the market.
- Successful salespeople respond to objections before they happen. Their preparation allows them to anticipate objections ahead of time and allows them to minimize customer concerns.
- Objections are welcomed in the meeting and great representatives make it easy for the customer to say "no." Objections help the great rep understand the customer's concerns and help the rep get to "yes."
- They are relaxed and attentive in the call. They never interrupt the buyer.
- If they have action items, great representatives always follow up. You can always count on them to perform.
- Truly great representatives seldom are hard closers. Instead, their skillful handling of the objections encourages the customer to close the deal themselves.
- They always tell the truth. No deal is worth compromising their ethics.
- They always say thank you verbally and often with a written note.

*Show up: Showing up and being accountable is step one. Avoiding the customer or problem is a characteristic of a poor salesperson.*

# 125. Legal Issues and Selling

"No law or ordinance is mightier than understanding."

**Plato (428 B.C. – 348 B.C.) Greek Philosopher**

Salespeople talk or send e-mails to customers and prospects all day long. They make sales presentations, handle objections, quote price and delivery, write proposals, and close orders. After a while it almost becomes automatic or second nature since this is what salespeople do. Yet, salespeople probably don't think of themselves as acting as a legal agent of the company.

Salespeople are legal agents for the companies that they represent. A salesperson has the legal authority to obligate the company to an agreement or commitment. Furthermore, the obligation does not have to be in writing. Yes, you can even talk your way into trouble by saying the wrong things. Put the wrong thing in writing and you may set your company up for a legal battle. The sad fact is that most salespeople freely make agreements without the blessing of management or legal counsel. Even worse, many salespeople don't understand the authority that they have as a legal agent of the firm. After all, they are "just" salespeople.

The Uniform Commercial Code (UCC) is a set of laws governing commercial transactions. The purpose of the UCC was to establish a uniform set of rules to govern commercial transactions, which are often conducted across state lines. The goal of the UCC law is to create a body of rules that would realistically and fairly solve the common problems occurring in everyday commercial transactions.

The UCC states the following:

- A sales presentation is an invitation to negotiate.
- Salespeople are agents when they have the authority to make offers.
- An offer happens when the agent (salesperson) quotes specific terms to the customer.
- A sale is defined as the transfer of title to goods by the seller to the buyer for consideration, which is price.

- An order happens when the offer is put in writing and both parties agree. However, it does not always have to be in writing to be
binding.

Salespeople do these things all the time. OK, I am not an attorney, but
the UCC tells us that the work done by salespeople is serious stuff and not
to be taken lightly. Yet, few salespeople look at their work with an attorney's perspective.

Agents have responsibilities and simply telling the truth is one of
their chief responsibilities. Exaggerating a product's capabilities or omit-
ting a serious drawback may seem like simple "puffery" but it can be
legally viewed as statements of fact or warranties. In other words, an
overzealous salesperson that misrepresents the facts to a customer can get
in big trouble quickly. The salesperson is the public persona of a company
and as such must be held accountable at the highest standards.

Selling is a serious business, so be careful about what you say and do
when dealing with your customers.

*Be specific: A good contract is a specific contract.*

# 126. Does Your Customer Trust You?

"The only way to make a man trustworthy is to trust him."

**Henry Stimson (1867 - 1950) Statesman**

Long-term customer relationships are built on trust. Trust is the single most important ingredient in a successful long-term selling relationship.

Trust is the belief that you will do your part, that you will deliver what you promise and that you will fulfill your obligations in the relationship. These commitments can be in writing, verbal, or inferred. They are your responsibility.

Sometimes, trust can be almost mammalian: we immediately trust some people because of their role, the way they look or act, or because of a referral. For example, if a fireman shows up at your burning house to help you and your family I would guess that you will immediately trust him even though you don't know him.

But, most of the time, trust is earned over time. Instinctively, we keep score on other people about how they fulfill their obligations to us. This is especially true for your customers. They are keeping tabs on you and your trustworthiness at all times.

The basic elements of trust include:

- Dependability: This is the customer's perception that you are accountable. Referrals can make you appear dependable. Punctuality for appointments is a factor; being repeatedly late makes you look undependable. Being late also infers that you don't value the customer's time.
- Competence: This is the customer belief that you know that you speak the truth. Customers will often test salespeople with questions to test their knowledge of the industry or their products. Some of these questions might trap you into revealing what you don't know, so don't BS. If you BS, you will get caught and this will break down whatever trust you've built thus far. Looking stupid or unknowledgeable is one of the biggest fears of salespeople,

yet making it up as you go along will only hurt you. If you don't know the answer, this is when the old standby of "I am not certain; may I research that and get back to you?" can be very effective.

- Customer Empathy: Understanding your customers' needs and how they feel is critical to building trust. If a salesperson is only focused on the sale itself and the potential commissions, this will look selfish and not empathetic. This will slow the development of trust.
- Telling the Truth: If you tell the truth, you will sleep at night without worry. Also, you won't have to remember anything, because the truth is always the same. Additionally, how you tell the truth is important. You must be sincere and tell the truth with reliability. If you get caught in a lie, you may never be trusted again.
- Rapport or Being Liked: You know what I mean. Some people are just more likeable and they are trusted from the beginning. But, a likeable salesperson who is not dependable or who does not tell the truth will lose this advantage quickly.

With almost everyone else, we choose to verify someone's trustworthiness by watching what they say and do. Instinctively, we track their promises and monitor how they perform to these commitments. We keep score. If someone follows through on their commitments, they can earn our trust. If someone breaks a commitment or tries to cover up the broken commitment, we learn not to trust that person. It is really rather simple.

This makes it hard for new salespeople to crack an account because trust is earned by experience and by sensing. It may take a while to earn a buyer's trust and get a shot at the business opportunity. How do you demonstrate trustworthiness?

Here are a few suggestions:

- Always deliver on your promises. Do exactly as you said you would. And, if you can, under-promise and over-deliver.
- Don't stretch or try to make things fit. If you do make a commitment which challenges you or your offering's capabilities, let the customer know that there is risk that you won't deliver. Be truthful.
- Demonstrate your commitment to the relationship and show how reliable you are by repeatedly delivering on your promises. Repeat as necessary.

- Choose your words carefully. Say "frankly" rather than "to tell the truth" or "honestly" since the latter two phrases sound as if you normally don't tell the truth.
- Use lots of eye contact. While it is true that liars have good eye contact, most people prefer doing business with someone who can look them in the eye.
- Speak slowly. Many people are suspicious of fast talkers.
- Listen. Repeat what the customer says. Say something like, "So, let me make sure that I understand. What is important to you is that I ….."
- If you miss a commitment, tell the customer immediately. Don't wait to get caught or try to cover it up. A trustworthy person will tell the truth. After coming clean about the missed commitment, make a new commitment and be sure to exceed expectations.

Trust is earned over time but can be easily lost—so do as you say.

*Trust me on this: Trust is a reward for doing what you promised.*

# 127. Ethical Selling

"The time is always right to do what is right."

**Martin Luther King, Jr. (1929 – 1968) Civil Rights Leader**

For most of us, knowing the difference between right and wrong is pretty clear, but sometimes doing the right thing is hard to do. Or, let's say we are challenged to make the right choices.

Our government helps us out by making laws that specifically tell us what is right and what is wrong. You must stop at all stop signs. It is illegal to shoplift. It is a legal requirement to properly label the ingredients on food products. While there is an occasional debate about the meaning of laws, we generally understand what is acceptable and what is not. Conveniently, these laws are enforced.

Ethical behavior is a slightly different matter, since ethics are established and maintained by the culture and they are not always written down or specifically communicated. If you find a wallet at a gas station that has $100 cash in it, the ethical thing to do is to contact the owner and return the wallet with the cash. If you go through the checkout line at a department store and the "new" cashier gives you back too much change, the ethical choice is to tell the cashier about the error. The challenge with ethics is that you are in charge of managing your own code of ethics.

Salespeople deal with ethical challenges all the time. Maybe you have faced issues like these:

- Should I tell the customer about my product's quality problems?
- My customer's purchase order had the wrong price on the order (it was higher than what you quoted). Should I tell them?
- My expense account is to be used for selling expenses only, but how would my company know the difference between a personal expense and a customer expense?
- Your product was not made to the customer's specification, but was shipped anyway. Do you tell them or do hope that they don't notice?

Your own code of ethics helps make the little decisions easier along with the big ones. When you always tell the truth you don't have to remember anything; it is easier this way. When you do the ethical thing, you have little regret or remorse about your choices.

So, what does a salesperson's code of ethics look like? Here are a few ideas:

- Always tell the truth.
- Don't lie through omission. Tell the whole story including the bad parts.
- Always do what you promise. If you can, deliver more than what you promise.
- When you fail to deliver on a commitment, tell the customer immediately. Don't wait for them to find out.
- When in doubt about a choice, seek advice from a mentor (I.E. someone you admire and someone you consider to be ethical).
- Put your promises in writing to hold yourself accountable. This will also document your good behavior when you deliver what you promised.
- Treat your customer like you would like to be treated.

For many, the most frequently confronted issue was the company's need for more sales versus the code of ethics of the individual salesperson. Others wrote about the day-to-day challenge of doing the ethical thing. It seems that the lines can blur when commission dollars are on the line. They asked how to tell if you are crossing the line.

Having given it more thought, please consider this list of questions to ask yourself when confronted with an ethical choice:

- Would you feel bad if this behavior was published tomorrow in the New York Times and you were specifically named in the article?
- Would you be uncomfortable talking about it during a performance review?
- Would your customer be worse off if you went forward with this decision?
- Would you be upset if someone did this to you?
- Would you fear being caught if you went forward with this decision?
- Would your mother or father disapprove of your behavior?

- Have others been reprimanded for this practice?
- Have you been spending a lot of time worrying about this issue?
- If you practice a formal religion, is the decision in keeping with its teachings?
- Would you be proud of yourself and the decision/behavior, even during private musings?

Candidly, if the answer is yes to any of these questions (except the last two), the behavior is probably unethical. Do the right thing.

*Ethical behavior: Ethical behavior allows you to sleep at night. Unethical behavior keeps you up at night with worry or regret.*

# 128. How Customers View Ethical Selling

"A liar will not be believed, even when he speaks the truth."

**Aesop (620 B.C. – 560 B.C.) Writer of Fables**

Let's turn the table and look at selling and ethics from the customers' perspective. Trust me, buyers know unethical behavior when they see it and they keep score. What does unethical selling look like if you are the buyer? Here is short list:

- Misrepresenting the product's specifications, warranty, or capabilities.
- Bashing the competition (warranted or not).
- Not listening to the needs or interests of the customer.
- Answering questions with BS (not knowing the answer but trying to fake it).
- Selling services or products that are not really needed by the customer.
- Lying by omission.
- Not following the chain of command for purchasing.
- Not accepting responsibility for problems by always offering excuses while blaming others for the problems.
- Not following through on commitments.
- Generally slippery behavior.

Conversely, what does ethical selling look like from the perspective of the buyer?

- Accurately describing the product's specifications.
- Not speaking on behalf of the competition or trashing the competition.
- Listening carefully to the customer to determine exact wants and needs. After this is complete, the salesperson can offer the right solution.
- If the salesperson does not know the answer to a question, he or she will admit it and then go find the answer. No BS allowed.
- Selling only what the customer truly needs and no more.

- Telling the whole story.
- Taking proactive responsibility for mistakes or errors right away and telling the customer when mistakes or errors happen.
- Always following through on promises.

Customers know when you are being ethical and when you are not.

*Unethical customers: Yes, some customers are unethical. If you come across one, don't waste your time with them. Life is too short.*

# 129. Objections: An Enabling Sales Technology

"Every sale has five basic obstacles: no need, no money,
no hurry, no desire, and no trust."

**Zig Ziglar (1926 – present) Motivational Speaker**

You have heard all the objections before: "I have no budget," "I have no need," "I am not interested," or "We are happy with our existing supplier." My favorite objection is "Maybe later." All these objections are the customer's way of saying "no."

It is in your best interest to have them object since most people have to say "no" for you to get to "yes." Seek objections at all steps of the sales process. Make it easy for them to object. Inexperienced salespeople finish their presentation and wait for the prospect's response. Experienced salespeople ask questions throughout the presentation.

Sales objections are defined as a customer's opposition or resistance to the information presented by the salesperson. They can come up at any time during your sales call; from introduction to close. Classical sales training tells us that you have to hear "no" before you can hear "yes." What this really means is that customers must purge themselves of all concerns, hesitations, and questions before they can buy. And if they don't get these things out their system they won't be able to go forward. These concerns manifest themselves as objections in the sales process. The astute salesperson is on the lookout for these and welcomes them.

When a customer objects, he or she is asking for you to help them better understand your offer. The prospect who presents objections is often more easily sold on your product. Let the customer know that sharing these objections is the right thing to do and that they are smart to do so. This may seem to be the opposite of what you might first think since many inexperienced salespeople run away or avoid objections. Often, objections are challenging and can end the sales process if handled poorly. Yet, closing your eyes and hoping they go away won't work either.

Some say that an objection is a request for more information and a request for help. Expect to hear no. Better yet, you should plan on it. Respond by being empathetic while also probing for more information. "No" is an enabling sales technology.

Let the customer know that "No" is an acceptable outcome because you are here for the long run and want to build a long-term relationship. This takes the pressure out of the sales process and allows the customer to explain more specifically his/her issues. This allows you the chance to provide a better solution.

Sometimes, you can ignore an objection. This can be a bit cocky because if the customer says it, then it needs to be handled sooner or later. I have found that this strategy works when someone hurls a volley of multiple objections at you. With this objection-handling strategy, you let him/her repeat the important objections and then you can address the important issues.

Other times, not addressing objections can be a mistake. It can result in the prospect not listening or shutting down or feeling that you are hiding something. It can give the appearance that you also feel it's a problem or that you're not able to answer because you do not know the answer. Worse yet, it can give the appearance that you are not interested in the prospect's opinion.

Some customers object on price because they feel that they have to. Oftentimes, this customer is a poor or inexperienced negotiator and feels that objecting once on price is enough or is an expected part of the process. Ignoring this objection can pay off with this type of buyer.

Most sales training suggests you turn around objections by restating them and taking the offensive. For example, the customer says the price is too high. You respond, "If the price wasn't too high could you agree to proceed with the service?" This seems a bit deliberate to me.

My thoughts are that objections are a part of a healthy sales process and are to be expected, if not desired, if you want the order. Greet them calmly and respond with calming words like "I understand how you feel," "I see," or "Others have felt the same way."

Next, probe more information with open-ended questions like:

- "How so?"
- "Tell me more?"
- "What else?"
- "Tell me about it."

Offer an explanation or more information to help the customer understand your offering's benefits. Then say something like:

- "Have I answered your question?"
- "Does that help?"
- "Does that sound better?"

Sometimes, the customer will continue to object. This means that they still need more information so you need to give them more. Then verify again that you have properly responded to the objection. If so, it can be appropriate to say, "Thanks for asking me that," "That was a great question," or, simply, "Thanks."

Consider discussing an objection before it is brought up by the prospect. Rehearse your responses and make the answers seem effortless. Salespeople often encounter the same objections from customer to customer. This provides good practice for the salesperson, a way to hone their skills. This helps make you an expert at handling objections. Be prepared by bringing data or information.

Remember not to take objections personally. Talking about these concerns is a healthy thing. All objections are fair. Objections help you find the way to yes, so welcome them. It is the customer's way of asking for help because "No" is an enabling sales technology.

*Don't waste time: "No" can mean that you are calling on the wrong customer or you skipped a qualification step. Learn from this and move on.*

# 130. The Doctor Is In

*"I am not feeling well. I need a doctor immediately.*
*Ring the nearest golf course."*

**Groucho Marx (1890 – 1977) Comedian and Actor**

Ever notice that when you go to the doctor, you get asked a lot of open-ended questions while the physician says little? Much like a doctor, salespeople help buyers with problems by asking questions and saying little. Rather, that is what the good salespeople do.

The patient replies with answers which are like objections. The doctor, ever inquisitive and wise, helps the patient make the best choices for a healthier life. At the end of the visit, the patient is given a prescription for medicine. The doctor's opinion is seldom challenged since we are taught to believe what the "good" doctor says.

In a similar fashion when a buyer and a salesperson meet, there may also be probing questions. The buyer talks the most while the "good" salesperson listens and takes notes. With the questions answered, the skilled salesperson normally offers a "prescription" to solve the customer's problem. Hopefully, the customer buys, but that is not always the case.

If the buyer is not buying the salesperson's medicine it generally means one of two things:

1. The customer doesn't think that he/she is sick.
2. The customer doesn't think that seller is really a doctor.

If the buyer does not feel sick it means that the salesperson has not identified the buyer's needs nor matched them with the benefits of the solution. Sometimes it means that the seller might not be selling to a qualified buyer.

If the buyer does not think the seller is a doctor, it means that they don't trust you or that they don't like you. This distrust of the salesperson is common since buyers have learned to distrust and even dislike salespeople. This is because of repeated negative encounters with other bad salespeople who don't listen and who talk too much.

Try acting like a doctor and not like a salesperson. Now cough.

*Your Prescription: Take my advice and call me in the morning.*

# 131. Giving Bad News

"Bad news isn't wine. It does not improve with age."

**Colin Powell (1937 – present) General and Statesman**

Sometimes in sales, you have to give bad news to customers. While this is never easy, a little preparation goes a long way to helping you get the job done. Start by gathering all the facts and preparing yourself emotionally. Put yourself in the customer's shoes and figure out how you would feel when delivered this bad news?

Here is a basic process to follow when delivering bad news:

- Define the situation: What must you communicate? How does this situation impact the customer? Do you need to provide all the background information? Where a strong emotional reaction is expected from the customer, providing reasons may only serve to fuel that reaction.
- Emphasize the positive points: Once you have presented the situation, are there positive points that you can emphasize to the customer? What will not change? Be honest with the customer to remind him/her what will not change in this situation.
- Be prepared to accept the customer's initial reaction: Try to predict the customer's reaction. How would you feel in this situation?
- Responding to the reaction: Prepare a possible conversation on what the buyer will probably say. Prepare your response. Restate positive points, if there are any.
- Express your expectations: How do you expect this situation to be resolved? Are your requirements negotiable? If "yes" then what is negotiable? What action, including deadlines, must be performed by this person and what is the deadline?
- Restate the basic agreement with a timeline: Confirm in writing and be specific.
- Follow-up action: Negotiate the best time for a follow-up meeting or phone call.

Delivering bad news is never easy, but a little preparation might help ease the pain (yours and theirs).

*Bad news can be good: Surprisingly, good things can come from bad. An honest delivery of bad news will be appreciated over hiding the truth. This straightforward method of communication will demonstrate that you are trustworthy.*

# 132. Selling on the Phone

"If the phone doesn't ring, it's me."

**Jimmy Buffett (1946 – present) Artist**

Selling on the phone can be drudgery, but this is how the money is made in sales. It all starts with a phone call. Whether you are a full-time telemarketer or CEO selling the company's vision, the telephone is the most potent tool in the sales tool bag.

Here are ten simple rules for selling on the phone:

1. Talk the customer's language: Talk louder, softer, faster, or slower; in effect, mimicking the client's voice using inflections and tones where the client is most comfortable.
2. Use words that they use: This sometimes is called mirroring and helps customers feel comfortable. For some of us it happens naturally.
3. Smile when dialing: People can sense your happiness and will react positively to your positive attitude. Try looking into a mirror as you speak to see if you really look happy and, therefore, sound happy.
4. Repeat the customer's name: This is "old school" selling. Use the customer's name at least three times during the presentation, and you will increase your chance of selling.
5. Customer "wants" trump "needs": Studies show that people don't buy what they need. They tend to buy what they want. Good salespeople sell to wants before needs.
6. Keep the word "I" to a minimum: It is not about you and it is all about them. People who talk a lot usually talk about themselves and come across as being selfish and egocentric.
7. Testimonials: Use testimonials or third-hand references since they are far more believable than anything you can ever say.
8. Be polite: Always say thank you and please.
9. Be punctual: If you promise to call at 2 pm, be sure to call at 2 pm and not a minute late.
10. Listen: Ask open-ended questions. Then stop and listen.

*Beware the telephone headset: Telephone headsets are the rage, but beware of the microphone quality. If you use one, make sure that it is a good one.*

# 133. Selling to C-Level Executives

"Be Quick – But Don't Hurry!"

**John Wooden (1910 – present) Coaching Legend**

C-level executives (I.E., CEO, CMO, CIO, etc.) need a different sales approach. Gone are the days when the sales rep could have "question and answer time" with the C-level executive to better understand "pains" and key initiatives. Today, this senior-level buyer has no time for such idle banter. The phone is ringing, the Blackberry is vibrating, and the in-box is bulging with unanswered e-mails. Instead, these senior buyers expect you to come in with answers rather than questions.

Therefore, you have to adjust your sales approach. Sometimes you only get one shot with this character, so you have to be prepared. This necessitates that you thoroughly research the customer prior to discussing business. This means scouring the website, the SEC documents (if the firm is public), and calling others in the firm to learn about the real issues at play.

Anyone at the firm can be a source of useful information. The best people to talk with may be the C-level executive's direct reports. Call them and confide in them that you are meeting the "big guy" in two weeks and that you are trying to figure things out. What are his hot points? What do they recommend that you do to prepare? Who else should you talk to before the meeting? Some of these people will actually coach you on how to proceed. It can be that easy.

When you actually get together with the C-level executive, the meeting becomes a forum for you to demonstrate your knowledge of the firm and of the executive's key issues. You need to provide value to have any chance of continuing the conversation. This will pave the way for a constructive conversation and help move the sale along. This approach is time-consuming, but worth it when selling products or services that require you to call on top executives.

C-level executives are tough to get in front of, but once they get convinced enough to do business with you, they like to take over the sales process. This is called "transferring ownership" and it is a wonderful thing.

It is a magic moment in selling when your customer joins you in the sales process while taking responsibility for the sale itself.

For whatever reason, the customer now owns the sale along with you. The value has been demonstrated to such an extent that the customer takes over and makes it happen. Objections are resolved and the questions have been answered. When the C-level executive has accepted the ownership of the sales process, let him take control because victory is at hand.

Unfortunately, turnover at the C-level is at an all time high, which makes selling to this crowd harder and harder. It seems that just when you get to know them, or just get them to return your phone calls, they are history.

A recent study by Spencer Stuart, the global executive search firm, estimates that the average Chief Marketing Officer (CMO) lasts on the job for only 23 months. When broken down by industry, the apparel industry tops the list with an amazing 10 month average stay while the longest-lived CMOs stayed 35 months in the financial sector.

Interesting enough, Spencer Stuart also suggests that an out-of-work CMO looking for the top marketing job at a big name firm could have a 12-24 month search. If my math serves me well, this means that same CMO needs to immediately start looking for a job after he or she lands one. For the record, CIOs are staying on the job for a 40 month average, while CEOs stay for an average of 54 months. Not a pretty picture.

What this means to us marketers who call on C-level execs is that we cannot pin our hopes on just one person to push our deals through, since there is a good chance that he or she won't be there later. Selling at the highest levels is becoming more and more a consensus sell with multiple coaches and advocates needed. Depending on one player to get your proposal approved is now a risky proposition.

Salespeople need many relationships at their key accounts. The mantra is "invest in relationship building now." That means sell up, down, and outside the corporate food chain because it is impossible to know which relationship will get you the contract. Also, be nice to the little people since they may be the only ones left.

*The next time you need to sell to a C-level executive: Make a list of all the decision makers at that company. Then work your way to the top.*

# 134. Is Selling Getting Tougher?

"To fly, we have to have resistance."

**Maya Lin (1959 – present) Artist and Architect**

Is selling getting tougher?

I get this question a lot from sales veterans who remember what selling was like before the Internet. My answer is that things are different with some aspects of selling harder and other parts easier.

The biggest change in selling is the rise of the better informed buyer. Prior to the web, buyers had fewer choices available and relied more heavily on salespeople for product information. Today, buyers come into sales meetings with significant knowledge of your product along with the competitive offerings, including pricing.

The days of the "canned pitch" are over. Seldom does the customer need to hear about your offering since they already know about it from their website searches which yielded product reviews, pricing tips from other buyers, and product comparisons. The focus of the conversation needs to be on customer needs and concerns. In this respect, this is just like the old days.

Identifying prospects is much easier today since just about any prospect can be found on the web. Social networks provide for a bonanza of information on just about everyone. Getting a hold of them? That is another issue. Caller ID, voice mail, Blackberry devices, etc. have made it much more difficult to have a live conversation. Often selling is reduced to an email game of tag.

Today's buyers are tougher negotiators. They come with a better knowledge of pricing and product trends. They know a good deal when they see one and the reverse is also true. Additionally, buyers have had negotiation training and know how to make salespeople squirm. On the flipside, salespeople have not had the negotiation training that many professional buyers have had. It is my estimation that pressures to reduce the cost of sales have not allowed salespeople to get this type of needed training.

"Cost of sales reductions" has also trimmed the support that old school sales had; including administrative assistants and marketing help in the field. Travel and entertainment budgets are greatly reduced. Instead, salespeople have productivity tools such as customer relationship management (CRM) systems better known as ACT!, Seibel, and Goldmine. The downside to these tools is that salespeople are required to enter ridiculous amounts of data into these CRM systems instead of selling. How stupid is that?

So, is selling harder? I think the answer is a qualified "yes." At the very least, selling today is much different from the good old days.

*What really matters: Although each business is different, creating loyal customers is what really counts. Loyal customers refer you to others.*

# 135. Selling is More Checkers than Chess

"The journey is the reward."

**Taoist saying**

The business trade press has published volumes about how selling requires intense strategy and calculated thinking. I think this is mostly hogwash. Stop trying to out-think your customers. Instead, try to understand the customers' wants and needs and then act accordingly. Selling is a lot more like checkers than chess.

Being understood by your customer may be the most important aspect of selling. If they don't get what you said, then you are setting yourself up for big problems which could include false expectations, confusion, resentment, or, even worse, a lost customer. Generally speaking, being misunderstood is avoidable.

Here are few ideas to help you be better understood by your customers:

- Speak slowly. Say what you mean and say no more. Don't fill the dead air with unnecessary words.
- Avoid clichés which can be misunderstood or misinterpreted.
- Slow down, stop talking, and listen. Listen to what the customer has to say about what you said. Give them time to react.
- Ask if they understand you. Pause and verify that they got it. If not, try again.
- Repeat what you said. Repeat what you said. Repeat what you said.
- Give examples of what you mean. Be specific.
- Tell stories. Facts tell and stories sell. Stories help the other person visualize what you mean. Stories are also remembered.
- Put what you said in writing. This helps avoid "he said, she said" situations. Written statements can also smoke out misunderstandings.
- Always tell the truth. This way you won't have to remember anything.

Think checkers, not chess.

*Don't complicate things: Stay in the moment and don't think ahead. Focus on what is being said or not said now.*

# 136. Selling With Questions

"It is better to know some of the questions than all of the answers."

**James Thurber (1894 – 1961) Author and Cartoonist**

A friend of mine reminded me that selling is not about what you say to the customer, but rather it is about the questions you ask. Many salespeople are in love with their own words and ideas. They are often described as having the "gift of gab" which means that they really just talk too much. Instead of asking open-ended questions and listening, talkative salespeople talk too much.

They ramble on and on about product features to fill the dead air (which is extremely uncomfortable for a talkative person). Worse yet, they invariably talk about themselves, which is the last thing that the buyer wants to hear.

Meanwhile, the buyer ultimately buys from the seller who best understands their problems or needs. Of course, you don't get to understand the buyer's needs by talking. Great salespeople ask questions to learn about the buyer's motivations, concerns, and desires. It is really that simple.

Ask questions to discover what matters most to the customer. If you must speak, then talk about what matters most to the customer.

*Good questions: Good questions are followed by silence. Ask the question and then refrain from speaking. Let the customer speak next.*

# 137. Selling to Difficult Customers

"He would make a lovely corpse."

**Charles Dickens (1812 – 1870) English Author**

Eventually, we all have to call on difficult customers. You know who they are. They are grumpy, angry, confrontational, cheap, lazy, critical, and picky. No matter how hard you try, it is hard to meet their expectations. Just picking up the phone to talk with them is a chore, so you avoid calling them whenever possible.

Most of the time, you find yourself "clicking" with the majority of your customers; it is as if they speak your language. You might have something in common like a hobby or passion for a sports team. Whatever it is makes doing business with that person a pleasure.

Occasionally, you find yourself on the other side of the table with customers who seemingly have come from another planet. No matter what you say or no matter how hard you try, you struggle to get along with them, let alone sell them anything. The good news in this situation is that you are aware that something is wrong. The hard part is doing something to improve the relationship, if that is possible. Remember, you don't have to be best friends to do business.

When selling to difficult customers preparation can help make things go smoother. Ask yourself what is important to them? What do they desire most out of a relationship with you? What do they value? What do they desire least? What do they want to get accomplished? Push aside your needs and put the focus on them.

Acknowledge that people may be different than you and that it is OK. You may be very "amiable" and relationship-focused, which is a terrific behavioral profile to have as a salesperson, but your customers may not be that way. While you are eager to show pictures of your kids or your last family vacation, some customers might find this photo sharing an incredible waste of time.

Some people are very "analytical" and prefer to look at spreadsheets and don't care about getting to know you. That is just the way they are.

They want to calculate ratios and evaluate trend lines. They are plodding in their decision making but absolutely resolute once they make up their mind. They don't say much, but you should listen carefully when they speak because they have been rehearsing this speech for a long time. They are seldom wrong or speak out of turn. More often than not, they are right.

Other customers may be "drivers" who want to get things done quickly. They likely will have a strong task orientation and have little need for relationships and small talk. They want to get down to business. Their office might be void of family photos and their desk might have a yellow pad of paper with a meeting checklist in front of them. They are ready for battle and know exactly what they want to get done.

Other customers might be very "expressive" and will need lots of talk time. They will have an intense need to let you know how they feel. For example, if your expressive customer is angry, ask them why? Shut up and listen. Make good eye contact. Take a few notes. When they are done with their rant try summarizing what they said and let them confirm that you "got it right."

Often this purging of the problem is all they really needed. By letting them blow off some steam, you can then get on with the meeting. But, if they have been holding on to this anger for a long time, they might need to repeat themselves a few times. Stay cool and let them finish. If you have some repair work to do, tell them what you will do and when you will do it. I suggest you put that in writing and then deliver exactly as you said you would.

More often than not, difficult customers are not being difficult just to spite you. Instead, they just do things differently than you. It is up to you to accommodate them and be flexible.

*Try to understand them: While some people are just plain crazy, most difficult people just need to be heard. Try not to be judgmental; instead ask questions to understand their point of view. You may learn something.*

# 138. My Sales Representatives Have Attention-Deficit Disorder!

"Pay attention when an old dog is barking."

**Anonymous**

Thom Hartmann, author of the book "Attention Deficit Disorder: A New Perspective," describes ADD as a genetic trait passed on for thousands of years to those who hunt. He says that a hunter is highly tuned-in to his surroundings and always on the lookout for threats or opportunities. Ever ready for action or new prey, the hunter can change plans at the break of a twig. The hunter is aggressive, cunning, and highly focused. The hunter is creative, spontaneous, and gregarious. The kill is everything to the hunter.

Then there is the farmer who also has evolved over thousands of years. The farmer is patient and nurturing. He tends the fields and is capable of waiting for long-term results. Farmers are friendly and work well with others, since farming is a group activity. The farmer values relationships and is not easily discouraged. The farmer can set long-term goals and patiently go about managing the tasks necessary to achieve the objective.

Is this sounding familiar? There is a great debate in the business press about what types of salespeople that are needed in sales organizations. Although most of us may have characteristics of both hunters and farmers, we probably lean one way or the other. Obviously, new business development favors the hunter characteristics, but after the account is sold, you had better get someone else to mind the store (like a farmer).

Ever met a sales rep that was incredibly likeable, showed up everyday, and patiently went about his business, but still did hit his sales objectives? I bet he was a farmer in a sales job that needed a hunter's disposition.

Sales managers hire the wrong people all the time. Guess why? Most successful sales managers have farmer characteristics, since it requires great patience to build and manage a sales team. Sales managers often hire people that they like (I.E. like themselves). By the way, hunters get promoted to sales manager jobs because of their new business success, but they typically don't last. Hunters are generally lousy managers since they are too impatient and aggressive and can't figure out the farmers.

Make sure that you hire the right rep for the job. Look for hunter characteristics if you want new biz, or look for a farmer rep if you need someone to mind the details and the relationships at the large account. Hunters hunt and farmers farm.

*Hire right: Think about the characteristics needed for the open sales position first and then look for the right person.*

# 139. Customers Remember Good Salespeople

"A dog is not considered a good dog because he is a good barker. A man is not considered a good man because he is a good talker."

**Chuang Tzu (399 - 295 BC) Chinese philosopher**

Years ago a very wise sales manager asked me, "What is the single most important factor in selling?" Dumbfounded by the question, I sat in awkward silence. Sensing my quandary, he answered his own query with two simple words, "Being remembered." I quickly nodded yes, but I did not really know what he meant.

Now, years later, I understand. In advertising, research tells us that "frequency of contact" is a must. Yet, the customer has grown numb from the thousands of messages delivered daily on the web, on radio, TV, and in print. But, alas, frequency alone is not enough since the same research tells us that contacting 10,000 of the right people ten times is far more effective than contacting 100,000 of the wrong people one time. In the ad game, these two factors are called "frequency and reach." You must contact the right customer with frequency to be remembered and you must be remembered before the customer will buy.

The same logic applies to selling. Customers need to be reminded that you exist and that you have solutions to their problems. How often you ask? You need to call on the customer or prospect enough that they not only remember your name and company, but they also distinctly remember the last conversation or sales call that you had with them. That is a tall order in the Internet age. To be remembered, you need to provide the customer a promise of value and you must be perceived as different.

Value is delivered when you provide the promise of a solution to their problems or fulfill some need. This promise helps you get the next appointment or propels them to answer your call or e-mail. This intention must be authentic, tangible, and available. Otherwise, there is little else to talk about. It is all about their needs or problems and it has nothing to do with you. It is all about them.

There is a thundering herd of salespeople that want the time and attention of the customer. To be remembered and to be valued, you must be different or you must do things differently. Although you could dress in a clown suit with a red nose and over-sized shoes to be different, the differences that are remembered are more subtle.

Here are a few things that will make you different from the other salespeople knocking on their door:

- Always be on time for the appointment; better yet, be early.
- Listen before you speak.
- Deliver valuable nuggets of information.
- Repeat the customer's name in your conversation since people are soothed by the sound of their own name; remember it is all about them.
- Focus on the customer's problem and not on your solution.
- Ask probing questions that begin with why and how.
- Always tell the truth.
- Acknowledge the customer's birthdays, anniversaries, and kids' names.
- For a repeat customer, anticipate their needs; be first to remind them about their dwindling inventory or an upcoming service.
- Keep your promises; if you plan to call back on a certain day or time, do it.
- If you can not meet a commitment or promise, tell them immediately. Don't try to avoid or hide the fact.
- When you make a mistake tell them and take responsibility for fixing it.
- Put a special quote in your e-mail signature that connects with your customer.
- Spell and grammar check everything you send to the customer.
- Send handwritten note cards as a follow up to your meeting. Include your business card.
- Write your cell phone number on the back of your business card so that they can contact you when they have an urgent need. Tell them to call you at any time.
- Always say thank you.

Put this list into practice and you will be different than 95% of the salespeople out there. And, you will be remembered.

*One more thing: Be remembered for doing well and not for dropping the ball.*

# 140. Customers Know Too Much

"Trust yourself. You know more than you think you do."

**Benjamin Spock (1903 – 1998) Pediatrician and Author**

With the proliferation of the Internet along with blogs, wikis, social networks, and online communities, buyers today are making superior purchase decisions based on information that is now readily available. Gone are the good old days when buyers depended on their salespeople to educate them about products and services. This newfound purchasing sophistication applies to both B2B markets and B2C markets.

I remember a 2000 Time magazine cover story that forecasted the "death of sales careers" (or, at least a re-engineering of how products and services would be distributed in the new millennium). Well, it is 2010 and the article was half right: the Internet has changed the landscape of selling.

But, what was not forecasted was the increased information that buyers now have at their fingertips. Buyers can now quickly "Google" a product or service to determine pricing, specifications, and sources of supply. Buyers are now very informed about current market conditions and about the alternatives (I.E. your competition). As negotiators, buyers are well armed.

So what are professional salespeople to do? They need to become "partners" who provide tangible value in the sales and distribution process. To provide this value, sellers need to be expert at helping buyers make the right purchase decisions.

A downside to the availability of all this information for buyers is the shear volume of data itself. In this case, the rep can assist the buyer in sorting through the options. The same information can help the seller be more informed and better assist the buyer.

Additionally, sellers need to take on the behavior of a valued partner by suggesting alternatives, price decreases, or specification changes before they are needed. A true sales partner thinks about the customer's long-term interests by helping the customer achieve cost savings and ordering efficiencies.

Meanwhile, the old behavior of the stereotypical sales rep who was prone to fast talking, bluffing, fibbing, and lying by omission is no longer acceptable. Of course, it never was acceptable, but now you will assuredly get caught.

When all is said and done, the Internet, blogs, wikis, social networks, and online communities have created new tools for the enlightened seller to better serve the customer.

*Talk is not enough: Avoid confusion by putting things in writing. It will keep you honest and will avoid "he said/she said" conversations later.*

# 141. How Top Salespeople Think

"Common sense is instinct. Enough of it is genius."

**George Bernard Shaw (1856 – 1950) Irish Playwright**

Ever wondered what is going on in the heads of top salespeople? Like most high achievers, top salespeople manage their thoughts with discipline and optimism. They do things differently from the rest of the team.

- They plan to win. For a top salesperson, losing is not an option. They visualize success.
- They have a positive dialog with themselves. They avoid negative thoughts.
- They make this intention to win a public testimony. They tell others about their intentions and commit to winning publicly.
- They focus on the needs of the customer and not themselves. Rather than focusing on commissions or themselves, top salespeople think about the customer's needs and issues. They understand that selling is all about the buyer.
- They take action. They take the first step and push themselves to make the next call. Sometimes, the difference between good and great is just one more phone call. They don't hesitate.
- They don't make excuses. If they make mistakes, they admit them privately and publicly. Yet, they don't dwell on them. Top salespeople are optimists and feel that problems are fixable.
- They self advocate. When they need help they ask for it. Unlike low achievers who try to hide their weaknesses, top salespeople confront them and ask for support or guidance.
- They track their progress. Top salespeople always know what they have sold year-to-date, how many calls they have made, and how this compares to last year. They often keep detailed records far beyond the organization's normal tracking requirements.
- They don't give up. They don't understand failure or apathy. Top salespeople are focused and know that by being persistent that they will hit their goals. Don't get in their way.
- They reward themselves. Company rewards and kudos are great, but top salespeople also reward themselves when they hit their goals. I know one salesperson that gave himself a Friday round of golf every time he hit plan for the month.

- They defend themselves. They are prideful and will stand up for what is right. They will fiercely defend their territory and actions.

*Self Advocate: Top salespeople ask for help or guidance, while others might stay quiet.*

# 142. Increase Sales with Reference Accounts

"My goal in life is to be as good of a person my dog already thinks I am."

**Anonymous**

If you ranked all the tools in the marketing tool bag, which includes product promotion, pricing, advertising, personal selling, and public relations, you will find that reference accounts top the list in effectiveness. Reference accounts are the most believed and trusted form of marketing. Let your happy clients do your selling for you.

When your firm is brand new, I encourage you to give away your product or service if that is what it takes to get a strong reference account. Consider doing business "pro bono" as my lawyer friends call it. Give it away and service the heck out of them in exchange for a good reference.

If your existing clients are happy, ask them to write it down or ask them for permission to have a prospect call them. Most of the time, they will be glad to help out. If they say no, they will be complimented that you asked.

Peer references resonate because prospects find them believable. Meanwhile, the prospect is disinclined to believe the sales rep, even though the rep may truly be expert on the subject and may know far more than the buyer. Since the sponsoring firm pays for the advertisements they are less believable. Likewise, the buyer knows that the rep is paid to sell. References provide a work-around for this trust problem.

By the way, the venture capital community understood reference accounts long ago. They frequently build portfolios of firms that sell to each other and act as reference accounts for each other. A little incestuous you proclaim? I agree. Nevertheless, it works and I guess all is fair when it comes to the VCs.

No better salesperson exists than the happy customer. Reference accounts are critical to the successful marketing effort at any business. (They aren't too bad on cash flow either since they pay their bills on time).

It is legendary that referrals can be the best method for new business development. Simply put, there is no better salesperson than a happy customer.

Here is a simple suggestion. Effective immediately, make it part of every customer meeting agenda to discuss referrals. Ask for three names, but don't stop there. The real goal is to get a personal introduction. While a name and email makes your database bigger, a warm introduction will be far more powerful than you personally lobbing in a phone call or email later.

Always attempt to enlist their help in introducing you. If you can, get them to do the introduction on the phone with you sitting in the room. I have done this many times and had the customer put me on the speaker phone to allow me to speak with the referral. When this happens my goal is to set up an appointment such as a lunch with the current customer, the referral, and myself. This may be the warmest referral that you will ever get.

This technique does not always work. Sometimes the customer says, "Let me think about it"—meaning who they might refer. This gives you a chance to call them back later and follow up. More often than not, they will be impressed with your follow up and persistence and will offer you the referrals.

On rare occasions the customer might say, "I am not comfortable doing this." If that is the case, you get the chance to ask them why this is the case. It might just open up a dialog about how you can do things better in the future. Guess who wins? You guessed it. You win because you asked for a referral.

*More on this: Referrals come easily when you do work or your product works. Concentrate on doing quality work and the referrals will come.*

# 143. Telephone Conference Calls

"Wise men talk because they have something to say; fools,
because they have to say something."

**Plato (424 B.C. – 348 B.C.) Classical Greek Philosopher**

For many of us in sales, it is an everyday occurrence to conduct sales meetings on a conference call with participants from multiple locations. While this can be a terrific way to communicate to multiple people in different locations, the call can be ruined by music on hold, shuffling papers, dogs barking, and background conversations. All this chatter devalues the message. Additionally, the host needs to manage the call and keep things on track by practicing some basic conference call etiquette.

For the presenter, here are a few suggestions:

- Introduce yourself. Start the call by giving your name and location and then have your audience do the same.
- State the purpose of the meeting. People are busy, so don't waste their time.
- Reconfirm the time required for the meeting and then stick to that schedule.
- Be on time. Nothing is more insulting than joining a call on time to discover that you have to wait on the host. Duh!
- Don't read the presentation. Your audience can do that without you. Instead, talk about what the slides mean.
- Send your PowerPoint in advance so everyone has a copy. This way you won't have to waste time resending or sending the slide deck at the front end of the meeting.

Request your audience (and the presenter) do the following:

- Turn off cell phones and pagers that might ring or make noise during the call.
- If you're using a multi-line phone, turn off all the ringers.
- Move your PDA away from the phone because it may make noise or cause interference.
- Land lines are preferred. You will get a clearer connection if you use a corded phone.

- Cell and cordless phones may cause an echo and static. If you must use a cell phone, be sure the battery is fully charged, and stay at a place where your signal is strong. I once had a cordless phone which beeped incessantly when the battery was low.
- Call in early. A few minutes before the conference call, dial the conference phone number and enter any user codes. This will give you adequate time to trouble-shoot if there are any issues with access.
- If you have a call waiting feature on your phone, disable it before calling into the conference by first dialing *70 and then waiting for the dial tone.
- Mute your phone. Muting keeps distracting sounds from disturbing the call. CONFIRM that you are on mute to avoid embarrassing yourself as you mutter to yourself about the ineptitude of the presenter, or whatever you say to yourself.
- If the call can't be muted, don't shuffle papers, type on your computer, or make any other distracting noises.
- Don't put the phone on hold. If you have to step away, don't put your phone on hold during the call or the other conference participants may hear your on-hold music.
- If you want to make a comment, be brief and concise. Don't ramble on and monopolize the conversation.
- Speak clearly. Be sure to speak slowly, enunciate your words, speak directly into the telephone mouthpiece, and speak loud enough to be heard.

Conference calls can be great for selling, but you need to manage them.

*It is worth the expense: Consider a telephone bridge line which can accommodate multiple callers in different locations. This will improve sound quality and make for better communication. Use a landline since cell phone quality remains a poor second choice.*

# 144. Selling With Integrity

"To know what is right and to not do it is the worst cowardice."

**Confucius (551 B.C. – 479 B.C.) Chinese Philosopher**

Marketing campaigns, sales quotas, and sales awards are soon forgotten. Yet, your reputation seems everlasting; it is the essence of what others remember about you. How will you be remembered?

Mark Twain said, "If you tell the truth you won't have to remember anything." This adage makes sense to me. I don't want to have to remember who I've told what or worry about who might find out what I did or did not say. You can see how this applies to selling. Telling the truth is an integral part of selling and a critical determinant of your reputation.

Salespeople get challenged daily to meet their customers' expectations or needs. It has been my experience that customer needs don't always fit your company's offering. Old school sales training challenged the salesperson to push harder on the customer to overcome their "objections." The customer just needed to be sold or convinced of your product's fit or superiority. In effect, the customer was ignorant or uninformed.

While this type of persistence may pay off, some salespeople have taken this message to the extreme by telling the customer whatever is necessary to get the deal, even lying. Of course, this behavior is dead wrong.

Besides showing poor self esteem and strong personal insecurity, these inflated claims or half-truths are unethical and will do more damage than good in the long run. Most customers will remember you and the falsehoods—good luck in ever getting their business again.

A half-truth is a whole lie and lies will ultimately damage your reputation. Instead, why not choose to sell with integrity by just telling the truth. You will be remembered as being honest, which is far better than any year-end sales award or commission check.

*Sleep better at night: Always tell the truth.*

# 145. No Hurry to Make a Decision

"To a quick question, give a slow answer."

**Italian Proverb**

"Let me think about it," says your customer. This is the dreaded "no hurry" response, which is one of the most frustrating selling situations that you can encounter in sales. You have answered all the questions, handled all the objections, and determined that the fit with your offering is good. Still, there is no decision.

There are many symptoms of a customer who is in no hurry. They can include:

- Concerns about price even though you had dealt with this objection earlier in the sales process.
- Deferring to a higher authority as you try to close the sale. Suddenly they can't make the decision anymore.
- Questioning the fit of your solution despite the fact that they had previously confirmed that everything was good.
- Changing their mind about what they need or changing their specification.
- Words like "I will get back to you," "I need some more time to think it over," or "let me run this by the boss."
- The customer has not been properly qualified.

What does no hurry mean? Candidly, it can mean many things. Most often it means that you did not qualify your prospect and you have been wasting your time by calling on the wrong customer. This happens to all salespeople, but it is the biggest weakness of an inexperienced sales rep. Another version of poor qualification is calling on the right account, but selling too low in the organization. Often this individual is a scout and is screening vendors for the boss.

No hurry can mean that you did not answer all their objections. This is a basic sales mistake since a no hurry objection can mean that you were rushing things. Slow down and ask your customer why? Remember that customers say "yes" only after all their objections are answered. If you skip something, no hurry is their way of telling you to slow down and help them. You should treat this stall as a request for more information.

Depending on the length of your sales cycle, things can change. If your offering has a long sales cycle, let's say 6-12 months long, don't presume that their needs are fixed. It is the sales representative's responsibility to continually verify the fit of the product with the customer. Changes at the customer could include new management, technology changes, decision process changes, and many others. You may only find out about these changes if you ask "if things have changed" since the last conversation. If you don't ask you may find them to be in no hurry.

Sometimes a customer may need an increased incentive to "get them off the dime." In this case, you might want to offer something extra for doing the deal now rather than later. Rather than offering a discount, make the pie larger with a tangible incentive. If this does not work, you may need to probe more deeply into why they are in no hurry.

No hurry can mean many things, but the response typically means that you did something wrong early in the sales process or that things have changed.

*Start over: When in doubt, start the sales process over by asking questions.*

# 146. Why Won't My Customers Call Me Back?

"What loneliness is lonelier than distrust?"

**George Eliot (1819 – 1880) English Novelist**

A common lament from many salespeople these days is the difficulty that they have in getting their customers to call them back. This applies to prospects and even regular customers. Salespeople worry that if they call too much they will be perceived as a pest or as unprofessional or, even worse, as a stalker.

This is a real dilemma and it seems to have gotten worse over the last few years. I think that there are many contributing factors, most of which you have already heard about. The factors include technology, the increased sophistication of buyers, and the re-engineering of the work day in the new millennium.

One more factor to consider: it is not their job to call you back. It is your job to call them. Let's address this first. Selling is a dance and it is the salesperson's job to lead. Don't expect them to call you back….ever. It is your job to call them, to inform them, and to serve them. Remember, it is all about them and not about you.

Let's return to the other factors that have made things harder for salespeople. Obviously, technology has made the salesperson's job tougher; this includes voice mail, the use of cell phones, Blackberry smart phones, laptops, and caller ID. Busy customers have figured out how to screen their calls and hide from salespeople thanks to technology. Caller ID may be the biggest culprit since your buyer can hide from you if they want to and many do. One way to handle this issue is use your cell phone's "block caller ID feature," which will keep them guessing who is calling.

With increased information available to buyers in the form of wikis, forums, and websites, buyers are relying less on salespeople to keep them updated about products and services. Candidly, this works against the buyer since they are not benefiting from the salesperson's superior knowledge. Think about it. You sell the same product day in and day out. When it comes to your product and how it works, you are one of the world's top experts. Meanwhile, the buyer buys your products occasionally (at best) and by definition knows far less than you do. What is wrong with this picture? To quote Forrest Gump, "Stupid is as stupid does." You have what the buyer needs, be sure to remember that.

I think the solution to this quandary is to position yourself as a "knowledge broker" rather than as a salesperson. Help your customer get as much information as possible about their problems and issues, along with the possible solutions (I.E. your offering). Keep them updated on other information resources such as wikis and forums. Become a source of knowledge and insight about their issues. This information will give you power.

The changes in the workday and workplace have been huge. Because of technology, people are working longer days and spend less time in the office. Nowadays, the new 24/7 work schedule allows people to work from home on their laptops away from the office phones. Many people prefer cell phones over land lines. In this case, take their cue and don't call them at the office and instead call them on their cell. If this is a problem, they will tell you.

How often should you call a customer while praying for a returned call? If I had to give you a ratio of your calls to theirs, a 5 to 1 ratio is good. I had a sales trainer tell me that once and it made sense at the time. After all, we don't want to overstep our boundaries. Or, do we?

Maybe a smarter answer is don't keep score at all. Remember customers get dozens and sometimes hundreds of emails a day, so your email can easily get lost in the milieu. The same applies to the voice messages that you have left. You can't expect them to leap for the phone when you call or even remember your last call with them. They don't keep score, so why should you?

A good strategy might be to mix up your approach. Try a blend of land line calls with cell phone calls, along with a few email messages. Text messaging works too. See what works best. When you are desperate to connect, try unconventional means such as sending a FedEx envelope because everyone opens FedEx packages. Call the operator at their work and have them paged; this one is surprisingly effective. Send a fax because people respond to faxes since so few faxes are now sent compared to ten years ago. Or, send flowers or a gift if budget allows, this will get their attention.

*Remember: It is your job to call them.*

# 147. Non-Verbal Communication

"If your dog doesn't like someone, you probably shouldn't either."

**Anonymous**

Non-Verbal Communication can be mightier than your words. This is especially true in-person. Your words are important, but your body language and "para-language" may transmit a louder message.

Studies have shown that people can "size up" another person in as little as three to four seconds. This judgment is a basic mammalian response that uses all our senses: sight, hearing, smell, touch, and taste. In addition, we call upon our past experiences with others to help us sort out friend from foe. If we had a bad experience with a tall, bald man once before, we might be wary of others who fit that description.

Body language may make up to 55% of communication. This includes posture, facial expressions such as smiling or frowning, hand and arm movements, and the tilt of your head. A hand moved in front of your mouth can indicate that you are uncomfortable or don't agree with the other party. Arms crossed can be a sign of aggression or disagreement.

Body language helps us communicate whether or not we are aware of it. A recent university study on how people receive information had the following results:

- 55% of what we learn from others comes from their body language (mostly from the eyes).
- 38% of what we learn from others comes from their tone of voice.
- 7% of what we learn from others comes from the words they say.

What this means is that our body language communicates a lot of information whether or not we try to manage it. This makes the initial greeting critical to the beginning of a new relationship. While people expect a firm and professional handshake, studies show that we make up our minds about people in the first three to four seconds.

Essentially, we make a judgment based on physical characteristics such as shape of the face, posture, eye contact, body type, voice, clothing, and smell. We quickly determine if the new person is friend, foe, or neutral. This mammalian reaction comes from thousands of years of learning to survive and thrive in a hostile world.

Beware that when you meet new customers or contacts that you are being sized up and categorized. To make the best first impression, a smiling face and direct eye contact helps get you off to a good start. A firm, uncomplicated handshake is best. Avoid a weak handshake or an overly aggressive grip. The goal is to be accepted not to dominate. Stand straight but relaxed.

Your voice should be steady and enthusiastic. A happy person has a higher pitch and fast pace, while a depressed or bored person speaks slowly in a monotone voice. An aggressive person can be loud with a deep voice (think growl).

Clothing matters. Have you ever noticed how a person who is dressed-up, even in older or out-of-style clothing, always commands more authority and respect? The impression you make and what you have to say is enhanced by your personal presentation. The goal is to fit in but not to draw extra attention, so beware of flashy or provocative clothing.

Additionally, good grooming is essential. Body odor is offensive in most cultures. Also, beware of overdoing it with perfume and cologne since this can also be offensive to some. Clean hands and well groomed nails are essential.

Akin to body language is the amount of space you maintain between yourself and others. While this space can be cultural and learned, it can also be an indicator of someone who is aggressive or unskilled socially. Standing too close to another person can make others very uncomfortable in western cultures, while in Middle Eastern cultures standing nose to nose is considered polite and a sign of friendship or trust.

Para-language is the use of intonation, sighs, and pauses in your speech. Studies have shown that para-language accounts for 38% of communication. Once again culture may play a big role in use of para-language. For example, Japanese businesspeople will use long pauses in meetings to reflect upon important points. These pauses show respect and wisdom and they also allow for time to think and help you avoid saying something stupid.

Para-language can be heard on the phone such as a sigh or an inflection of voice. Our listening for these signals is more acute when on the phone. In person, you can actually see a sigh which involves a deep breath and its release.

Our words may say one thing while our body language and para-language may say another. For example, on a job interview you may try to say the right things while your nervous hands and sweaty brow may communicate another. The interviewer will know that you are nervous despite your confident words.

Another example is the behavior of a liar. Typically someone who is lying is stiff and uses few arm and hand movements. They avoid eye contact and they will turn away or turn sideways. Sometimes they unconsciously put things between you and them such as a stack of magazines or some other object to hide behind.

For businesspeople, the best advice may be to "be yourself" since you cannot hide behind words.

*One more thing: "Take it from the scientists. Thirty-seven years ago, the late anthropologist and professor of communications Ray L. Birdwhistell demonstrated that less than 35% of the message in a conversation is conveyed by spoken words—the other 65% is communicated with facial expressions and body language. Says Matthew Lombard, a professor at Temple University and president of the International Society for Presence Research: 'Without the visual, you miss most of the nonverbal cues.'"*

*Source: Business Week Online 2/16/07*

# 148. Fear of Rejection

"A rejection is nothing more than a necessary step in the
pursuit of success."

**Bo Bennett (1972 – present) Businessman**

The single greatest cause of sales "failure" is the fear of rejection, which is that creeping feeling that customers will tell you "no." It can be so paralyzing that rookie and veteran salespeople will go to great lengths to avoid that word. This fear disables you from cold calling, closing, and from getting up in the morning. You see a lot of salespeople killing time at Starbucks. It is fear that makes them drink the coffee, not the caffeine.

It is legend in sales that selling starts with the word "no" or starts with an objection, which is sales vernacular for a reason not to buy. Objections are really requests for information. It is the sales representative's job to help the buyer understand the product better. Objections help the sales rep move the sales process along; thus, no can be an "enabling sales technology." Yet, the word no can be disabling for many.

Buyers will automatically say no even when they mean yes. Ever walk into a shoe store and have a sales rep ask, "Do you need any help?" Invariably, we say, "No." Then we turn to the shoe rack and pick out a shoe and then ask the same sales rep for help. Shoe salespeople learn that this cat and mouse game is all part of the sales ritual. It all starts with no.

While not all of us are cut out for sales, fear of rejection can be overcome by a simple technique called systematic desensitization. Oddly enough, the more you do something the easier it becomes, while conversely the less you do something the harder it becomes. The single best way to confront our fear of rejection is to do what scares us the most. In the shoe salesperson's case, he or she confronts the fear by continually asking the question, "May I help you?" The sales rep becomes desensitized to the rejection through repetition.

Another example is the fear of public speaking. Some studies have shown the fear of public speaking to be greater for some people than the fear of death. They avoid speaking publicly at all costs. Yet, the best way to beat the fear of public speaking may be by speaking publicly. Toastmasters

International, the world renowned public speaking training organization, advocates making speeches weekly to conquer this fear. They believe that only with repetition can this fear be truly beaten.

Here are a few tips on confronting the fear of rejection:

- Look for no. Keep a record of how many times you hear no in a day. Try to beat yesterday's tally. Track weekly.
- Visualize your customer saying no, but tell yourself it means they have questions.
- Let the customer know that "no" is an acceptable answer, since you are interested in a long-term relationship with them. Watch or hear them exhale with relief. The pressure is off. Ask them to tell you about their concerns.
- Remember that in selling it is not about you. Rather, it is all about the customer; focus your thoughts on them and their needs. The commissions will come later.

Frankly, not of all us are cut out for sales, but most salespeople can beat this fear. It can be conquered by a simple technique called "systematic desensitization." This is a fancy term that describes how you can beat your fear by confronting it repeatedly. That's right. The more you confront the fear, the more you will minimize it. You do it again and again until you lose your fear.

Conversely, if you do nothing and if you don't confront the fear, you make your fears even larger. If you don't make cold calls, they will become harder to do.

As it is says on the shampoo bottle: lather, rinse, and repeat.

*Fear not: Most fears are based on a lack of information.*

# 149. Smile While Selling on the Phone

"The shortest distance between two people is a smile."

**Anonymous**

People can "hear" you smile when you talk with them on the phone. A recent study confirmed that you sound different or better when you smile.

Smiling affects how we speak. Listeners can actually detect your smile based on sound alone according to a new study by the University of Portsmouth. The study determined that some people have "happier" voices than others. All in all, people prefer to listen to people with happier voices. Thus, they are more receptive to listening to a sales pitch from a happy voice on the phone.

In a nutshell, when we listen to speech we hear the general pitch and people associate a rise in pitch with more "smiley sounding voices." We might also be picking up on more subtle cues like how intense the voice is. A person with a naturally short vocal tract may therefore sound more smiley than others at all times. The research adds to the growing body of evidence that smiling and other expressions pack a strong informational punch and may even impact us on a subliminal level.

What this means to people selling over the phone is that the customer is more aware of our engagement and disposition than what was previously thought. Does this mean if you smile while selling you will sell more? It may be so.

One technique that I have used over the years when selling on the phone is to look at a photo of a person. Don't laugh, but I had a photo of President Reagan posted on my office wall and used his picture as the image for my customer. His smiling face made me smile back, which must have made me sound happier.

Can you tell that I am smiling as I write this book?

*Try the picture trick: Place a photo of a smiling person by the phone and look at it when you are on the phone.*

# 150. Personalize Your Offering

"One must talk little and listen much."

**African Proverb**

Understanding your customer's needs is a critical step in the sales process. If you understand this, you are empowered to construct the best possible solution for their problem. Without this information, you are just doing guesswork.

With this knowledge, you can personalize your solution by emphasizing the fit of your offering with the customer needs. More than just generic features and benefits, this personalized offering is tailor made and only they can design it. The challenge is for you to get access to the right information and then match that information with your offering's benefits.

To personalize your offering with the customer's needs, you need to do the following:

- Slow down, it is not a race.
- Ask them open-ended questions that begin with "Why…" and/or "How…"
- Ask them to give you examples.
- Listen and don't offer solutions (just yet).
- Reconfirm your understanding of their needs or problems by repeating their needs or problems. Say something like, "If I understand you correctly, you need…"
- This may sound trivial or overly deliberate, but you might have missed something or misunderstood.
- Make sure that they confirm that you got it right. This will often trigger them to think of other things that are also important to them.
- Having created a confirmed list of the needs, take a deep breath. (Sometimes this next step happens at the next appointment, depending on the complexity of the sales cycle.)
- You can now describe your offering by talking about specific benefits rather than generic features.
- Slowly describe the benefits of your solution while matching each benefit with their need.
- Seek confirmation after each benefit that it matches their need.

By tailoring your solution to the clients' needs, closing the sale is easy. More often than not, the customer will take over and start talking about the order, in effect, selling themselves. When this happens, you have the deal.

*Slow down Grasshopper: You might miss something.*

# 151. Phone or E-mail?

"The problem with communication is the illusion that is has occurred."

**George Bernard Shaw (1856 – 1950) Irish Playwright**

E-mail communication with customers can be efficient and easy, but it is easy to fall into a bad habit of only using e-mail to handle customer inquiries. If your goal is to build better relationships with your customers, the telephone may be a better tool.

While talking on the phone can be stressful or distasteful in some instances, I find that most of the time you end up doing a better job helping the customer. A byproduct of this personal contact is a more evolved relationship, which can be more satisfying for provider and customer.

My auto mechanic runs a busy shop. Yet, he always finds the time to call me about the status of my car when it is in his shop. His friendly call comforts me that the job is getting done and it is smart marketing on his part because I end up referring my mechanic to many of my friends since I know that he will treat them equally well.

An opposite example is my relationship with Google. I recently had a problem with my Google AdWords account which had been infected with malware (corrupt software from an Internet pirate). I have had 30 e-mail messages back and forth with the help desk at Google and still have not resolved my problem. I am not happy and I have to wonder how easily this would have been resolved by a simple phone call.

*The moral of this story is simple: call your customer whenever possible. It will make you feel better.*

# 152. Handling Difficult or Angry People on the Phone

"Speak when you are angry and you will make the
best speech you'll ever regret."

**Lawrence J. Peter (1919 – 1990) Educator**

If you deal with difficult or angry customers on the phone, you know that the biggest problem is that they tend to go on and on, don't listen, and dominate the conversation. There is just no easy way to get into a conversation with these people. This consumes lots of time, and, of course, it's hard to help a customer who won't let you talk.

There's a simple technique that you can use on the phone to get the customer to stop talking. It's called "silence is golden." Like any kind of conversation, telephone conversations have rules. One of those rules is that when one person is talking, the other person sends signals to the "talker" that they are listening, and still there. This is necessary because the parties can't see each other.

The only way to know there is a person on the other end is if the other person makes some sort of noise, usually "yes," "uh-huh," "I understand," etc. Consistent with our self-defense principles, you do not want to follow this rule.

The best way to get a person to stop talking on the phone is simply to say nothing at all. If you can avoid breathing into the phone, or if you can exclude any noise getting through from your end, this is even better.

Eventually, the person on the other end will stop, and say something like "Hello, hello, are you there?," and pause for a moment. This gives you the opportunity to say something like, "Yes, I was listening to you. Let me see if I understand what you are saying…." By repeating back what the difficult or angry customer said, not only are you back in charge, it also gives the customer time to cool off.

Now that you are back in charge, you can help fix the problem.

*What angry people want: Angry people want to be heard—so let them speak.*

# 153. Managing Customer Conflicts

"Conflict cannot survive without your participation."

**Wayne Dyer (1940 – present) Self-Help Guru**

Customer conflict happens. It can happen with new customers, with prospective customers, or with major accounts. From time to time in a customer/supplier relationship, disagreements can happen over quality, failure to meet commitments, or interpersonal dynamics. When problems like this happen, you can quickly get stuck in a stalemate.

Until the problem is resolved, you probably won't be able to go forward or do business. While conflict can be uncomfortable, it can also help you solve problems. The key to managing conflict is to avoid making accusations and personalizing problems. Try to focus your comments on yourself and your feelings by using "I-statements" like "I feel" or "I felt" instead of "you statements" like "you did this" or "you said that."

For example, if a customer breaks a commitment to give you a contract extension, maintaining your cool is essential. By all means, don't say "you broke your promise to me" or "you lied to me" (even if that is what happened). Pinning the blame on the other party likely won't solve the problem and might seriously injure the relationship and your chance to do business in the future.

Instead, say "I feel let down and disappointed by not getting the contract." By using an I-message the emphasis is focused on you and your feelings (not the act or omission of the other party). This gets the message across without blaming or pointing fingers at the buyer.

I-messages state a problem without blame. By not personalizing the problem, it allows the other party to help you solve the problem. If they were wrong or erred, it allows them to "save face" and make things right. Also, you may have misunderstood the actual commitment or something might have happened that was out the other party's control. Thus, the I-message confronts the issue without blame and acts as a request for information or explanation.

It takes both bravery and restraint to confront a problem with a customer, while not personalizing the issue. It is my experience that confrontations with I-statements can help you get to the heart of the matter without injuring the relationship. Often, this disarming self-disclosure about your feelings can help build a better relationship while solving the problem at hand.

Customer service representatives need to maintain their cool even when customers push all their buttons. Keeping cool is a matter of keeping your self control while helping customers get through their rants. Here are a few ideas on how to maintain your composure when the heat is on.

Be sure to breathe. Silly as it sounds, make sure that you are breathing and sending enough oxygen to your brain. Monitor your breathing the next time you are upset. I am willing to bet that you are breathing shallowly or not at all. No wonder you get red faced.

Avoid sharing your anger in e-mails, voice messages, or notes. These messages may come off very heavy handed, yet when the same messages are delivered in-person with eye contact and body language they may appear constructive or helpful.

Consider the use of the expression "I understand." This phrase will support your goals when the tension is high and when you need to find common ground to form compromises or agreements with the other party.

Monitor you own emotions. When you feel threatened, try not to defend yourself or to shut down when the other person is trying to communicate. The other person may have something that you need to hear (they might even be right!).

Try mirroring the other party's words. Repeat the exact words that the customer is saying to you; this keeps you focused and helps demonstrate your openness. Say something like, "Let me see if I heard you correctly. When I do this…"

When you feel like blowing your top or saying something you might regret, take a break. Put those feelings aside and deal with the issue later. You will be surprised how often the issue is minimized by doing this.

Throwing a fit in the workplace seldom does any good. More likely, people will not feel safe around you. You could be labeled as unpredictable and people will avoid you and your nasty behavior. Before long, your reputation will impede you from getting things done.

Stay cool with hot-headed customers by managing your own emotions.

*It's just business: Be sure to not take this business stuff personally.*

# 154. Gifts and Bribes

"You can only get what is yours by giving the other person what is his."

**Wallace Wattles (1860 – 1911) Author**

Gift giving practices vary from industry to industry, but an appropriate gift is a great way to say thank you and can help solidify a relationship between customer and provider. The operative word is "appropriate."

Appropriate gift giving has these key elements:

- The gift is well timed.
- The gift is meaningful or relevant to the recipient.
- The gift is memorable for the giver or the brand.
- The recipient can and will accept the gift.
- Nothing is expected in return.

Without these elements, the gift may be inappropriate or may be considered a bribe. For definition's sake, a bribe is money or a favor given or promised in order to influence the judgment or conduct of a person in a position of trust. The gift could be seen as a bribe if you're trying to obtain a new client's business or if you have contract talks underway.

The timing of a gift is critical. The element of surprise brings a certain drama to the exchange that will flatter the recipient. Other times to give a gift include:

- Holidays, promotions, graduations, etc. While these are obvious times to give gifts, you may be one of a herd of gift givers.
- When you want to strengthen your business relationship with a client.
- To celebrate a business associate or employee's promotion or retirement.
- To celebrate a personal event of an employee, such as marriage or the birth of a child.

Gifts need to be meaningful and relevant to the recipient. I remember getting a golf bag from a vendor which I graciously accepted. The only problem is that I don't golf, so I promptly gave it to my brother who does. My brother remembers the gift fondly while I don't remember the name of the giver who gave it to me first. I guess that makes me a "regifter."

One way to make the gift memorable is to personalize it with engraving or embroidery. It could read something like "To: Tom Chaney. Congratulations on your promotion to Vice President. From: Jack Thomas, May 16, 2010." The date is also an interesting touch.

Just because you think it's an appropriate occasion does not mean that the recipient can accept it. You might want to call his or her company to discover whether it allows employees to accept gifts or if it places a dollar-value limitation on gifts received. Many large corporations have strict gift policies. Avoid an embarrassing situation of a returned gift by checking first.

You also might want to consider whether religious or personal issues prohibit him or her from receiving holiday gifts. A canned ham might not be appropriate for Islamic or Jewish business associates. Also, don't send flowers to someone who is allergic to them. Being remembered is what really counts, so be remembered for a gift that is acceptable.

But when does a gift become a bribe? Having done a fair amount of business internationally, I am very aware of the gift giving protocol in Asia, the Middle East, and Eastern Europe. I accepted this practice as part of doing business abroad. I gladly complied. And, I got gifts in return (nothing of substance, but gifts nonetheless). No big deal, I thought. Maybe this is your experience as well.

So what is a gift and what is a bribe? From my point of view, a gift is something of value given without the expectation of anything in return and a bribe is the same thing given in the hope of influence or benefit. Gifts and bribes can be actual items, or they can be tickets to a sporting event, travel, rounds of golf, or restaurant meals. Thus, the difference between a gift and a bribe is simply the expectation that comes with it.

A recent study by Transparency International, a non-profit organization dedicated to ending global corruption, surveyed 11,000 business executives. The survey studied the business ethics of the world's top 30 exporting countries. The end result of the study was a stacked ranking of the nations most likely to offer bribes.

The top ten countries most likely to offer bribes are as follows:

1. India
2. China
3. Russia
4. Turkey
5. Taiwan

6. Malaysia
7. South Africa
8. Brazil
9. Saudi Arabia
10. South Korea

According to the survey, there is an obvious direct correlation with poverty with emerging export powers India, China and Russia ranked among the worst. Anecdotally, you can presume that poorer countries are the most likely to bribe. It is safe to say that these countries also had the least amount of government regulation regarding corruption.

Is it ethical to accept a gift? The answer is yes, but when it comes with strings attached you have crossed the line. In this case, accepting the bribe is as bad as offering it. Let's also say that you will know a bribe when it is offered. It just won't feel right. I challenge you to consider the worth of a business relationship that begins with or is based on bribery. This type of relationship is a house of cards at best.

So, how can an entrepreneur, who is desperate to begin a new business relationship, avoid bribes? First, each country has its own cultural norms regarding gift giving and its own laws regarding corruption. The issue of corruption is particularly thorny when selling to foreign governments. Take the time to prepare before you travel by researching the gift giving practices ahead of time and by consulting your attorney (if not your priest or rabbi). Second, consider the adoption of a gift policy for all employees at your firm. This can act as a good compass for doing business internationally and might provide a safety net when you are put in an uncomfortable situation.

I can only advise you to proceed with caution and to only give and accept gifts. Beyond that, it just is not worth it.

*You should know that: The IRS currently allows businesses to deduct up to $25 for gifts you give to any one person per year. There is no limit on how many people you can give business gifts to during the year, nor on how much you spend for those gifts, although your business gift deduction is limited to $25 per recipient. Be sure to check with your accountant on this one since the IRS likes to change the rules periodically.*

# 155. Two Wolves: One is Evil and the Other is Good

"One evening an old Cherokee told his grandson about a battle that goes on inside people. He said, 'My son, the battle is between two 'wolves' inside us all. One is Evil. It is anger, envy, jealousy, sorrow, regret, greed, arrogance, self pity, guilt, resentment, inferiority, lies, false pride, superiority, and ego. The other is Good. It is joy, peace, love, hope, serenity, humility, kindness, benevolence, empathy, forgiveness, generosity, truth, compassion and faith.'

"The grandson thought about it for a minute and then asked his grandfather: 'Which wolf wins?'

"The old Cherokee simply replied, 'The one you feed.'"

**Cherokee Author Unknown**

I think I was about 12 or 13 years old when I became aware of the two wolves that battled inside me. Like the Cherokee parable, one wolf was good and the other was evil. Like a lot of young men, I made good choices and I made bad choices. Sometimes, the evil wolf made me lie to get what I wanted. Most of the time, the good wolf encouraged me to do the right thing. I did the best I could while not truly understanding this duality within me. I never told anyone about the two wolves because, for me, it was a private angst.

As an adult I have learned to manage a truce with the two wolves, but from time to time my desire to win at all costs was prodded on by the evil wolf. My corporate life found me battling many other evil wolves; some were my bosses and co-workers, while others were my customers. They challenged my ethics and begged me to do whatever it took to "succeed." It seemed that the higher that I climbed the corporate ladder, the more I was challenged to compromise my personal ethics so I could do what the corporation needed. I regret that I made some lousy choices and hurt others in the pursuit of money and position while being subservient to the evil wolves at bay.

Because of these ethical challenges and my desire to take control of my work life, I eventually left the large corporate work world for my current life as an independent writer, consultant, and teacher. I wanted to better manage the wolves within me and make better choices. This may sound lofty or presumptuous but I wanted to teach others how to make better ethical choices.

Yet, even today the two wolves are still at war within me. I must feed the good wolf daily to keep him strong since the evil wolf still lives.

*I found the "Two Wolves" story on the web: I am not sure of its real source, but the message resonated with me.*

# 156. Do You Have an Affinity for Marketing?

"It takes a long time to grow an old friend."

**Anonymous**

Affinity marketing is marketing and promoting to a group of customers that have common interests. It usually involves getting other people or other firms to help you sell and promote your business. It can be as simple as an endorsement from one firm for another firm's products. In exchange for this effort, the other party gets compensation or value. The effort or campaign to get another party to help is often called an "affinity program."

An example of an affinity program would be an automobile mortgage company which markets its financial products with the endorsement of a thrift lender, which does not offer auto loans. The customers are shared and have common interests. In this relationship, the two firms promote each other's products to a shared audience. The relationship is reciprocal.

Similar affinity programs can be created for most any business, entrepreneurial or not. Here are a few tips for setting up an affinity program:

- Establish the rules of engagement: determine who does what, what you get for doing it, and how to measure success.
- Designate a champion at your firm and at the other firm to be responsible for the success of the program.
- Treat the other firm like a customer or a member of a special team. Communicate regularly to maintain and create mind-share. Share success stories. Be generous with kudos and rewards.
- Brand the program by giving it a "mantra," a three to four letter name. Make it easy to say and spell. Make it clever and memorable. Blanket the earth with the mantra.
- Avoid affinity partners which directly compete with your firm; this can be trickier than it sounds. The risk is that the partner might decide to enter the business with you. Instead, establish non-compete agreements which discourage this behavior.
- The pay off has to be mutual or the affinity program won't work; you need to address the question: what is in it for me?

Affinity marketing can be a very powerful method to ramp your brand awareness and sales. It can be like having two sales forces.

*Partner wanted: Who might be a good affinity partner for your business?*

# 157. Inside the Buyer's Head

"We don't see things as they are—we see them as we are."

**Anais Nin (1903-1977) Author**

Salespeople are taught to manage and control the sales process by moving the customer from qualification to presentation to close. While this process accurately describes the activities of the salesperson, there is a separate and equally important process at play. That other process is the one in the buyer's head.

In my view, there are eight steps in the buying process:

1.  Attention: It all starts when the buyer has an initial contact with the offering. This contact could be an advertisement, a phone call from the seller, or a referral. Somehow the buyer identifies the offering amongst the thundering herd of products and services.
2.  Interest: The buyer sees the possibilities of the offering and begins to understand the benefits. "Hmmm," says the buyer.
3.  Desire: At this juncture in the buying process, the buyer starts to visualize the product helping to solve a problem, provide some utility, or bringing happiness. Things are clicking.
4.  Conviction: Clearly the offering makes sense. The research is done and the decision to go forward to buy is imminent. This could really work.
5.  Action: Bingo! The buyer steps up and secures the offering. All systems go. We have lift off.
6.  Confirmation: The product is used, tested, and appreciated first hand. The seller's value proposition is fully vetted.
7.  Satisfaction: The votes are in and the product is a winner. Repurchasing it is an option.
8.  Loyalty: The highest level of happiness with a buyer. At this stage the buyer is actually referring the product and the seller to others. The buyer is an advocate.

Not all buyers reach loyalty. Many never buy while some who do buy have remorse. Yet, this path is real and tangible for the buyer. Unfortunately, many salespeople are oblivious to the buying process which is a result of antiquated sales training, selfishness and plain old ignorance.

When you are selling you need to ask yourself what is going on in the buyer's head.

*Stop and think: Next time you are selling something, stop and think about what is going on in the buyer's head. What might he or she be thinking?*

# 158. Fire Your Bad Customers

"If there were no bad people there would be no good lawyers"

**Charles Dickens (1812 – 1870) Author**

Not everyone should get the honor of being your customer. Life is short, so why spend your valuable time with customers that are rude, slow to pay, or overly price sensitive?

Recently, I had a new client verbally abuse one of my team members. My teammate was mortified at the experience and was not sure how to handle it. After investigating the situation, it became clear that our client was a bully and would be impossible to satisfy. I terminated the relationship. End of story.

The essence of niche marketing is to create an intimate partnership with a market segment that is under-served or not served at all. The entrepreneur provides a carefully crafted solution to this customer segment, but only after intense research and testing.

Through this special relationship the customer gets what they needed and, in return, the entrepreneur gets customer loyalty and higher profits. And, thus, the competition does not really matter.

But, this niche market success is dependent on the right mix of customers. So, what does the right customer look like? I call this the "preferred customer profile." Create a list of the criteria that are most important to you and your business. That list might include:

- Proximity to your office or shop.
- Pays bills on time.
- Easy to do business with.
- Future need for your product or service.
- Profit margin.
- Fun relationship.
- Size of customer.
- Industry.

Rank your current customers based on these factors. When my clients have done this ranking, it is frequent that some of their customers score very high, while other customers may score very low. The question then is how can you raise the score of the low ranking customers or how soon can you replace them with customers which better fit you and your business?

Why exhaust your resources trying to serve customers that don't pay their bills on time, that are difficult to work with, or don't fit with your future product plans. Focus your energies on your high scoring customers. Direct your marketing efforts and new business development on finding new customers that fit your preferred customer profile.

Life is short.

*Say goodbye: Raise the prices for your bad customers and say goodbye.*

# 159. It's Not About You

"Wherever you are, be there."

**Anonymous**

Many of us spend a lot of time thinking about what we want. This is true for career planning, negotiation, marketing strategy, and lunch. We are the center of the universe, or so we think.

In marketing and sales you must let go of what you want and put the focus first on the customer, or better said on the market. The needs, issues, and dreams of the market (I.E. a collection of customers with common interests) should be what drive your marketing strategy along with your day-to-day decisions.

Of course, a business needs to make money and grow and meet the stakeholders' expectations, but these are downstream rewards given by your satisfied customers. They come after you have delivered value or solved the customers' problems.

To get these rewards, the focus must start with the customer. Sounds simple and it largely is. Here are a few examples:

- Your marketing messages need to include the customer and not you. For example, the tag line for McDonald's for many years was "You Deserve a Break Today." The message was about you getting burgers and fries and not about making them money.
- Automaker Jeep just came up with a new ad campaign that reads: "Have fun out there." Yep, you need to have fun, so go drive a Jeep.
- Your e-mail subject lines should include the customer and a benefit for them. A good example is "You can save 50 percent on airfare." The call to action is for the reader to open the e-mail so he or she can learn more about how "You" can save money on airfare.
- Salespeople need to focus their presentations on the customers' needs and desires. Product pitches are dead. Put away the PowerPoint presentations and canned pitches. The customers want to talk about their needs and issues. Shut up and listen.

- Advertising must include the customer. Apple very cleverly had a dancing silhouette of an iPod user dancing to the music. Yes, that is you having a great time spending $300 on a MP3 player.

Public relations efforts should focus on stories of successful customer engagements and not about your new product announcements or new technologies. Human interest stories get read, while company announcements get trashed or deleted.

It is all about them and not about you.

*Write it down: When you see a tagline that you like, write it down. This will help you write your own.*

# 160. How to Earn Customer Loyalty and Referrals

"The question is not whether you're loyal; it's who you're loyal to."

**Anonymous**

The best salesperson is a happy customer. It may sound trite, but a happy customer is much more believable than your best sales pitch. If only you had more of them.

Loyal customers keep on coming back. Loyalty is earned after the sale has been made and after the product or solution has been delivered. It is all about their perception of value. This perception is the reward that you get for delivering what you promised in quality, service, and responsiveness. More than just satisfied, a loyal customer refers you to other potential customers. They value the relationship with you and they want your business to succeed.

A loyal customer often pays more and they won't stop to haggle when placing an order. They are confident in your product or solution and they feel that you need to be fairly compensated. Since you know them and their special needs, servicing this customer is easy. The sheer repetition helps.

Referrals resonate because prospects find them believable. Meanwhile, the prospect is disinclined to believe the sales rep, even though the rep may truly be an expert on the subject and may know far more than the buyer. This also explains why advertising is such an inefficient tool: it is obviously paid for by the sponsoring firm and is not believable. Likewise, the buyer knows that the rep is paid to sell. References provide a workaround for this trust problem.

Now let's be clear about a few things. Just because a customer says that they are happy does not mean that they will buy from you next time. The sad truth is that satisfied customers change providers all the time. Maybe it will be because of price or a lack of attention by the sales rep or some new feature offered by a competitor.

Satisfied customers are great, but they can still be teased by a competitor's lower price or product features. Loyal customers are not swayed by the sweet talk from your competitor since they are committed to doing business with you. The acid test for loyalty is referrals. If your customer refers you to their friends and colleagues, they are loyal. It is as simple as that

Customers who refer your firm to someone else seldom change providers. If you can only ask your customer one question to determine his or her level of satisfaction with your product or service, you need to ask, "Have you recommended our company to a friend?"

If you ranked all the tools in the marketing tool bag which includes product promotion, pricing, advertising, personal selling, and public relations, you will find that reference accounts top the list in effectiveness. Reference accounts are the most believed and trusted form of marketing. Let your happy clients do your selling for you.

It is one thing to say that you will refer someone and another thing to actually do it. Real advocates are people who actually recommend your firm to their friends. They are not people who just talk about it.

Creating this type of customer loyalty is hard work, but it can be done. Here are a few tips:

- Always say thank you. I recommend personal note cards as a follow up to every order or after a meeting. This personal touch is almost lost as a business practice; do this and you will be noticed, if not admired.
- Always ask for feedback on the buying experience. Do this in-person and by survey. Make your firm easy to do business with; eliminate inefficiencies and problems today.
- Consider a service or product guarantee. This will take the anxiety out of the purchase. In practice, they are seldom exercised, but when they are you are being told that you have big problems to fix.
- Measure everything. Monitor all your customer facing processes. Catch problems before they fester.
- Try to anticipate customer needs. Call them first and remind them if they are low on stock. Let them know of product changes or improvements.

- Hold quality meetings with your staff. I bet they know where things could be improved; sometimes, you just need to ask them. Let them know it is OK to give you negative feedback. Create incentives to improve your products and processes.
- Welcome customer complaints. A customer who complains is giving you a second chance to make things right. If you can fix things, you could end up with a customer for life.
- Offer incentives to customers who refer you to other customers. Reinforce this great behavior. It won't take much either; it might cost you a lunch or tickets to the theater. It is worth it.
- Never over-commit. If you cannot meet a customer's expectations, don't take the order. The downside risk too great.
- On the flipside, always exceed expectations. Deliver sooner or better or more than quoted. Be excellent!
- Finally, whenever a customer compliments you on a job well done, say thanks and ask for a referral. If they cannot think of anyone, it means that you have more work to do.

*End all customer meetings with this question: Do you know anyone that would like our product or service?*

# *161. Special Events for Loyal Customers*

"Cocktail party:  A gathering held to enable forty people to talk about themselves at the same time.  The man who remains after the liquor is gone is the host."

**Fred Allen (1894 – 1956) Comedian**

For a small business such as a retail store or a service provider, special events can help propel the company and its brand to the next level. Unique events can provide a great perk for loyal customers while differentiating your business from the competition.

Often I am asked, "What can a little business like mine do that my customers would consider special and actually attend?" The better questions to ask are: "What is important or interesting to your customers?" and "Why do they use your services or buy your merchandise?"

A special event for a haberdasher (a men's clothing store) is a "trunk sale" which is an after hours sale. New merchandise is offered for the first time at special prices for invited customers only. This works because of the exclusivity of the event and it provides what the loyal customer wants: special treatment and the right product.

Here is another example that may be a bit arcane but really works. Omar's Exotic Birds is a California retailer of exotic bird species such as Macaws, Amazons, African Greys, and Cockatoos along with cages, food, and supplies. They have a great reputation and provide their customers with much needed support and information about these challenging pets.

Omar's Exotic Birds decided to announce an after hours "singles event" for parrot owners in effort to build their brand and provide a unique event for their customers. They call it "Omar's Singles Sunday." The premise was simple: the people coming to this event are single and want to meet other single parrot owners. Please bring your parrot.

This is just brilliant. Think about it. Parrot owners are a special breed since owning a large bird is a huge commitment of time and energy. It requires very special knowledge; these large birds are very smart, need lots of training, and some can live for 60 years or more.

Just as important is why do people buy large parrots? My guess is the unique relationship that you can get with this special pet. For some, parrots are surrogate children like dogs and cats are for other people. And there is a certain novelty of owning an exotic bird (I have a 24 year old Amazon Parrot named Billy). What could be cooler than hanging with a bunch of people who share your passion who also desire to meet you?

Special events are a great way to reward loyal customers and to position your business as different.

*Visit: http://www.omarsexoticbirds.com.*

# 162. Special Customer Service Touches Make the Difference

"It's never crowded along the extra mile."

**Wayne Dyer (1940 – present) Self-Help Guru**

It is a cliché that the little things you do make the difference with your customer, but it is true.

I read a story the other day by author Mac Anderson about a grocery store "bagger" (or a box-boy as I grew up calling them), who had devised an idea to make his customers happy. Much like a fortune cookie, he would drop a small piece of paper with a positive or happy quote in each customer's grocery bag as they left the store. On the back of the note was his name.

This special touch went on for a few months before the store manager discovered it. The manager noticed that the line for the register where the special bagger worked was always longer. As it turns out, customers wanted to get their special quote of the day even if it took a few minutes longer. By the way, it is worth noting that the bagger had Downs Syndrome.

The quote was a small act of kindness, but it made a huge difference. It made me think of the ways that others have made me happy or made me feel special. One that came to mind is my Pharmacist at Rite-Aid named Anna. Although Anna must fulfill prescriptions for hundreds of different customers every week, she always greets me with, "Hi, John." Candidly, I don't go to the pharmacy that often, yet she always remembers not only my name, but also the names of my wife and kids. I cannot tell you how she does this memorization, but I will say it does make me feel special. And, I always look for her when I go into the store.

Another special touch came from my dentist and life-long friend Dr. Dave Primac. The other day I had a crown on one of my molars come loose just prior to a week-long business trip. Schedules would not allow me to get into the dental office that day, so I agreed to keep the crown and go in to see him when I got back from my trip. About an hour later there was a knock at my door and there was my dentist. He had a major appointment cancel, so he jumped into his car and drove to my house with his dental instruments and glue. He popped the crown back in my mouth and I went on my business trip with smile.

What can you do to make a difference?

*When you see it: When someone does something exceptional, be sure to tell them thanks. Maybe they will do it again.*

# 163. Say Thank You!

"The deepest craving of human nature is the need to be appreciated."

**William James (1842 – 1910) Psychologist and Philosopher**

Thank You. I cannot think of a more powerful phrase that is never said enough to our customers: thank you. And, it is so easy do.

Here are a few ways to tell your customers thank you:

- Call them. Yes, you will get a voicemail, but go ahead and leave a message. Say something like, "I am calling to say thank you for your business. Your ongoing support means a lot to me. Thanks." Trust me this small gesture will be remembered since so few people do this.
- Send a postcard with the same message next time they place an order. Be sure to handwrite on the envelope and use a real stamp. Receiving a card like this is a rare event and will be appreciated.
- Set up a lunch with your favorite client in appreciation of their patronage. The purpose is to say thanks, so be sure to do your selling another time. If they want to talk business, that is up to them.
- Include a Post-it note on your next invoice with a handwritten note of appreciation. As simple as this seems, Post-it notes get noticed. Consider getting a Post-it note printed with your name and contact information on them.
- Send an e-mail with a photo of you holding a sign that says thank you. A little goofy but it works.
- Send a FedEx package with chocolates and a thank you card. This is a special treat for a special customer.
- Make a donation to your customer's favorite charity in their name. While we do this for sad occasions like a funeral, think about how impactful this would be as a simple thank you.
- Send flowers or a plant. Be sure not to over do it since many employers have limits on accepting gifts.
- Send them a discount coupon for future use. Easily done.
- Send them tickets to the movies.

As your mother told you, it is the thought that counts.

*To my readers: Thank you for buying this book. It means a lot to me.*

# 164. Accounts Believable

"Money frees you from doing things you dislike.  Since I dislike doing nearly everything, money is handy."

**Groucho Marx (1890 – 1977) Comedian and Actor**

You know it's a tough market when the marketing and sales staff spends an inordinate amount of time managing collections. With cash so important during hard times, it can be a virtual tug-of-war with your customers to get the cash which is due and payable.

Here are few thoughts on how to manage your accounts receivable in a down market:

- Manage the terms on the front end. Be sure to put all terms and conditions in writing up front and take the time to discuss them before accepting the order.
- Do credit checks. Although a poor credit history may be a lagging indicator of a company's health, it is best to know who you are doing business with and how they pay their bills.
- When a net 30 invoice goes unpaid, call them right away. This sends a signal that you are on top of things and won't tolerate late payments.
- Talk to your late paying customers. Often when a customer falls behind on payments they become the enemy; it is common for communication between vendor and customer to stop. This is exactly the wrong thing to do. Instead, keep an active dialog with them and treat them humanely. Generally, this approach will insure that you get paid.
- Put someone in charge of accounts receivable. While larger firms may have an accounts receivable manager, most small firms don't. Appoint someone with the honor of managing your collections and give them special incentives to help usher the money home.
- Focus on the biggest fish. Prioritize your collection calls on the biggest dollars first. I know that this sounds silly, but it is common to work a collection list by the alphabet.
- Have the sales department push credit card purchases for the smaller orders. This is guaranteed cash.

- Call on Monday. This is only anecdotal, but it is my experience that the best time to call is Monday morning. People are generally happier and more optimistic on Mondays. Get their attention before the Friday check run.
- Consider the creation of a promissory note. This may best apply to a large customer who is behind on multiple payments. In this instance, the party owed renegotiates all the outstanding receivables with the slow payer. This typically elevates the discussion with the management of both parties. Do this only with someone who is likely to stay in business and eventually pay.
- Consider a cash only relationship for firms that consistently miss payments. It may be harsh but you may not have other options.

Cash is king, so make sure to get your fair share. Believe me when I say it is your number one priority in a down market.

*Start here: Create a list of your top debtors and call them every Monday. I mean every Monday until they pay. Let them know that you are not going away until they pay. Be nice but be persistent.*

# 165. Networking Basics

"Am I not destroying my enemies when I make friends of them?"

**Abraham Lincoln (1809 – 1865) Statesman**

For many people meeting someone new can be an awkward experience. What do you say to break the ice and begin a conversation? The answer is simple: focus the conversation on them and remember that even the shortest conversation has a beginning, middle, and a closing.

Let's say that you are at a cocktail party for a convention. The first thing you need to do is make eye contact with the other person. Studies show that up to 70 % of communication is non-verbal and most of that is done with eyes. Also, scientific experiments have confirmed that you need less than four seconds to make a good first impression, so be ready. Add a smile to the eye contact and you will send a positive message that will be hard to refuse.

Next, say hello. If they have a name tag on, say the person's name. You've probably heard the old saying that there is no sweeter sound to the human ear than the sound of one's own name. Next say your name and something like "pleased to meet you." Pretty simple so far isn't it?

Now we come to the part that tends to trip people up. This is not a time to be overly clever or to start talking about you. Instead, find something that you both have in common. It could be the long line at the bar or the music in the background. The goal is to get the conversation started and all it takes is a simple observation or question about something shared. That shared experience can be all it takes to get the conversation going.

Current events make great conversation starters. It might be a headline news story or the keynote speaker's comments. Remember to ask the other party how they feel about it. Ask their opinion first before you launch into a tirade or rant (on second thought don't do the tirade or rant). You might offend or put off the other party with your position or opinion, so see how they feel first.

In professional settings, asking the other party about what they do for a living is a reasonable and easy question. Listen and act interested in them.

Now you can say what you do, but don't over do it. Try to flip the conversation back to their interests.

Look for a way to help them either personally or professionally. Who do you know that can help them? It could be a former boss or a friend from your country club. What resources do you have that could be useful to them professionally? Maybe it is a website that you frequent. Suggest that you might be able to help them and will follow up.

All good conversations come to end and it is often better to do so earlier than later. Offer your business card and the gesture will almost always be greeted with reciprocity. Suggest that you will be back to them later with that introduction or website. Say good-bye with a smile, with good eye contact, and a firm handshake. Leave them wanting more.

Always follow up with a hand-written note card, an e-mail, or a phone call. It is best to do this within 48 hours or you will be forgotten. Deliver as you promised and you will have made a new friend.

Strangers are friends that you have yet to meet.

*Be open: Say hello to strangers. Be interested in them. Listen.*

# 166. Name Tags at Big Events

"Do you suppose I could buy back my introduction to you?"

**Groucho Marx (1890 – 1977) Comedian and Actor**

Conferences, Trade Shows, and Conventions are a great time to brand yourself and your company with your name tag. The last thing you want to use is one of those peel and stick labels, which often fall off in a matter of minutes.

Instead, take the time to get a preprinted name badge, which is engraved or printed especially for you and your business. This badge should include your name, title, company, and logo. Adding your tagline would be great. Other info to include could be your website address and some eye catching phrase or slogan. Make sure that the font size is big enough for everyone to easily read your message.

Add a compelling question on the badge like, "ask me about what I did yesterday?" Your answer could be a story about how you helped a customer save time and money with your new technology. Yes, it is a set-up, but people look for conversation starters and this technique works.

I recommend the badge be pinned on your lapel or shirt on the right, since most of us shake hands with the right hand. Be sure that the badge is even and does not droop to one side or the other.

You might want to have multiple versions made so that you can vary your "presentation" based upon the audience. You can have badges with different messages depending on the people you might meet.

*Consider the purchase: Get a permanent nametag made for yourself which won't peel off and that includes your website address along with your company name.*

# 167. Social Media or Social Networking?

"What's in a name? That which we call a rose by any other name would smell as sweet."

**William Shakespeare (1564 – 1616) Playwright
(from Romeo and Juliet)**

What is the difference between social media and social networking? These terms are kicked around by bloggers, the press, and consultants as the salvation for marketing and relationships. But, are they the same thing?

The terms are fuzzy and used synonymously and often erroneously. I can argue that terms are still developing context or meaning, but here is my best shot.

The word "social" refers to the interaction within groups of people who share common interests or needs, which the sociologists refer to as cohorts. These shared interests could include almost anything such as age, hobby, health, or history. Regardless of the commonality, the group desires to communicate with each other. The dinner table on Sunday night with the family is an example of a cohort group. A weight loss support group is a cohort group.

"Social Media" refers to the vehicle or method to communicate this information. This could be email, a chat room, YouTube, radio, and TV. Social media is a channel of distribution. The operative word is media.

"Social Networking" refers to the process of how a cohort group shares information with each other. This proactive process of communication is with others we know or new people who share our interests. This could be phone, email, video, or others.

In short, we use social media to do our social networking. Implicit in today's culture and jargon is the use of "social networking sites" such as Facebook, LinkedIn, and MySpace. Or, it could be as simple as your buddy list in your Gmail or Outlook email applications.

*Bookmark this: Be sure to bookmark your networking sites and make reading them a part of your morning ritual like we used to do with the morning newspaper.*

# 168. Social Networking is a "Must Do"

"Keep your friendships in repair."

**Ralph Waldo Emerson (1803 - 1882) US poet & essayist**

Facebook, the social networking firm, now has a user base on the verge of topping 200 million people. Amazingly, this lofty number is driven by a largely North American demographic. If you are waiting for social networking to catch on, you need to know that the train has already left the station!

And there are many other social networks to choose from including LinkedIn, Twitter, Plaxo, MySpace, DirectMatches, Ryze, Bebo, Friendster, Habbo, Meetup, Orkut, and Xanga. The reason that you may have not heard of some of these social networks is because they may have originated or are used exclusively in Asia, South America, or Europe. Nonetheless, they all have millions of users and potential "friends" for you to meet.

In my opinion, LinkedIn is the most "business friendly" social network with Facebook coming in a close second. If you are not a member of these two sites, I highly recommend you do so now. Using social marketing tools such as Facebook and LinkedIn provides a great way to reach new groups of people. Employers are actively data mining both of these sites for talent. Additionally, entrepreneurs are looking for partners. LinkedIn is business-friendly in that it allows users to keep an online resume formatted profile in a business-like format without features that traditional social media offers such as picture albums and music options.

Twitter is friendly to companies with the ability to broadcast recent news and events to their respective following. "Facebook pages" are business friendly also, while "Facebook Profiles" are simply for personal use. The new Facebook rules highly regulate against promoting a business using a "personal page."

For example, I used the term "Angel Investor" in my own Facebook profile and was recently contacted by a start up that was looking for money. The company founder was doing a search with the term angel investor and found me with a simple web search. While I did not invest in the firm, I was able to refer them to someone to help them out.

Here are a few tips on using social networks:

- Use your "personal profile" to introduce yourself to others. Take the opportunity to make friends with people who have similar interests as you.
- Use your business "profile page/s" to introduce what your business does and how and why they plan to use social media.
- Make sure that all business profiles are consistent throughout in terms of look, feel and concept.
- Add valuable content that will be of interest to your visitors. Many of these networks have a blog function which gives you yet another way to build your personal brand.
- Keeping your profile updated with frequent content will help increase the traffic to your profile. An easy way to do this is to learn how to use RSS feeds to auto update your accounts simultaneously.
- Beware of adding too much personal information, which you might regret later. One of my former employees recently included bachelor party photos on one of his public pages. While he seemed to be having a great time in the photos, they could be images that he might not want to show a prospective employer.
- Take some time to visit other profile pages to get a feel about how other people brand themselves. This might inspire you to update your profile.
- Leave comments wherever you can. The more comments you offer (and receive), the more likely it is that your profile will show up in the search engines. This really only applies to blogs and bookmarking sites.
- Join and participate in as many groups as you can. I anticipate that they will all get acquired and merged anyway.
- Do not spam users.
- Update blogs and content on your profile frequently. This will keep it interesting to your visitors and keep them coming back.

Networking is more than handing out business cards at cocktails parties. Social networking on the web is the new thing. It is the tool that helps build the relationship that may be started at a cocktail party.

*Join: Please subscribe to my blog at www.firstbestordifferent.com.*

# 169. Social Media: The New Water Cooler

"I am a deeply superficial person."

**Andy Warhol (1928 – 1987) Painter**

Facebook, MySpace, LinkedIn, Twitter, and the other social networking websites have supplanted the water cooler as the place to go when you need a break from your work day. I suppose for many of us in this increasingly virtual world having a chat with a cyber friend brings some meaning, if not a respite from the grind of work.

Yet, I am stunned at the time that my social network friends spend on these sites. They must be spending many hours every day posting goofy photos, useless links, and smarmy comments about others. If only their bosses knew.

Actually, their bosses do know. Increasingly, companies are monitoring the behavior of employees who post regularly on social networks. Human Resources, with help from the guys in IT, can data mine the social websites to find prospective employees. Additionally, they can function as a data source for background checks, so beware what you post. The world is watching.

I agree that the social networks provide business and monetary benefits to the individual. With that in mind, here are a few tips:

- Be friendly but don't be stupid. Be careful about who you allow in your network since friendship is about quality not quantity.
- Keep your profile page simple. Try not to overload the page with goofy widgets, bells, and whistles.
- Post tasteful photos only. Pictures of you and your friends in a drunken stupor from last weekend could prove to be hazardous to your career.
- Avoid trashing your friends, classmates, and employers.
- Use spell-check and write in English. Text-speak can be unbecoming to a professional.
- Always respond to your friend's requests and messages.

- Be sure to set your privacy settings so that only people approved by you can see your profile and photos.
- Never use profanity.
- This might seem obvious but never bash your current, potential or even last job as horrible as it might be or might have been. People have lost opportunities because of this type of carelessness.
- Beware your company's Social Media Employee Policies. Some firms have disallowed all social media references about the company. In some cases, unauthorized use can cause immediate termination.

*Update this: Be sure to update your profiles on the social networks you are on—people read these. Avoid getting embarrassed by deleting personal information that might be misunderstood by someone who does not know you well.*

# 170. Social Media and Ruthless Self Promotion

"Brevity is the soul of wit"

**William Shakespeare (1564 – 1616) Playwright**

For some, the sole purpose of social media is ruthless self promotion, if not outright narcissism. At the very least, they consider social media an outbound marketing tool. It is my opinion that that they are missing the point of social media: social media is all about two-way communication.

For example, we all know that Twitter is populated with many vain and useless comments. Still, if you use the search option on the Twitter page, you can "data mine" some very interesting stuff. Essentially, you can use Twitter as a very specialized search engine within your own personal network. Facebook is also beta testing a similar search function with a beta name of "Mashable."

Facebook and LinkedIn allow you the ability to ask questions of your network. Call it basic market research. Depending on the size of your network and their response rate, the results could prove to be significant from a statistical perspective.

Maybe the greatest benefit of social networking is the opportunity to help others. You could help a colleague find contacts for a job search. Or, you might be able to recommend a solution for a problem that someone is having with their email marketing campaign. When you help others, you will be remembered and rewarded some time in the future (OK, maybe only in the afterlife).

Social media allows for a dialog that might not happen in traditional communication channels. Turn down your personal volume and listen to your social network.

*Be social: Be sure to join Twitter, Facebook, and LinkedIn.*

# 171. Social Networking: The World is Watching

"One loyal friend is worth ten thousand relatives."

**Euripides (480 B.C. – 406 B.C.) Greek Playwright**

Facebook, LinkedIn, and MySpace: The opportunities to join the wave of social networks are seemingly endless. Not wanting to be left behind, I jumped in feet first and joined all the popular social networks and posted all sorts of information about my likes and dislikes.

Like many people I joined Facebook as a way to connect with old friends and to make new connections. I populated "my page" with information about where I live, my gender, my marital status, my desire to meet new people, my birth date, hometown, political views, religion, my favorite activities, favorite TV shows, favorite films, music preferences, contact information, and a simple bio. All this stuff is for my "friends" of whom I now have hundreds, most of whom I have known from work.

In much the same way, I have done this for LinkedIn. I now have 500 "friends" on this more "business-like" network. My work history is openly displayed and all you have to do is search for my name and you too can know too much about me. A number of colleagues have given me recommendations and they are openly posted for the world to see.

I also have dabbled with MySpace and even added special music and photos of my car to make me seem cool for the younger folks (of course, that did not work and I am still an old geek). My kids just laugh at my MySpace page.

I got a call from a recruiter who viewed my "public" profile and wanted to talk to me about a CEO position at a startup. The truth is I am not looking for a job and I am very happy with my portfolio of entrepreneurial activities: writing, consulting, teaching, and my other assorted businesses. Yet, this call is clear evidence that social networking works.

Yes, you can say that I am a real player in the social media space. But, here is the rub. The recruiter already knew all about me…. I mean everything. He knew where I had worked before, my interest in horses, co-workers that had recommended me, and my current activities. Candidly, he knew too much about me and it is my own fault. I had disclosed all this stuff on these networking websites. Yep, I am really a player or, should I say, I am really a chump.

You need to ask yourself, do you really want new friends (I.E. strangers) to have access to your vacation pictures, political views, and thoughts about religion? What if the reader is a web pirate building up a dossier in preparation for identity theft? Be aware that there are bad guys out there who prey on those who put themselves out on the web.

Or, in my case, a potential employer who might view photos of yours truly in compromising positions while vacationing in Cancun? OK, I have never been to Cancun, but you get the picture.

Speaking of pictures, a former employee of mine and a "friend" just sent me a Facebook "news feed" showing pictures of her at a bachelorette party stuffing dollar bills down a male stripper's thong. She seemed to be having a great time, but what image does this portray to a potential employer doing a background check? Might it kill the job offer? I think it might. Be mindful that although there are ways to safeguard your photos by setting the security preferences of the photo albums that are put on social networks, you cannot control what preferences your friends or even enemies might setup on theirs. Also keep in mind that once anything is posted on the web it will be there forever. Don't post anything that you wouldn't want your great-grandkids seeing.

My recommendation is to make sure your public profile on these websites is purged of any information that might be controversial or extreme, since your next employer might be viewing it. Or, maybe a web pirate might be watching. Mashable has a great guide to follow to make your profile acceptable in the eyes of future employers, which includes not posting any particular views in terms of religion or politics. Many of these guidelines are simple etiquette when meeting someone for the first time. The key is to use the same caution on your profile where an employer might get their first glimpse of you.

*Check out: Got to www.mashable.com to learn more about social media.*

# 172. YouTube, the Vatican, and New Media

"Be well, do good work, and keep in touch."

**Garrison Keillor (1942 – present) Author and Personality**

You may have heard or read the headlines about Google buying YouTube for $1.65 billion, but secretly asked yourself, "What the heck is YouTube?"

It is a fair question since YouTube was founded only in February 2005. YouTube is a consumer media company for people to watch and share original videos worldwide through a Web experience. Everyone can watch videos hosted on YouTube both on YouTube.com and across the Internet since everyone can include a YouTube video on their site. People can see firsthand accounts of current events, find videos about their hobbies and interests, and discover the quirky and unusual. A key attribute of YouTube is that it is mostly uncensored. It allows for people to broadcast freely and assists in democratizing media.

As more people capture special moments on video, YouTube is empowering them to become the broadcasters of tomorrow. YouTube is a place for people to engage in new ways with video by sharing, commenting on, and viewing videos. YouTube originally started as a personal video sharing service, and has grown into an entertainment destination with people watching more than millions of videos on the site daily. The site lured 129 million unique visitors in November 2009 according to Nielsen Online.

If you are still not convinced that YouTube has gone mainstream then consider this. Pope Benedict XVI launched his own channel on YouTube. Supposedly this was done so the Catholic Church could connect with a younger audience. The church recognizes that the future rests on the shoulders of the younger generation. Church elders have been painfully aware of a disconnection with their younger members of the flock. Candidly, this move seems brilliant.

"With the YouTube platform, we now have the capacity to give young people direct access to the thinking, to the thoughts, to the words and deeds of the pope," said Monsignor Paul Tighe, secretary of the Pontifical Council. "That allows them to share with their friends."

I love the use of the term friends since it sounds so much like MySpace. Using the proper lingo was a smart thing for the Vatican to do. The Vatican plans to use its YouTube channel mainly as a Catholic news channel featuring the pope's daily activities and speeches, and it will provide links to other Catholic TV sites around the world.

Thus, the Pope understands the value proposition of YouTube. How about you?

*When time allows: Be sure to check out http://www.youtube.com/ vatican.*

# 173. Viral Marketing or Astroturfing?

"I heard it through the grapevine."

**The Funk Brothers**

Viral marketing is very hip and everyone says that it works. Yet, my experience is that few people can define what viral marketing really is or give tangible examples other than to say, "Like YouTube." So, let me take a crack at it.

Viral marketing is not new. In fact, it has been around for ages since it really is just someone passing along some information to a friend about something that they heard or saw. More specifically, the term "viral marketing" describes online or offline techniques to increase awareness about an offering or an event using existing social networks. True viral marketing is voluntary and relies upon the recipient to pass on the message to his or her friends. That message could be text, audio, video, or images; it could be as simple as a story told to another. The originator of the message has no control over the message's destinations, but relies upon the intelligence of the social network to find the right recipients.

The most famous example is the launch of the free e-mail application called "Hotmail," which relied upon happy users to tell their friends about it. Launched in 1996, Hotmail now has over 230 million users. The technique has been copied by Google's Gmail, which allows you to invite up to five friends to join.

Word-of-mouth campaigns require that the offering or event be interesting, valuable, or funny to the recipient to such an extent that they will refer it to a friend. This is where most viral campaigns fail. Most are valuable to the recipient and there is no reason to pass it on.

MySpace has opened up a new channel for viral marketing. I have a friend named Rudy Chavarria who runs American AMP. American is a specialty advertising, marketing, and promotion firm. He promotes movies and special events using MySpace and other social networks. Prior to formal release of a movie, Rudy's team will build multiple sites on MySpace promoting the event hoping to create a buzz. The different sites might target a slightly different demographic or "friend" as they call them on MySpace and other social networking sites. In all cases, it is the passion of people involved that propels the viral message on its way.

Another viral marketing trend is the use of free e-books to create a buzz for an author or expert. Typically, the e-book is a short summary of a print book. The e-book is passed along to build a brand for the book with the hope that the reader will want to buy the printed version.

Advertisers figured out that an odd or entertaining video might be just the vehicle to carry an advertisement. In my opinion, some advertisers are pressing the envelope of ethical advertising when using this technique. More commonly known as "Astroturfing," some advertisers are using YouTube and other media sharing sites to distribute viral ads that are disguised (I.E. misrepresented) as an amateur video. In this example, the consumer is deceived or lied to about the authorship of the video; it is represented as being real. I am the first one to enjoy a clever joke, but I don't want to be lied to or duped. How about you?

Advertising has grown less and less effective over the last decade because of the continuous bombardment of advertisements, which increasingly relies on shock value and sensationalism. These ads use a "spray and pray" methodology that is based on the assumption that, if you spend enough money and contact the customer a gazillion times, the prospective buyer will eventually get the message and buy the product. This is, of course, absurd. This deluge of "Madison Avenue advertising spam" destroys the brands of the sponsors. Our brand awareness is raised, but so is our distaste for the brand and product in general.

What is left for the unscrupulous advertisers to do? Answer: deception and outright lying to the consumer. Under the guise of a good joke or a clever presentation, viral marketing is a great way to enjoin the customer in your marketing efforts. Be sure to position the message as a commercial effort and identify it as coming from you.

*Read a classic: "Babbit" was written in 1922 by Sinclair Lewis about business culture and ethics—see how little has changed.*

# 174. How the Web Was Won

"Fast is fine, but accuracy is everything."

**Wyatt Earp (1848 – 1929) Wild West Legend**

If the Internet is the Wild West, then search engines are the gun-slingers and they are the ones that decide what sites will be visited or not. If the search engines don't like your site, you just won't get found.

If you look at the market share of the search engines, Google is by far the most dominant. U.S. search engine market share numbers have been released my market researcher ComScore. There were 137 billion search queries in the U.S., 85 billion of which done through Google. It is speculated that Google's share will continue to increase.

The market share breakout for 2008 is as follows:

1. Google 63.5%
2. Yahoo! 20.5%
3. MSN 8.3%
4. Ask 3.9%
5. AOL 3.8%

In fact, these five search engines account for the whole of the market. The other firms, of which there are many, don't show up on the scoreboard. The spiders love only the top five. A spider is the name of the software robots that crawl around the web looking for and evaluating websites. Google has two main spiders. Googelbot is the spider that records the location of the websites and the content that is found. The second spider is Freshbot which looks for updates to websites. Generally, Google spiders will visit the average site twice a month.

The reason that this is relevant is that 80% of Google users prefer organic results for a search rather than using a directory or direct entry of the URL or other means. So, the question becomes, how do you maximize your Google ranking?

Here are a few things that you can do:

- Page Tags: Every page needs to be named with the appropriate Meta tag names.
- Page Names: Every page on your site needs to be named with keywords.
- Relevance: Relevance is how closely the keywords in your copy match the keywords in a search.
- Keyword Density: The new rule of thumb is 7 keywords per 100 words of copy.
- Inbound Links: A link from a site outside of your site that directs traffic to your site.
- Relevant and Fresh Content: Daily updates are best. This explains why blogs are so effective at increasing a site's rank.

Manage these things and your search rank will increase.

*You cannot please everyone: So be sure to please Google since they are the biggest dog on the block when it comes to search.*

# 175. Privacy on the Web

"Privacy is not something that I'm merely entitled to,
t's an absolute prerequisite."

**Marlon Brando (1924 – 2004) Actor**

Privacy on the web does not exist. Surprised?

According to Rebecca Davis O'Brien of Parade.com, "When you search for information online, you're not the only one who learns something. Microsoft retains data identifying your search—including the words and sites you searched for, and the time and date—for 18 months. Google keeps this data for nine months."

She continues, "In response to pressure from privacy advocates, Yahoo! recently dropped its data-retention time to 90 days. Because searches can be traced to you by name through your computer's IP address (the unique identifying number assigned to all computers to access the Web), Internet search companies have a detailed profile of your personal interests and tastes. Experts worry that this private data could be misused."

What this means is web users are vulnerable to loss of privacy. Look for this issue to grow with government regulation around the corner. In the meantime, your website must have a posted privacy policy. No exceptions please.

With e-mail marketing the most practiced form of customer communication and the most common way that contact information is gathered, a privacy policy needs to explain what you plan to do with customer contact information. A privacy policy is a clear description of how your company uses the e-mail addresses and other information you gather via opt-in requests for newsletters, company information, third-party offers, or other functions.

If you rent, sell or exchange your list to anyone outside your company, you should say so in your privacy policy. (For the record, I don't support or recommend the renting, selling, or exchanging of e-mail lists since most opt-in subscribers don't want you to misuse or peddle their contact info).

State laws may also compel you to explain your privacy policy, where to put the policy statement so people will see it, and where the policy should be displayed. As you might suspect, California has the toughest laws on this issue. On the left coast, the law mandates privacy policies on any web site that can be viewed in their state.

Make it easy to find. Place it wherever you collect names and e-mails. I recommend a prominently displayed button on the website to house a statement about privacy.

Do this or you will be called a spammer. Worse yet, you may be breaking the law. For more information, consult your attorney.

*Protect yourself: Add a privacy policy to your website.*

# 176. Drive Website Traffic With Online Activities

"I hooked up my accelerator pedal in my car to my brake lights.
I hit the gas, people behind me stop, and I'm gone."

**Steven Wright (1955 – present) Comedian, Actor, and Writer**

The best way to drive traffic to your website is with online activities. While some techniques are better than others, it is best to employ a mix of the different methods since things change so fast on the web. What worked last year may not work next.

Here are some ideas about how you might drive traffic to your website using the web:

- Pay per Click Advertising: This can be done with Google, Yahoo!, MSN, and many others. If done right, this is cheap and effective.
- Article Marketing: Write short articles for article directory sites such as EzineArticles.com. This improves search rank and creates frequency in a search. This is one of my secrets to success in web marketing.
- Free Online Classified Ads: Post ads on free online classified ads sites, such as Craigslist and Kijiji. These sites get incredible traffic and you will be found.
- Blogging: My web business strategy is based on this method. It really works. Write with keywords.
- YouTube: YouTube can be extremely important to your business. A clever video can drive monster traffic to your site. If you have not been to YouTube recently, you are putting yourself at a great disadvantage.
- Forums and Social Networks: Pick forums related to your industry and site, and put links in your signature line so it appears in all your posts. These can be stand-alone sites, or "groups" on sites like MySpace, Facebook, LinkedIn, etc. Both forums and social networks are great web tools that have come of age, but you have to be a player to get the benefits. Get involved.

- Blog Comments: Visit blogs that cover your industry or space and leave comments with your URL. Position yourself as a thought leader by commenting back to other bloggers.
- E-mail Newsletters: While you may forward these to existing customers, they will get forwarded to buddy lists. This is viral marketing at its best.
- Content Aggregators: Submit your content to aggregators. The easiest way to do this is to burn your feed to FeedBurner and enable the feature to distribute your feed to blog aggregators. There are many others. Do a search for content aggregators.
- Blog Sites: Subscribe and post to blog sites like Digg and Delicious.

This is just a small list of the on-line activities that will that drive traffic to your site.

*Try article marketing: Visit www.ezinearticles.com.*

# 177. Offline Activities Drive Website Traffic

"Traffic signals in New York are just rough guidelines."

**David Letterman (1947 – present) Comedian**

When you think about methods to drive visitor traffic to your website, I bet you mostly think of web related activities. These online activities are great, but don't overlook the offline methods which can be surprisingly effective.

Here are a few ideas:

- Signage: If you have a brick and mortar business, include your URL on the outdoor sign.
- Invoices: Always include your website address on your printed bills. Make it easy for your customer to find you.
- Promotional Items: T-shirts, coffee mugs and pens are frequent choices for logos; be sure to include your URL on all of them.
- Bumper Stickers: I hate these, but they work too.
- Post Flyers: For a small business, the bulletin board at the community center, church, or school is a great way to remind people about your site.
- Business Cards: This is a no brainer, but frequently small business owners forget to put their URLs on their cards.
- Tattoos: For those of you who are really committed to driving traffic to your website, consider getting a conspicuous URL on your forearm? Count me out on this one.
- Leave Fliers: Leave fliers for website at your local university library, restaurants, or stores.
- Letterheads and Stationery: Create a letterhead to use for all your off-line communication. List your website address on all forms of company correspondence.
- Outdoor Advertising: Advertise on bus benches and billboards—they are amazingly effective on local audience.
- Newspaper Ads: They're often pretty cheap and local papers can have a circulation of thousands.
- Wear Your URL: Make a custom hat or shirt with your URL on it.

- Stickers: Stickers can be very useful especially if you sell to a young demographic.
- Direct Mail: You can print up some postcards (with your web address very visible on them) and send them to specially selected customers.
- Press Releases: Send a press release to all of the media outlets in your area, including newspapers, radio stations, and television stations.
- Printed Newsletters: With a newsletter, companies can communicate with existing and potential customers on a regular basis.
- Wrap Your Car: Some people sell advertising space on their car to make some money but you can advertise your own website on your car and it really works and drives traffic to your website. You can find car wrapping services in your city and pay them to wrap up your car. The rear windshield is the most important part.
- Give Lectures: Target city community centers, schools, colleges and universities.
- Letters: Write letters to the editor. Just have a very small byline at the bottom of your article and introduce your website. If you are a good writer, it will be a great way to drive free traffic to your website.

As you can see, there are many off-line ways to drive traffic to your website. I think you get the picture.

*Visit the local library: Volunteer to speak on a subject that you are passionate about and that is related to your business.*

# 178. Getting Found on the Internet

"Lost time is never found again."

**Benjamin Franklin (1706 – 1790) Founding Father and Inventor**

Getting found on the Internet is what really matters in web marketing. No matter how great your offering is, you are nowhere if they cannot find you. To be found you need "rank" and "frequency."

According to marketing writer Seth Godin, when there are 2 million Google matches for a search, the number one match gets 10,000 times more traffic as the number 40 match. With an average of 10 search results per page, this means you literally must be found on the first page of the search results. This is called "rank."

"Frequency" is the number of times you are found in a search. For instance, do a Google search for "Pepsi" which is a unique brand name. Be sure to filter it by putting quotation marks (I.E. "Pepsi") outside the word Pepsi. On the first page of the search results you will see that Pepsi gets multiple matches or hits. Thus, the searcher sees the brand name multiple times which increases brand awareness.

Getting both rank and frequency is done by doing web marketing basics well. They include:

- Article Marketing: Submitting articles for distribution by article directories which published on e-zines.
- Blogging: Frequency of blog submissions will please the search engine spiders.
- Forums: Helps make a site relevant and fresh.
- Pay per click advertising (PPC): The ad placement is determined by key words which are purchased in a bidding process.
- Keywords: Writing with words that searchers will use to find you. Add no more than 10-15 keywords per page to keep the search engines attention. Any more and the same search engines will flag your site for keyword spamming. Prioritize your words. Great copy is more important than keywords.
- Fresh Website Content: Maybe the number one criteria in the search engine algorithms.

- Banner advertising: Online ads purchased on other websites which link to your website.
- Sponsored Links: Similar to PPC, but listed at the top of a search result.
- Reciprocal links: Shared links between two sites.
- Triangulated links: A common third party link shared by two other sites.
- Relevance: Offering something that people want. Duh.
- Web Directories: Getting registered on all pertinent directories, paid or not.

While there may be many other web marketing best practices, if you do these I can nearly guarantee that your website will get both rank and frequency. Be sure to use multiple methods to drive traffic to your site since individual methods fall in and out of favor. For example, PPC has been the rage for the last 18 months, but recently it has been criticized with the increase of click fraud.

*Go blogging: visit all the major blog sites for your industry and leave well thought out comments with links to your site.*

# 179. *Swahili Spoken Here*

"Words have meaning and names have power."

**Unknown**

The language of the web sometimes resembles Swahili and this is especially true with domain names. Coming up with a domain name with a .com suffix that matches your company name or offering is darn near impossible.

The first thing you have to ask yourself is should your business or product name match your URL? Conventional wisdom says yes, yet if you do a Google search for some of your favorite brands you will discover that many do not match. For example, if you enter the word "iPod" you get directed to http://www.apple.com/itunes. OK, that makes sense.

Most people will do a Google search for a company or product instead of entering a URL. I have seen estimates that up to 80% of companies are found by web searches instead of directly entering a URL. There is a good argument that a perfect match does not really matter much anymore.

My personal take is that it makes sense to have a domain name that reflects your site or business. It is easier for your customers to remember. Now here is the hard part. Just about every two and three word combination for a .com URL is already taken. Don't believe me? Go to Godaddy.com and enter any three word combo and you will discover that these URLs are already owned by someone else. Amazingly, this applies to the other web suffixes (.net, .org, .biz, etc.) as well. They are almost all gone.

Unbelievable but true. This explains the trend of inventing company or product names. For example, www.Kijiji.com is an online classified ad website that competes with venerable Craigslist. "Kijiji" is Swahili for the word "village." If you don't believe me, go visit www.kijiji.com.

An alternative to Swahili or fabricating words is the use of long domain names. Kijiji could have used www.onlineclassifiedadwebsite thatcompeteswithCraigsList.com. I didn't check but I am pretty sure this URL is available—cheap. But, can your customers remember it?

There is some evidence that longer URLs are easier to remember than single word inventions. Yet, it took me a few years to quit confusing Yahoo! with Wahoo; I just love their fish tacos or is it their pay per click advertising? No matter.

Hyphens or underscores can help you create shorter domain names but they confuse me and where is the underscore key on the key board anyway? Maybe you feel the same way.

Another workaround you can try is to add "the" to the beginning of a URL. I think this trick works if your business is known as "The BirdDog Group" which is the name of my company. In this case, "the" has meaning and is logical.

The final challenge is to choose between .com, .net, .org, and the many others now available. Candidly, .com still has cache and is the suffix of choice for businesses. For those that do enter a URL in a search, 99 times out 100 they will enter it with a .com prefix. The choice for you is made easier since most .com URLs are already taken.

Also, searchable terms or words now get a premium in Google search rankings. For example, www.internetsearchengine.com will get a premium over made up names such as www.google.com. I know this seems crazy, but Google keeps on changing the rules.

I wish you all the best in your domain name search. As we say in Swahili, "Hakuna matata" (which means no worries).

*Update:*    *Google is giving a boost in website rank when searchable*
         *words are used in a URL.*

# 180. Does Search Engine Optimization Fool the Search Engines?

"Fool me once, shame on you; fool me twice, shame on me."

**Chinese Proverb**

Google, Yahoo!, MSN, ASK, and AOL are getting smarter. Trying to fool the major search engines is getting harder to do as the major search engines continue to upgrade and refine the search algorithms to determine rank on web searches.

Most website owners rely upon the expertise of Search Engine Optimization (SEO) consultants to help them maximize their rank. This makes good sense because keeping up with the changes of the different algorithms is a full time job. Yet, many of the SEO firms try to trick the search engines with workarounds and gimmicks.

Sooner than later these tricks get caught by the search engines and the algorithms get changed and your rank drops. It is my argument that these SEO efforts represent wasted money and the wasted effort of everyone involved.

Here are a few of the tricks and gimmicks being used by SEO firms and website owners to temporarily fool the search engines:

- Hidden Links and Invisible Text: This is when website pages use white text on a white background. These messages are visible to the search engines but not to people.
- Dedicated Search Engine Pages: These special website pages are not a part of your main website. They are made solely for search engines and are not valuable to the reader.
- Cloaking: As is sounds, cloaking provides web content to web spiders that is not seen or needed by the reader.
- Duplicate Website Pages: Content is duplicated on the site but may have different file names. This is visible to the reader.
- Link Spamming: Excessive use of linking to other sites that are not relevant or of any value. This is also referred to as link farming.

- Keyword Spamming: This is the excessive use of keywords on website pages. This is also referred to as keyword stuffing.

While these techniques may work for a while, the algorithms get changed. Then you and/or your SEO firm have to go back to the drawing board. This will require more money and time.

Wouldn't it be better to create a website with real value in the first place?

*Educate yourself: Do some research on search engine optimization.*

# 181. Search Engine Optimization Is No Longer Optional

"Reputations are made by searching for things that
can't be done and doing them."

**Anonymous**

As a "solopreneur" who writes, speaks, coaches, and consults on the subjects of marketing and sales, I find myself spending more and more time working on my website since it is my main channel of distribution. My website and blog help me build my brand with people who don't know me personally. Generally, my website (or my blog) is the first point of contact with my target customer.

The challenge on the Internet or in the blogosphere is how to be found. If you have a website it must be optimized to be useful. This means that your website must be designed to be found by the major search engines, especially Google.

Search engine optimization (or, SEO as it is more commonly known) means many things and is a source of confusion and angst for many entrepreneurs. Search engine optimization is the process of increasing the amount of visitors to a website by ranking high in the search results of the major search engines. The higher a website ranks in the results of a search, the greater the chance that that site will be visited by a user. It is a common practice for Internet users to not click through pages and pages of search results, so where a site ranks in a search is essential for directing more traffic toward the site (this definition comes courtesy of web-inspect.com).

Okay, so how do you optimize your website for search engines? The answer is that there are many ways to optimize your website and the methods are changing everyday. Here are some things that you can do to optimize your website with the help of your web designer:

- Your website title should be between 6 and 12 words and should contain your key words. In fact, titles should contain multiple key words (this is sometimes called key word density.)
- Your title should have a Meta tag (this is like an HTML street address).

- Your home page should have between 7 and 48 keywords.
- Your Meta tag description should have between 12 and 24 words. These are HTML "names" that describe the content of each page on your website. Search engines hunt and record Meta tag names and locations to allow for quick searches. Your web designer can help you build-in these "street numbers" to insure good traffic to your site.
- Place keywords in your copy on every page of your site. These are the words, terms, and phrases that your customers use to describe you and your business when conducting a search. These keywords are sought by the major search engines, which use robotic software called "spiders." Spiders crawl around the Internet 24/7 looking for keywords to assist people in their searches.
- Your page headlines should contain your keywords.

You will note that most of the ideas listed above are managed "under the hood," which requires that you write HTML code or that you have your website designer do it.

There are also other things that can be done without the website designer. Here are a few:

- Blog your brains out and make sure that other bloggers reference your blog on their site or on their blog.
- Visit the blogs that relate to your offering. Link your comments on the other blog sites to your site by using the trackback and permalink functions (this is like a digital bread crumb trail back to your site).
- Make sure that your content gets tagged by everyone; this could be the inclusion of links to Digg, Flickr, Del.icio.us, etc.
- Submit articles to e-zines with your URL link.
- Create reciprocal links with other websites.
- Add great content everyday. The search engines are looking for new and rich content. Your rank goes down with old and out-of-date content. Your site must have lots of content that is relevant to the searches that people make. Nothing is more important or keeps people coming back than content.
- Consider pay per click advertisements located near the search results. Located off to the right on a Google search with lots of white space, these ads get the visitor's attention. When the visitor clicks on the advertisement, the advertiser is billed. This works and is very cost effective.

- You can go directly to Google or Yahoo! to do this, or you can seek out a search marketing consultant to help you. It is really not that hard.

Try this: Here is a free diagnostic tool that was advertised on Google the other day. It can give you immediate feedback on what you can do to optimize your website. This is not a commercial endorsement, nor am I paid to suggest this tool. I just found it useful.

*Free tool: http://www.web-inspect.com/search-engine-preparation.php.*

# 182. Websites Need SEO

"I feel like I am diagonally parked in a parallel universe."

**Anonymous**

To be successful online and generate profit for your company you must have lots of customer traffic and it needs to be the right people. Yet, getting your site the right visitors is no simple task. An incredible looking website is useless if the web designer did not consider search engine optimization (SEO) when building the site or if they lacked the knowledge to successfully implement a SEO strategy.

As odd as it sounds, artistically designed websites can be totally ignored by the search engines. Worse, they are a waste of time and money. Yes, they may be beautiful, but if no one finds it, nothing is really accomplished.

So, how can your company avoid wasted effort and become a major player online? It's a lot easier than you might think. First, contact a qualified search engine marketing firm and have them take a look at your existing web site or discuss your needs for developing a new web site. They should be able to explain all SEO techniques currently used to gain page rank for your site. This can save your company time, dispel numerous myths about search engine algorithms and help you understand how algorithms are actually used to index your website for "Search Relevancy."

Major search engines like Google, Yahoo and MSN utilize algorithms to sort through millions of websites to identify the most relevant match to a user's search query. If your company has done a good job at identifying the product features and services that you intend to market online, a SEO professional can tweak your website's code to let the search engines know your website is in business. It's that simple.

The hard part comes in developing an effective SEO strategy that will continue to keep your website listed at the top of the search engine results pages. This is where the proper selection of keywords, the creative use of domain names, the building of external links and the inclusion of unique content can set your company's website apart from the rest.

There are literally hundreds of techniques that may be implemented including validating and minimizing code, renaming pages, writing quality web copy, making good use of heading tags, etc.—most of which the average web designer knows almost nothing about.

My recommendation: fire your brother-in-law who has been working on your website part time and hire a professional web developer who is also a SEO expert.

*Hire an expert: If your web designer asked you to write the copy for your website, it means that he or she does not understand SEO web copy. Find someone who does.*

# 183. Eye Tracking and Web Design

"My eyes are an ocean in which my dreams are reflected."

**Anonymous**

The state-of-the-art for website design continues to evolve as does the sophistication and experience of the website visitor. This discriminating surfer has pushed the web designer to reconsider what really works for the visitor instead of what looks cool. This new website design criteria is based on eye tracking research.

Eye tracking is a term used to describe how the eye moves along a web page. This eye movement is part cultural, part physiological and part learned. For example, Westerners will normally read a web page from the top left and then follow a downward sloping "s-curve" to the right. The curve will then move back to the left bottom and so on. This is why Google AdWords and Yahoo! Pay per click ads are on the right.

Recent studies now offer other conclusions. For example, text may draw attention before graphics or other images. We are taught at an early age that words are powerful and to be reckoned with. STOP signs say "STOP" and we hit the brakes, yet a STOP sign without the words will only confuse us.

Our eyes easily fatigue from ornate or decorative fonts. Welcoming and easy-to-read fonts include Arial, Times New Roman, or Sans Serif. Bold face and capital letters catch our attention but they lose impact if we use it too much. Bold face and capital letters scream for attention and should be used sparingly.

Our eyes prefer shorter paragraphs and shorter sentences. Also, people tend to read the lead sentence in a paragraph and then scan the rest of the page. This may account for the popularity of Hemingway or People Magazine, but I digress.

White space is good. Just look at the Google website and you will see what I mean. We also like simple formats such as a one column page layout since this is easier to read than a multi-column format. White space has a calming effect on the reader and helps them focus on what is important.

Website buttons and tabs work. They help us navigate around the site and we are comforted by them. Left and top navigation both work, but the top is preferred. Having a simple dashboard is essential for website usability. Busy websites create stress for the visitor and can send them away.

Design your website for ease of use; looking cool or stylish may be hard on the eyes.

*Review your website: Is it designed with these points in mind? If not, why not?*

# 184. How Search Engines Work

"The voyage of discovery lies not in finding new landscapes,
but in having new eyes."

**Marcel Proust (1871 – 1922) French Novelist**

Search engines enable your customers to find you on the web. But, how do they do that and what is important to them?

The prime objective of any website owner is to be found by the search engines; if it cannot be found, your website is a waste of time and money. The big three search engines (Google, Yahoo!, and MSN) deploy automated software robots (sometimes called spiders) to find you. The spiders jump from hyperlink to hyperlink crawling all over the Internet looking for new content and new websites, while verifying the old content on existing websites.

This page by page crawl by the search engine spiders goes on 24/7 all over the web. This information is stored in a giant database and is indexed, which provides the search engine a roadmap back to the information by keyword, hyperlink, and Meta tag. These databases contain the locations of billions of documents for future reference.

With this database created, the search engine responds to the requests for information made by the users of search engines (I.E. your customers, you, and me). These requests for information are submitted in the form of keywords or phrases and are matched up with the indexed documents. A search engine then provides a listing of the matched results. Depending on the search, the results might yield hundreds or thousands of possible matches.

To make the reading of the search results easier, the search engines ranks the results. Relevance is the key criteria in the ranking and the results are provided in descending order. This ranking is created by algorithms that are constantly monitoring relevance. Relevance can include the age of a document, the number of links to a document, and the keywords in the document. All this is done in fractions of a second.

To please the search engine gods, be sure to offer the following on your website:

- Unique content that is frequently updated (weekly at a minimum).
- Make sure that your content bursts with keywords.
- Provide free content for visitors.
- Include numerous links to other sites and other content.
- Remember that search engines cannot read graphics or photos.

*Question: If search is free, how does Google make money? Answer: Advertising.*

# 185. Organic Search or Pay Per Click?

"There is nothing in a caterpillar that tells you
it's going to be a butterfly."

**Buckminster Fuller (1895 – 1983) Architect, Author, and Futurist**

There are two methods for web surfers to find your website using the major search engines: organic search results (also known as natural search results) and pay per click advertising. Organic search is defined as text listings on search engine results pages that are listed by their relevance to the search terms. These results are non-biased which means that the search engine publishers such as Google, Yahoo!, and MSN will not take any money to influence the rankings. This can be contrasted to pay per click advertising which is the advertising on the search results page on the top or on the right. Both help drive traffic to your site.

It is very significant to note that organic search is used 80% of the time by web searchers to find websites. While natural search results seem the logical first method for being found on the web, the algorithms used by Google and the other search engines are constantly changing to the consternation of the web developers and search engine optimization experts. Much like a game of cat and mouse, the search engines continue to refine the criterion of what is important in the ranking of search results. This criterion is also a closely held secret. Thus, getting a high ranking is not always plausible nor is it easily retained if you get it.

Natural search results are free in the sense that you cannot buy your ranking. Yet, you can spend a lot of money building a website with clever features and compelling content. If you are in a competitive space with many other websites vying for the same visitors, it can be difficult to get on the first two pages of search results. If your ranking is beyond those first two pages, the likelihood of being found by your customers diminishes greatly.

Also, in some cases it may take weeks to be found by the search engine spiders. These spiders are the software robots which crawl around the Internet looking for new websites or for new content on previously visited websites. The typical website once found is visited every two to four weeks by the spiders. Thus, it can be laborious process to get found naturally.

It can be generalized that organic search is more trusted than pay per click advertising. You can compare it to the credibility of an editorial in a newspaper versus that of a paid advertisement in the same paper. The sophisticated user will know that the pay per click advertising is paid for and thus is less believable or trusted.

Still, pay per click advertising is quite effective and the results can be immediate. After you create a pay per click campaign, your ads will often start appearing within minutes. It is also a snap to monitor which keywords bring visitors to your website. This tracking allows you to spend your advertising budget efficiently by using the best keywords.

Unfortunately, the best keywords may also be the most expensive. When pay per click advertising first was introduced in 2000, spending $.10 to $.25 per click was common. Today, keywords can cost multiple dollars with $10.00 or more per click common for the more competitive search terms. Additionally, every click costs even if the click is in error by the searcher or if the search term is just too broad. This makes pay per click advertising too expensive for many.

Additionally, organic click rates are three to four times greater than paid listings. Searchers can begin to recognize your pay per click advertisement and will choose to avoid it. Thus, they learn not to trust the advertiser.

If your budget allows for it, there is an argument for a mix of both pay per click advertising and organic results. You can begin by creating traffic to your site right away through pay per click. In parallel, you can you build organic search rankings through search engine spider friendly web designs, embedded keywords, and good content. As your site starts to climb in ranking you may decide to reduce or eliminate your pay per click advertising.

If money is tight, I would recommend putting your efforts into building a compelling website design which is keyword rich and search engine friendly. This favors the use of a search engine optimization (SEO) specialist to insure your site is designed properly and maintained to meet search engine requirements.

*Research this: Do a search for "Organic SEO or Pay per click Advertising."*

# 186. Keywords and Your Website

"I had some eyeglasses. I was walking down the street when suddenly the prescription ran out."

**Steven Wright (1955 – present) Comedian**

Keywords are how people find you on the web. They function as the language of online search and are a must have feature on your site.

The critical question to ask is what are the keywords used by your customers and prospects when they want to find you? The process to determine these terms involves reviewing actual searches from live data bases. This helps make a good understanding of the actual keyword phrases and patterns of search used by your customers. This information helps you decide on website content creation and pay per click advertising with Google Adwords, Yahoo! Search Marketing, and others.

A great website is optimized by adding heavily used keywords that relate to your business. You need to be sure to integrate your top searched keywords and phrases into the content of your site. The words must be relevant and read as normal copy. Don't get overly creative since the search engine spiders are smart and will see through a ploy to stuff keywords in your web content.

If you think your copy does not make sense when you read it, you will need to fix it. To verify the readability of your copy, have an unbiased third party verify that your copy reads well.

Keywords are great but don't overdo it.

*Investigate this: Go to Search-based Keyword Tool site at http://www.google.com/sktool/ to determine your best keywords.*

# 187. Websites Need to Be Different

"If you do things well, do them better.
Be daring, be first, be different, be just."

**Anita Roddick (1942 – 2007) Businesswoman**

People buy products and services for their differences, not because they are the same as everything else. This also applies to your website. The proliferation of websites has raised the bar when it comes to making your customer experience unique and meaningful.

Although all good websites must have the same basic things such as up-to-date content and ease of use, the similarities should stop there. After you deliver the basics, you need to make your website different.

Consider adding the following unique elements to your website:

- Start with an eye catching header. Know that the colors of your header communicate your website's theme or mood. This may be the first contact with your brand, so make sure the image is consistent with the message that you want to communicate. I recommend having the header professionally designed.
- Color choices are critical to web design. See the chapter in this book called "I See Colors."
- Consider adding video clips to your site. Digital video is now easy to create by yourself and it can add a personal touch to your site. If done by you, it can add a warm, homemade feel, even if it is amateurish in style. Alternatively, some B2B sites might need the production values of a professionally done video with narration (this is not cheap).
- Even easier than adding video is the addition of audio clips. Once again the software is free and all you need is a microphone and something to say. Like the homemade video, the self-made audio clip can add a very personal touch.
- Add a blog to your website. Blog software is free and is an easy addition to your website. It is an efficient way to add fresh content to your website since blogging does not require the help of the web designer. It is also one of the best ways to communicate personally with your customers.

- Forums provide a community for your customers to exchange ideas with each other. Again the software is free and easy to add to your site. Forums can be self monitoring, but since it is your site I recommend you edit it. Forums give your customer another reason to visit your site.
- How about live chat on your website? This can provide answers to your customers' questions. Consider it an instant message system for all your customers. It can be a great way to provide "after the sale" support and it can build credibility for your firm.

These additions can help make your customer website experience unique and memorable while differentiating your site from the others.

*Take a tour: Go visit the websites of your top competitors. How are there websites different than yours?*

# 188. Women on the Web

"Remember, Ginger Rogers did everything Fred Astaire did, but she did
it backwards and in high heels."

**Faith Whittlesey (1939 – present) Ambassador**

A study by Yahoo! and Starcom/Mediavest Group offers some interesting insights about women and how they interact with the web. The survey interviewed 1,199 women about how they use the Internet. Here are a
few of the findings:

- The Internet is the preferred media among women and is the 4th
  most time intensive activity behind work, sleep and time spent
  with the family.
- The content most popular with women includes subjects relating
  to news, weather, finance and games - items not found in most
  popular women's magazines.
- Women's online spending habits are increasing and they are also
  using websites extensively to make decisions before purchasing
  in the offline world.
- Average time spent actively online each day was 3.3 hours.
- If offered only one choice as to a source of news, information and
  entertainment, 65% of women surveyed chose the Internet.
- 43% of the women surveyed make regular online purchases.
- 58% stated convenience as the major motivator for shopping
  online.
- The web is not a spare time activity for the women surveyed and
  it is accessed at various times of the night and day.

What this means to marketers is that women need to be recognized
for the dominant decision maker in consumer and B2B markets that they
are. Women outnumber men 51% to 49%. Women make the major decisions in households 75% of the time. Women account for more than 50 percent of stock ownership in the US and by 2010 they will represent 50
percent of the private wealth in America, or about $14 trillion. By 2020 that
number is expected to rise to $22 trillion.

*Take another look at your website: Is it woman friendly? Better ask a
woman.*

# 189. Marketing to Baby Boomer Women

"Women who seek to be equal with men lack ambition."

**Timothy Leary (1920 – 1996) Writer, Psychologist, and Futurist**

Author Marti Barletta recently coined the phrase "Prime Time Women" to describe women over 50 years old, which she says "was an attempt to move away from the misleadingly negative connotations of phrases like "mature women" or worse, "middle-aged women."

Here is some quick math from her book "Marketing to Women": "From 1992 to 2020, the number of people age 50+ is expected to increase 76%, while the number under age 50 will decrease 1%. Americans 50+, while "only" 27% of the population (36% of adults 18+), nonetheless control 50% of the discretionary spending. Per capita, they spend 2.5 times as much as younger consumers. They own 70% of all the financial assets, including 80% of all the money in U.S. savings and loans, and 66% of all the dollars invested in the stock market."

Our aging society is a major marketing mega trend. Hidden within that expanding demographic is the fact the money is also shifting (or, has already shifted) to women. In fact, it is estimated that 80% of the spending decisions in the typical dual earner household are controlled by women, regardless of age.

More compelling is the longer life expectancy of women (currently, women now live 80.1 years, compared to men at 74.8 years per the Center for Disease Control). This puts them in charge of the bulging estates created by the passing of their male spouses, along with the wealth from "baby boomer" parents (parents of babies born from 1946 to 1964) who are slowly dying off. In a nutshell, baby boomer women are in charge of most of America's personal wealth.

This means that the prime time customer for many businesses is now baby boomer women. This includes financial services, real estate, health and medical, automobiles, consumer goods, etc. Yet, most firms don't get it since many are still messaging their products and services for the man of the house (I.E. the older, infirm fellow in the rocking chair wearing "Depends" diapers who looks to the lady of the house to make all the financial decisions).

For the entrepreneur, this shift of money and power to boomer women is a major trend that is ripe with opportunity. If you sell to consumers and are not targeting boomer women, you need to reconsider your marketing strategy.

Get it?

*Your lobby: If you have a brick and mortar building with a lobby, what magazines are available for your customers to read? Are any of them targeted at women?*

# 190. Boomer Cemeteries Full

"A person's maturity consists in having found again
the seriousness one had as a child at play."

**Friedrich Nietzsche (1844 – 1900) German Philosopher**

A new millennium marketing mega trend is the retirement of the "Baby Boomers" (people born in the US from 1946-1964). They will change our landscape and will create new opportunities for marketers. Little did I know that this trend would impact the available space at cemeteries (and literally change the landscape).

A while ago the mayor of a village in southwest France threatened residents with severe punishment if they die, because there is no room left in the overcrowded cemetery to bury them. In an ordinance posted in the council offices, Mayor Gerard Lalanne told the 260 residents of the village of Sarpourenx that "all persons not having a plot in the cemetery and wishing to be buried in Sarpourenx are forbidden from dying."

The mayor added, "Offenders will be severely punished." The mayor said he was forced to take drastic action after an administrative court in the nearby town of Pau ruled in January that the acquisition of adjoining private land to extend the cemetery would not be justified. Lalanne, age 70, is standing for election to a seventh term in this month's local elections, said he was sorry that there had not been a positive outcome to the dilemma. "It may be a laughing matter for some, but not for me," he said.

With nearly 80 million "Baby Boomers" now venturing into retirement, the mind reels at the changes that our society will have to make. The U.S. Bureau of Labor Statistics projects 330 people are turning 60 years old each hour; there's clearly a change on the horizon with marketing implications all around.

Although cemetery shortages may not be the most appealing of opportunities, it is clear evidence of the impact of this new millennium marketing mega trend.

Land speculation anyone?

*P.S. Background information is courtesy of Reuters France.*

# 191. The New Auction Culture

"You don't have to burn books to destroy a culture.
Just get the people to stop reading them."

**Ray Bradbury (1920 – present) Author**

My sixteen year old daughter asked me the other day, "Dad, can we trade in Tara for a new puppy? We can sell her on eBay." Tara is our eight year-old, slightly annoying, yellow lab. I was aghast at the suggestion. How could my daughter even consider trading in the old dog for a new puppy?

Welcome to the "new auction culture." Cell phones are traded in every year or so. PCs last a couple years before we discard them and trade up to a faster microprocessor and bigger hard drive. Cars are leased for three years and then traded back in for a new model. When our e-mail address starts getting too much spam, we just abandon it and get a new one (I should know, since I have nine different email addresses).

College students don't keep their text books. When the semester is over they list them on websites that resell books, such as Amazon (http://www.amazon.com). No sense hanging on to that unnecessary stuff when you can get cash instead. For that matter, college students also auction their old CDs, surf boards, and iPods. Who needs that stuff anyway?

Flash back a few years ago and you will remember when we repaired broken appliances and kept them for decades. My mom had an IBM typewriter and it was built like a tank and it worked for 30 years! We have a sewing machine that is over 60 years old and my wife doesn't sew, but it is a family heirloom which is cherished. I think it is tucked away in a closet.

Daniel Nissanoff, author of the book "FutureShop," suggests that a new "auction culture" will change the way we buy, sell, and use our possessions. According to Nissanoff, we have had an "accumulation society" for many years where permanent ownership of a product was very important. Today, we are adjusting to "temporary ownership" where we buy or lease the goods we want (some at prices we can't even afford), and then sell them for optimal resale value when we tire of them.

Gone are the days of saving for years to make a special purchase and keeping it to pass down to the next generation. Instead, we just go buy it, use it, and discard it when the thrill is gone. No worries. Some might say this also applies to our jobs, since all we need to do is visit monster.com (http://monster.com) and get a new one. Or, if you tire of your current spouse, go visit eharmony.com (http://eharmony.com) to find a better one who is more compatible—can you say Sagittarius?

Welcome to the new normal. For my daughter's generation, this is all they know: everything is disposable and replaceable—even the dog.

*Time to purge: Look at your current direct marketing materials. Is there anything worth keeping?*

# 192. Hispanics Have Clout

"We need to help the Hispanic community feel more
comfortable when they call 911."

**Erica Ramos Hispanic Activist**

Hispanics have the power.

Hispanics accounted for about half the growth in the U.S. population since 2000, according to a recent US Census Bureau report. The nation's largest minority group is increasing its presence even faster than in the previous decade. Contrary to popular belief, births have overtaken immigration as the largest source of Hispanic growth. If you are not marketing your products with this "minority" in mind, you are making a big mistake amigo.

It appears that iTunes understands the Hispanic consumer because they recently announced "iTunes Latino," which is an area on their online store which is dedicated to Latin music, videos, audio books, and podcasts. The iTunes store is the world's leading digital music outlet with 1.5 billion songs sold since its launch.

Rather than just a knee jerk reaction, iTunes says that this expansion was a response to the growing market for this genre of Latin digital products. They believe that half of Hispanics are Internet users and that this number is increasing. I think they smell the money.

The biggest minority in the US has muscle. Are you marketing to Hispanics? You had better consider this market pronto, amigo.

*Opportunity: Hispanics are overlooked and underserved. Don't believe me? Name a movie produced this year with a Hispanic actor in the lead role? Name a television drama with a Hispanic actor in the lead role? Name a state governor with a Hispanic last name? A U.S. senator?*

# 193. Green is the New Black

"Don't blow it—good planets are hard to find."

**Unknown**

Green marketing—what is it really?

The marketing mega trend of the decade is unquestionably the need to be "green." Call it what you like: clean-tech, low carbon footprint, environmentally conscious, eco-friendly, the impact of global warning, or just common sense. It's for real and it represents a major marketing opportunity, while some might say it will be a political necessity. Sooner or later, it will be mandated by law.

To be green denotes that the offering is good for the environment or at least does not harm it. Many suggest that if we converted to bio-fuels, we would have a better planet. Or would we? A new study from The Nature Conservancy and the University of Minnesota finds that many bio-fuels — seen by many as a potentially low-carbon energy source—can emit more greenhouse gases than the fossil fuels they aim to replace.

While it is true that use of the word "green" or "natural" has been largely unmanaged and often abused, it should be used as an expression of the provider's commitment to a better environment and a healthier planet. It can also be measurable; for example, we can measure the impact of an electrical appliance which uses less electricity, paper products which are made of recycled paper, or the impact of using alternative fuels such as ethanol.

From a political perspective, conserving oil is a unilateral political party platform agenda item for political elections (thanks to former U.S. Vice President Al Gore). All major candidates are eco-friendly, at least in rhetoric.

This is where good marketing kicks in and saves the world. It starts with the right messaging from smart marketers like you and me to create the awareness with the consumer. Interestingly enough, a recent Gallup poll of U.S. voters ranked the war in Iraq, healthcare, and the economy to be greater issues than the need to become carbon neutral. This is particularly vexing when you think that two of the three top issues are directly related to oil; namely the war in Iraq and our current economic malaise.

It is up to us marketers to help the consumer understand the benefits of leaving behind a carbon neutral footprint because it leads to cleaner air, less dependency on foreign suppliers of petroleum products, less waste to bury or burn, and a healthier environment for our children and their children.

The spoils earned by the providers who commit now to a greener earth will be the chance for increased sales and profits. The market is ready for this message. Go green or watch your business erode.

Spiraling fuel prices and global warming fears hog the headlines of newspapers and blogs. Savvy advertisers have adopted green campaigns but consumers are increasingly confused over what it means to be "green," according to a recently released study by Landor Associates.

Allen Adamson, managing director at Landor says, "It is easy to say you are green, but consumers are skeptical. And because everyone wants to jump on the green bandwagon, all of a sudden it is noisy in this space, and it is hard to break through."

The study found that 64% of those who responded couldn't name a "green" brand; even 51% of the respondents who are considered to be environmentally conscious were unable to name one. "As much as the term green has been tossed around, many people are unclear as to what it means," the study reported. The words "eco-friendly, fuel efficient, biodegradable, natural, and organic is used in different categories to emphasize green, but can confuse and cloud the mind of consumers."

Still, green means profits as consumers gravitate toward the messaging while corporations use it to create profits. Green is good for the planet and for the firms touting it.

Green is the new black.

*Visit Home Depot: Look for green consumer products. You will be amazed at the quantity.*

# 194. Online Everything

"The Internet is the world's largest library.
It's just that all the books are on the floor."
**John Allen Paulos (1945 – present) Math Professor**

Everything is online. If this is not the case for your business, it probably means you are going out of business. Since you are reading this book, you are probably on the right track. Here is my story.

Call it mid-life crisis, but a few months ago I was desperate for a red Corvette. The first thing I did was research the car thoroughly so that I could become an informed buyer. I did an online search for "corvette" and found a forum called the Corvette Forum (http://forums.corvetteforum.com), which is an online community for Corvette enthusiasts. Chock-full of information from hundreds of Corvette owners from all over North America, I was ready to take the next step.

This meant that I had sell my old car, which was a red 2004 Nissan 350Z with only 7,000 miles (yes, you may be seeing a trend here). I advertised my "Z" on AutoTrader (http://www.autotrader.com/), which is the largest online car site with over 2 million used vehicles listed. I sold my car in three weeks to a buyer who lived 300 miles away; he had been searching for my "Z" for about a week.

Money in hand, I started my search for a red 2005 Corvette with a six speed manual transmission, a removable hard top, and a Z51 performance package. Low mileage was a must since low miles is the single most important factor in preserving resale value for a used Corvette. Conveniently, most "Vette" owners choose to drive their cars only on weekends; the weekend drive is done only after the car is washed, waxed, and polished. More than one Vette owner that I talked with referred to their cars as their "baby," which tells you a lot about the psyche of the Corvette owner.

I did my search for my "baby" with the Internet. It turns out that there are car dealerships which only sell and service Corvettes. But, my research showed that buying the car from a private party was probably the best way to go. I located a number of Vettes within a 100 mile radius of my Orange County home, and the fun began: I got to test drive the different cars for sale. Hot dang!

The actual purchase was easy since there were so many low mileage Vettes in near perfect condition. The ultimate seller lived about 75 miles away and was moving to Europe and had to sell her 2005 red Corvette with only 6000 miles. Call it destiny or whatever, but I found my car in a matter of minutes in perfect condition and at the right price.

As far as new car financing, I did a web search for used auto financing and chose to go with Well Fargo (https://autofinance.wellsfargo.com/home.jsp) for their competitive rates and ease of doing business with them. I did this all via the web.

With the transaction made, I decided to upgrade the floor mats and ordered them from an online store in Houston, Texas (http://www.corvette sofhouston.com). Now my Corvette was really perfect. Also, I needed to change my insurance, so I emailed my insurance agent (who lives in San Jose by the way) to drop the Nissan and add the Corvette.

The point of this story is about the process I used to buy and sell my cars. It was virtually all online with help from others located all over North America. Had this been even five years ago, I would have bought and sold my car locally and relied upon local merchants, local buyers, and local inventory. I am positive that the web delivered a quicker and better transaction.

*Everything is online: Is your business up to the challenge? Go look at your competitors' websites to see how you compare.*

# 195. Market Online or
# Go Out of Business

"The Internet is becoming the town square for the
global village of tomorrow."

**Bill Gates (1955 – present) Founder of Microsoft**

If your business is not actively engaged in web-based marketing, it is likely you are going out of business.

One of the best examples I can describe is the book business of which I am an active participant. The era of the brick and mortar retail store is quickly being eclipsed by the online or virtual bookstore. The traditional bookstore is a "hits" or "best seller" business and cannot begin to carry all the titles that the readers desire.

Instead, traditional bookstores stock only the top 1-2% of books published leaving the rest of the titles to the online booksellers like Amazon. In fact, when I visited Amazon today their book titles totaled an amazing 19,382,861 individual titles. The real statistics on the book business are rather startling. 75% of U.S. adults haven't been in a bookstore for the last 5 years and bookstores sell only 45% of all books sold.

The majority of books are now purchased online and the trend is increasing. The consumer is voting with their keyboards and is demanding more titles. The only way to deliver the other book titles is through the efficiency of the online store.

Another example of how businesses are embracing the web is that of the retail cookie store in the shopping mall. My friend, Ryan Paules, who owns two cookie stores, tells me although the aroma of cookies is a powerful stimulant for walk-in purchases, the website contributes up to 30% of his sales and many of his customers are not local.

Ryan attributes this high percentage of online sales to aggressive e-mail marketing, sound e-mail list management, and a good website. Direct mail is a contributing factor too. Much like the traditional bookstore, the cookie store is changing with the times. Also, most of his telephone orders come from people who first looked at the website.

Books and cookies are just two examples about how the web has changed businesses. Change can be good.

*Google this: Go to Google and do a search for "search engine optimization" to learn more about how to please the search engines and get a higher rank.*

# 196. Change While You Can

"Don't fight forces, use them."

**Buckminster Fuller (1895 – 1983) Visionary**

Even the best marketing strategies need to be revisited, if not revised. Changes in the market environment can dramatically change the marketing mix and your product plans. Marketing strategy should be viewed as a process, which means that the best laid marketing plans will change sooner or later.

Strategic change can be caused by many forces; sometimes change is a threat while other times it can be an opportunity. It all depends on how your product or business is defined; additionally, how you react may be the biggest factor in your future success.

Sometimes the market evolves and the demand for an offering changes. For example, obesity is on a dramatic rise in North America; because of this people are becoming more "food label savvy" about calories, fat grams, sugar, carbohydrates, and protein. Fast food restaurants have had to respond with salad bars, better disclosure of nutritional information, and leaner products.

Another source of strategic change is technological innovation. As microprocessors increase in speed and processing ability, older personal computers quickly become obsolete. A more disruptive technological change might be the creation of the MP3 format and downloadable music. Music is now purchased one song at a time instead as albums of songs.

Occasionally, a market is redefined. This is often driven by competition or customer demand. Today, our fast paced culture demands a more personalized relationship with information, which has created wikis, blogs, and the birth of IPTV (Internet Protocol Television). This new information content business allows the reader or viewer to get "personalized content" when they want it and where they want it.

Also, marketing channels change. Today the Internet has changed the relationship of customers with providers. No longer dependent on the provider for education on products and services, the new consumer is more informed and sophisticated than ever. In fact, the consumer is more powerful and will get what they want or they will find another provider.

For the marketing strategist, the challenge is to anticipate the changes and take control of their destiny. The alternatives of delaying action or getting surprised can lead to business failure.

A wise friend of mine told me once that all good things last two years. It sounds a bit cynical, but I think what he meant was that there is a life cycle to all things including products, jobs, companies, and ideas. Implied in his message was to not rest on your laurels or revel in your past glories too long, since change may be just around the corner.

Tower Records, my favorite bricks and mortar music retailer, was a victim of a shift in the marketplace. A few months ago they were liquidated with 2,700 jobs eliminated along with a nearly 40-year legacy. Six years ago Tower Records founder Russ Solomon was quoted saying, "The Internet will never take the place of stores (like Tower)." Meanwhile, Internet retailers like Amazon.com proliferated and Wal-Mart slashed prices with its massive purchasing power. Small record stores closed right and left. Tower hid behind bankruptcy protection in 2004, but emerged unchanged and did not embrace the digital music revolution.

This same phenomenon applies to marketing in an entrepreneurial setting. Things can change quickly, which can dramatically change the needs of your target customer and thus challenge you to quickly change your product or solution. My experience is that these changes generally come with warning signs or cues (as is the case with Tower Records), which will allow you time to adjust. Your intimacy with your niche will provide you a competitive advantage, but it will be up to you to positively greet the changes rather than sticking to your existing methods or designs. And that can be hard to do.

And it is not just Tower Records that had resisted this major shift to digital music downloading with MP3 formats. For decades, the music industry has fought tooth and nail to protect their intellectual property on records, then on tapes, then on CDs, and now digitized on the iPod. Over the last five years, the music industry has been forced to change their entire business model to accommodate the changing needs of their customer.

In this case, technology was the driver of the change with the new affordable MP3 format which allowed digital music to be downloaded legally (or otherwise) to a low-cost portable MP3 player. The technology allowed customers to get exactly what they wanted, which was the ability to listen to the individual songs from their own customized, portable music players.

While the court battles raged between the giant music companies and the technology makers, the customers voted their preference for the MP3 format. Case closed. For some in the music business, this has allowed new packaging and marketing opportunities. Meanwhile, iTunes was created out of nowhere and the customer got what they wanted.

The lesson is simple. Don't fight battles which cannot be won. Instead, use the market shifts to your advantage and be a player in the new game.

*Confront your demons: Write down the current and future threats to your business. Consider a strategy to understand them, if not embrace them.*

# 197. Mutant Guppies Still Haunt Me

"Suspicion always haunts the guilty mind."

**William Shakespeare (1564 – 1616) Playwright**

Bear with me on this one and please excuse the odd title of this chapter.

When I was a kid I had an aquarium in my bedroom that housed dozens, make that hundreds of guppies and neon tetras. They seemed to multiply almost daily and I was quite proud of them. While I enjoyed watching the pretty little fish, I did not enjoy cleaning the aquarium (much to my mother's chagrin).

The stink got so bad one day that my mom took it upon herself to clean it for me. Her cleaning agent was Clorox bleach, which did a great job eliminating the bad smell. Unfortunately, after the cleaning I had a mass die-off of the guppies and neon tetras. In a week or so I was left with 5 mutant guppies. As near as I could tell they were all blind, scarred, and unable to reproduce—they also swam kind of funny.

Needless to say, my mother felt horrible. As for me, I learned a lesson from my negligence and the importance of acting now rather than later. The truth is that I am still haunted by the image of the 5 mutant guppies swimming awkwardly in the tank by my bedside. Poor little guys!

Companies can also be negligent and slow to change. Change is hard and companies will often wait until they have to change. Then they are left with little choice but to react very aggressively. Sometimes management will overreact with over-zealous layoffs or they will layoff the wrong people.

With sales declining and profits gone, firms will often call for a "new strategy," which is business-speak for "make changes now." While the changes may be needed, the timing is poor. The best time to change a strategy is when things are working, not when things are falling apart.

For example, General Electric takes pride in continuously changing the firm's strategy. A key to the firm's success is a constant review and revision of people, practices, and products. While the GE culture can be criticized for being a bit bombastic, it is hard to argue about their resilience. Former GE CEO Jack Welch had a mantra that still resonates in the hallways, "Change before you have to."

Like the dirty aquarium, firms need to routinely clean house and review strategy. If not, you may end up with a bunch of mutant employees scarred by the management's swinging ax and desperate reinvention.

*Listen to your customers: Do a customer satisfaction survey. Look for weaknesses in your offering. Fix the problems now.*

# 198. Top Ten Marketing Mistakes by Entrepreneurs

"Good judgment comes from experience,
and often experience comes from bad judgment."

**Rita Mae Brown (1944 – present) Writer**

One way to achieve entrepreneurial success is to not make the following marketing mistakes:

1.  Trying to sell everything to everybody: Trying to do everything is a prescription for a marketing disaster. Being the best requires commitment and focus. Pick that one thing and pass on the rest.
2.  Cost-based pricing: Most small firms don't have a good handle on cost accounting and they invariably underestimate their costs. If pricing is cost-based, the end result is often an underpriced products. Instead, price on perceived value. This is pricing which reflects the potential savings, the highest satisfaction level, or the maximum use that a client will receive from the purchase and the use of the product or service.
3.  Inconsistent branding: Your business cards say one thing, your website says something else, and your brochures tell yet another story. Branding is a promise of value which requires consistency. Tell one story only.
4.  Over reliance on one big customer: Many small companies become hostage to one large customer. When that customer goes away, your firm is toast. How big is too big? I suggest no bigger than 25% of annual sales. Take care of this important customer, but focus your marketing dollars on finding some other customers. Do it now.
5.  Selling product and features: People don't buy products and features. They buy solutions to their problems. It is not about you. It is all about them.
6.  No market research: Many successful entrepreneurs rely on their "gut" and experience to make strategic decisions. That may be a good compass, but take the time to verify your assumptions with market research; sometimes your instincts are wrong.

7. Not giving things time to succeed: Building a brand and selling customers takes time and money. Set conservative goals and make sure you have funds available to promote new products; you might get lucky, but generally success is hard earned.

8. Lousy websites: Dead links, out-of-date copy, and old web designs will drive your customers away. Websites need to be refreshed constantly with new rich content and you need to maintain your site's optimization for the major search engines. This is a requirement of doing business in virtually all industries today.

9. Out-of-date customer lists: Your current customers are in the accounting system, your holiday card list is in Excel, your prospects are in Outlook and your former customers are in the file cabinet. Your customer list should be treated like a treasure chest. Keep this list meticulously updated in one file and back it up. Let me repeat: back it up.

10. Not updating your marketing plan: Even good marketing plans need to be updated. Things are changing quickly. The promise of Internet advertising is finally coming true. The Yellow Pages are dead. We have entered an era of personalization. One size does not fit all anymore. Review your plan quarterly and update annually.

*Dust off your marketing plan: If you have a marketing plan, bring it up-to-date. If you don't have one, write one now.*

# 199. Expressing Gratitude in a Thankless World

"The smallest act of kindness is worth more than the grandest intention."

**Oscar Wilde (1854 – 1900) Irish Playwright**

It seems that we live in a thankless world and this void seems most pronounced in day-to-day business. The ever increasing pace of commerce in the new millennium seems to leave little time for a thank you or even common courtesy. Global competitiveness seems to have sapped us of empathy and compassion. Yes, this is a cynical view of business today, but I fear it is true. It is my opinion that we are mired in a deep dark thankless funk that rivals the world of Ebenezer Scrooge from Dickens lore.

One only has to turn to YouTube or most anywhere on the web to read the smear campaigns that mocked political candidates in our 2008 Presidential race. Barack Obama was a victim of a Republican smear campaign which spread false information about his family history, religion, birth certificate, and background using a false Wikipedia citation. This is an example of negative advertising at its best with lies included. Regretfully, this negative viral message spread like crazy, misinforming thousands of readers.

Presuming that you buy into my harsh view of current affairs in the world, what should you do?

I suggest that you do the opposite. Greet the world by saying thank you to your customers, colleagues, suppliers, and competitors. Be different than the rest and look for the good in things and be grateful. At the very least, it will make you feel better. I can only imagine the shock on people's faces when you greet them cheerfully and express good tidings.

William Arthur Ward said that "Feeling gratitude and not expressing it is like wrapping a present and not giving it." Give the gift of your gratitude. Give often.

Thanks for reading my book.

*Practice this: See how many times you can say thank you today. Keep score.*

# *EPILOGUE*

"To make a prairie it takes a clover and one bee,
One clover, and a bee,
And reverie.
The reverie alone will do, if bees are few."

**Emily Dickinson (1830-1886) American Poet**

# BIBLIOGRAPHY

Allen, Kathleen, LAUNCHING NEW VENTURES: AN ENTREPRE-NEURIAL APPROACH, Houghton Mifflin Company, New York, 2006.

Anderson, Chris, THE LONG TAIL: WHY THE FUTURE OF BUSINESS IS SELLING LESS OF MORE, Hyperion, New York, New York, 2006.

Barletta, Marti. MARKETING TO WOMEN: HOW TO UNDERSTAND, REACH, AND INCREASE YOUR SHARE OF THE WORLD'S LARGEST MARKET SEGMENT, Dearborn Trade Publishing, Chicago, Illinois, 2006.

Boirac, Emile. L'AVENIR DES SCIENCES PHYCHIQUES, Paris, 1917. Translated as The Psychology of the Future, London, 1918.

Burg, Bob, ENDLESS REFERRALS: NETWORKING YOUR EVERYDAY CONTACTS INTO SALES, McGraw-Hill, New York, 1994.

Butler-Bowdon, Tom, FIFTY SELF-HELP CLASSICS: FIFTY INSPIRATIONAL BOOKS TO TRANSFORM YOUR LIFE, Nicholas Brealey Publishing, Incorporated, Yarmouth, Maine, 2005.

Carson, David, Stanley Cromie, Pauric McGowan, and Jimmy Hill, MARKETING AND ENTREPRENEURSHIP IN SMES: AN INNOVATIVE APPROACH. Prentice Hall, Upper Saddle River, New Jersey, 1995.

Christensen, Clayton M., THE INNOVATOR'S DILEMMA, Collins Business, New York, NY
2003

Clifford, Jr., Donald K. and Richard E. Cavanaugh, THE WINNING PERFORMANCE, Bantam Dell Publishing Group, Westminster, Maryland, 1991.

Covey, Stephen R., THE SEVEN HABITS OF HIGHLY EFFECTIVE PEOPLE, Simon & Schuster, Incorporated, New York, 1989.

Ferrazzi, Keith and Tahl Raz NEVER EAT ALONE: AND OTHER SECRETS TO SUCCESS, ONE RELATIONSHIP AT A TIME, Double Day, New York, 2005.

Fugere Brian, Chelsea Hardaway, and Jon Warshawsky WHY BUSINESS PEOPLE SPEAK LIKE IDIOTS: A BULLFIGHTER'S GUIDE, The Free Press, a division of Simon & Schuster, Incorporated, New York, 2005.

Gerber, Michael E., THE E-MYTH REVISITED: WHY MOST SMALL BUSINESSES DON'T WORK AND WHAT TO DO ABOUT IT, Harper Collins, New York, 2001.

Gladwell, Malcolm, THE TIPPING POINT: HOW LITTLE THINGS CAN MAKE A BIG DIFFERENCE, Little, Brown, and Company, New York, 2000.

Godin, Seth, ALL MARKETERS ARE LIARS: THE POWER OF TELLING AUTHENTIC STORIES IN A LOW-TRUST WORLD, Penguin Group, New York, 2005.

Godin, Seth, PERMISSION MARKETING: TURNING STRANGERS INTO FRIENDS AND FRIENDS INTO CUSTOMERS, Simon & Schuster, Incorporated, New York, 2001.

Gordan, Kim, MAXIMUM MARKETING MINIMUM DOLLARS, Kaplan Publishing, Chicago, 2006.

Hartmann, Thom, ATTENTION DEFICIT DISORDER: A NEW PERSPECTIVE, Underwood Books, Nevada City, Nevada, 1997

Helgesen, Sally, THRIVING IN 24/7: SIX STRATEGIES FOR TAMING THE NEW WORLD OF WORK, The Free Press, a division of Simon & Schuster, Incorporated, New York, 2001.

Hiam, Alexander and Charles D. Schewe, THE PORTABLE MBA IN MARKETING, John Wiley and Sons, New York, 1992.

Jackson, Bradley. FIRST, BEST, OR DIFFERENT: WHAT EVERY ENTREPRENEUR NEEDS TO KNOW ABOUT NICHE MARKETING, Dog Ear Publishing, LLC, Indianapolis, Indiana, 2006.

Kaplan, Jack and Anthony C. Warren, PATTERNS OF ENTREPRE-
NEURSHIP, John Wiley and Sons, New York, 2007.

Kawasaki, Guy, THE ART OF THE START: THE TIME-TESTED,
BATTLE-HARDENED GUIDE FOR ANYONE STARTING ANY-
THING, Penguin Books, London, 2004.

Kotler, Philip and Gary Armstrong, PRINCIPLES OF MARKETING,
Prentice Hall, Upper Saddle River, New Jersey, 2005.

Kotler, Philip and Kevin Lane Keller, MARKETING MANAGEMENT,
Prentice Hall, Upper Saddle River, New Jersey, 1995.

Kragen, Ken, LIFE IS A CONTACT SPORT: TEN GREAT CAREER
STRATEGIES THAT WORK, William Morrow and Company, Incorporated, New York, 1994.

Kuratko, Donald F. and Richard M. Hodgetts, ENTREPRENEURSHIP:
THEORY, PROCESS, AND PRACTICE, Thomson South-Western,
Mason, Ohio, 2007.

Levinson, Jay Conrad, GUERRILLA MARKETING FOR FREE:
DOZENS OF NO-COST TACTICS TO PROMOTE YOUR BUSI-
NESS AND ENERGIZE YOUR PROFITS, Houghton Mifflin Com-
pany, New York, 2003.

Lodish, Leonard M., Howard Morgan, and Amy Kallianpur, ENTRE-
PRENEURIAL MARKETING: LESSONS FROM WHARTON'S
PIONEERING MBA COURSE, John Wiley and Sons, New York,
2001.

MacPherson, Kim, PERMISSION-BASED E-MAIL MARKETING
THAT WORKS!, Dearborn Trade, Chicago, 2001.

Morgen, Sharon Drew, SELLING WITH INTEGRITY: REINVENTING
SALES THROUGH COLLABORATION, RESPECT, AND SERV-
ING Berkeley Publishing Group, New York, 1997.

Nissanoff, Daniel, FUTURE SHOP, Penguin Group (USA), New York,
2006

Porter, Michael, COMPETITIVE STRATEGY: TECHNIQUES FOR ANALYZING INDUSTRIES AND COMPETITORS, The Free Press, a division of Simon & Schuster, Incorporated, New York, 1980.

Reichheld, Fred, THE ULTIMATE QUESTION: DRIVING GOOD PROFITS AND
TRUE GROWHT, Harvard Business School Press, Boston, Massachusetts, 2006

Rogers, Everett M., DIFFUSION OF INNOVATIONS, The Free Press, a division of Simon & Schuster, Incorporated, New York, 1995.

Rogoff, Edward, BANKABLE BUSINESS PLANS, Rowhouse Publishing, New York, 2007.

Scott, David Meerman. THE NEW RULES OF MARKETING AND PR: HOW TO USE NEWS RELEASES, BLOGS, PODCASTING, VIRAL MARKETING AND ONLINE MEDIA TO REACH BUYERS DIRECTLY, John Wiley & Sons, Inc, Hoboken, New Jersey, 2007.

Seligman, Martin, LEARNED OPTIMISM: HOW TO CHANGE YOUR MIND AND YOUR LIFE, Vintage Books, London, 2005.

Sharp, David J., CASES IN BUSINESS ETHICS, Sage Publications, Incorporated, Thousand Oaks, California, 2006.

Surowiecki, James. THE WISDOM OF CROWDS, Random House, New York, 2004.

Underhill, Paco, WHY WE BUY: THE SCIENCE OF SHOPPING, Simon & Schuster,
New York, 2000

WIKIPEDIA: THE FREE ENCYCLOPEDIA
http://en.wikipedia.org

Seligman, Martin, LEARNED OPTIMISM: HOW TO CHANGE YOUR MIND AND YOUR LIFE, Vintage Books, London, 2005.

Sharp, David J., CASES IN BUSINESS ETHICS, Sage Publications, Incorporated, Thousand Oaks, California, 2006.

Underhill, Paco, WHY WE BUY: THE SCIENCE OF SHOPPING, Simon & Schuster,
New York, 2000

WIKIPEDIA: THE FREE ENCYCLOPEDIA
http://en.wikipedia.org

# *Index*

# "Déjà New Marketing"

- Visit the author's websites at http://www.dejanewmarketing.com, http://firstbestordifferent.com, or http://www.thebirddoggroup.com.
- Start a conversation with John Bradley Jackson on his blogs at http://dejanewmarketing.com/blog, http://firstbestordifferent.com/blog, or http://thebirddoggroup.com/blog.
- Give the author a call at 714 777 2033 or write him an email at johnbradleyjackson@gmail.com. He will respond!
- Follow "Déjà New Marketing" on the Facebook page called "Déjà New Marketing."
- Follow John Bradley Jackson on Twitter, Facebook, & LinkedIn.
- Check in on the website for new ideas and tips that will give your business a boost.
- Have the author give a speech about all the concepts in this book and more!
- Read the author's first book "First, Best, or Different" which is available at http://firstbestordifferent.com.


"Still around the corner there may wait a new road or a secret gate."

**J.R.R. Tolkien, Author**

CPSIA information can be obtained at www.ICGtesting.com
Printed in the USA
BVOW020026010312

284086BV00002B/21/P